PORTRAIT
GALLERY

BOOKS BY AGNES DE MILLE

Dance to the Piper
And Promenade Home
To a Young Dancer
The Book of the Dance
Lizzie Borden: Dance of Death
Dance in America
Russian Journals
Speak to Me, Dance with Me
Where the Wings Grow
America Dances
Reprieve
Portrait Gallery

PORTRAIT GALLERY

AGNES
DeMILLE

A Peter Davison Book

HOUGHTON MIFFLIN COMPANY / BOSTON

1990

I wish to thank all those who have faithfully typed my manuscript: Mary Green, Matthew Gilmore, Anthony Fernandes, and Denise Cogan for researching and typing; and those who have advised and instructed me: Isaac Stern, Igor Youskevich, Barbara Barker, Lillian Libman, Richard DeMille, Lee Freeson, Jonathan Prude, and Carlheinz Ostertag; and the staff of the Dance Archives of the New York Public Library, who have been tireless in opening their remarkable archives and serving my needs. My thanks and affection go above all to my editor, Peter Davison, for his faith and kindness, for his patience in guiding and correcting my often floundering taste, and beyond all else for his enthusiasm.

Library of Congress Cataloging-in-Publication Data

De Mille, Agnes.
Portrait gallery / Agnes de Mille.
p.   cm.
"A Peter Davison book."
Includes index.
ISBN 0-395-52809-7
1. De Mille, Agnes.   2. Dancers—United States—Biography.
3. Choreographers—United States—Biography.   4. De Mille, Agnes—
Friends and associates.   I. Title.
GV1785.D36A3   1990
792.8′092—dc20
[B]   90-4620
CIP

Printed in the United States of America

HAD 10 9 8 7 6 5 4 3 2 1

The author is grateful for permission to quote from "A Cup of Coffee, a Sandwich and You," by Joseph Meyer, Billy Rose, and Al Dubin (page 217). Copyright © 1925 Warner Bros. Inc. (renewal). All rights reserved. She would also like to thank the Dance Collection and the Billy Rose Theatre Collection of the New York Public Library at Lincoln Center, Astor, Lenox and Tilden Foundations, for permission to use the photographs on pages 3, 38, 51, 95, 107, and 118.

The following chapters first appeared in different form: "Isadora Duncan," in the New York Times Magazine; "Alicia Markova," in the Atlantic Monthly; and "Alicia Alonso," in Dance Magazine.

The names of all persons employed in the author's household, as well as those of Jonathan Prude's and Alice George's friends, have been changed.

CONTENTS

LIST OF
ILLUSTRATIONS

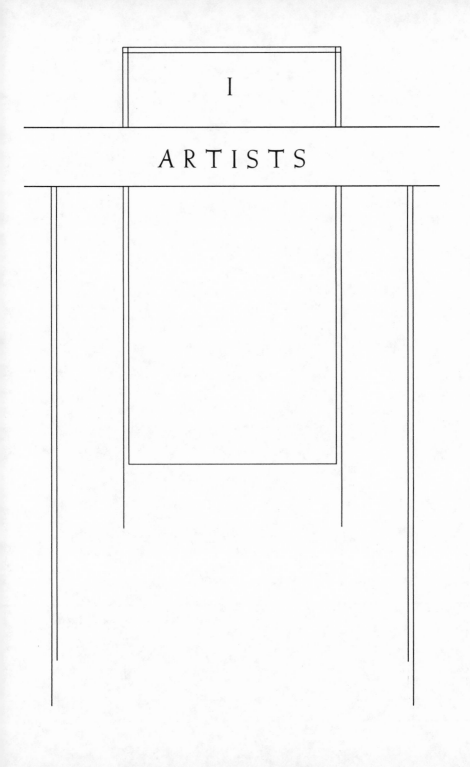

I

ARTISTS

ISADORA DUNCAN

SIXTY-THREE YEARS have passed since Isadora Duncan's death. Although she worked in the most ephemeral of all the arts, and although she was seen by a relatively small number of people—nothing like the multitudes that acclaimed Pavlova and the latter-day ballet companies, not to mention the latest rock star—her reputation stands today brighter and more illustrious than ever. She is still a force revered and cherished by all dancers, notwithstanding they have only a handful of solos to study and not one foot of film to preserve the genius that changed their métier.

When Isadora's autobiography, *My Life*, appeared in 1927,

it created a shock. It was "the first statement in our literature of woman as an artist," said Alfred Longueil of the University of California. It is written with passion, clarity, vehemence, and color. It is not written with humor. Whether Isadora had humor I cannot say. Her followers have none and rise to her defense as though she were even today a beginner and dependent on their personal support. But if her book proves anything, it is that humor is not the most desirable attribute in art. The response of the Anglo-Saxon public to the volume signified exactly how tired we all had grown of hollow wit, and how we longed for what was passionate, even if outrageous. But at the time it proved dreadfully unnerving to the young. Several virgins of my acquaintance went directly astray in the hope of becoming great dancers — a mistaken notion. They found, not surprisingly, that the one condition did not follow automatically on the other.

No, what Isadora guaranteed was a change in vision. What she provided was a point of view, an orientation, a sense of dignity and passion, where before there had been none. Isadora placed dancing on a par with religion and considered it not only the mother but the greatest of the arts, and since she herself was an artist hailed by the greatest people of her time, her words took on the force of prophecy and fiat. The change in the status of dance amounted very nearly to a revolution in moral values. Before Isadora, dancing was not considered important or dignified except by the people who practiced it. After her, it came to be. This, in brief, is her contribution. It seems a simple fact to state, but I suppose, in point of historical significance, that no one except Chaucer or Dante single-handedly worked such an astonishing change in the popular reception of an entire art.

Since Isadora's time there have been good dancers and bad dancers, but dancing per se has not been considered as it was before, a theatrical entertainment of inferior order, at best frivolous and diverting, at worst an adjunct to prostitution. Isadora made possible the work and the recognition of such great figures as Ruth St. Denis, Martha Graham, Mary Wigman, and Doris Humphrey, as well as the ballet renovators Michel Fokine, George Balanchine, and Antony Tudor and the performers Anna Pavlova, Vaslav Nijinsky, and Tamara Karsavina. After her came the Diaghilev repertoire, Pavlova's "Dying Swan" and "Bacchanale," and the whole school of Middle European dance. The body of educated, dedicated, intelligent choreographers who have given their lives to finding new ways of moving came not before but after her. She broke and remade patterns in her art, and she broke all known patterns of her sex.

Isadora Duncan was born in San Francisco on May 27, 1878. Her mother, Mary Dora Gray, came from a fairly wealthy family who disapproved of her marriage to a man thirty years older and not very stable financially, but Dora was an independent spirit and a nonconformist, part of that post–Civil War generation that questioned everything: dress, diet, medicine, aesthetics, religion, pedagogy, and matrimony. Nonconforming was one of the hallmarks of that generation, and young people, both men and women, were bursting with new ideas. Dora was one of the leaders of her community, believing strenuously in self-expression and self-education.

Dora was free enough in spirit to marry against her parents' advice, and she was free enough in spirit to divorce when her husband proved unsatisfactory. The crisis was reached when Mr. Duncan got into bad financial troubles because of unscrupulous dealings in his bank; he was brought to trial four times, was acquitted, and departed San Francisco and his family of four children, two girls and two boys. Dora was forced to earn their keep, which she did by teaching the piano to children and playing for the social dancing that her daughters, Mary Elizabeth and Isadora, taught—jigs, reels, waltzes, polkas, mazurkas. To Dora's playing of Schubert and Chopin, Isadora began to invent her own kind of movement. She derived from this almost daily practice a sound grounding in classical music and a deep love for the finest in musical literature.

The Duncan children were fairly familiar with the arts, but they were thought by the neighbors to run wild, without parental supervision or care as to home, training, and clothes. In fact, according to legend, the leaves blew through their domicile. But Dora was busy teaching all day, and when she came home she gave her entire attention to her children's reading, their interest in music, their interest in the arts. The father had abandoned them, but he did not forget them. Two years after he left, in 1893, he provided a home at Sutter and Van Ness streets, where they taught their classes. After another two years he had a second financial reversal.

During her childhood, Isadora observed very closely what it was like to be dependent on a man and bound to him by legal ties, and she decided quite young to have none of it. She also began to feel that she could be a very great artist and a revolutionary. From the time she was a child she believed in herself. Not all great artists have. Cézanne, for instance, never believed in himself at all, but Isadora did, and she was quite right in her self-appraisal.

When Isadora was in her late teens, she and her mother came east, and after holding various jobs Isadora got a position in Augustin Daly's stock company as a fairy in *A Midsummer Night's Dream*. But the prospect of being a sprite under some oversized leaves did not tally with her idea of art, and she left to pursue higher ideals, embarking with the rest of her family on a cattleboat bound for London. There she studied with Katti Lanner, who had once been prima ballerina of the Vienna Opera and who was the daughter of Joseph Lanner, who wrote the great waltzes. Isadora had done preliminary ballet training with Maria Bonfanti in New York, and there are some early photographs of her actually standing on pointe—not very well, but up in ballet shoes and trying to balance. The arms, head, and torso were, as always with Isadora, wonderfully beautiful.

In London all the family starved. They starved until they reached Vienna, where Isadora was taken up suddenly and hailed as a genius by the élite. From then on her story is one of wildfire success, particularly in Austria and Germany, and later in Paris, although she was never, alas, hailed in America, because Americans, she said, did not have the soul to understand. (It must be noted that it was largely American money that made her subsequent methods of life and her extravagances possible.)

She had two very famous lovers: the first Gordon Craig, son of Ellen Terry and a remarkable designer; the second an American multimillionaire, Paris Singer, heir to the sewing machine fortune. She also had unnumbered casual lovers and liaisons. In fact, it became fashionable to boast of having had a week with Isadora, whether true or false, the chance of contradiction being slight.

Along the way Isadora conceived three children. The last died in childbirth; the first two—Deirdre, the daughter of Gordon Craig, and Patrick, the son of Paris Singer—were drowned in a tragic motor accident. After that her life was rootless, and she drifted, forming liaison after liaison and taking up project after project. She finally went to Russia at the request of the commissar of education, Anatoly Lunacharsky, to form a school, and stayed there for nearly four years. During this time she married a young Russian poet, Sergei Yesenin, who was frequently deranged with vodka and who resented her fame and publicity. She was forced to leave him because his rages became uncontrollable, and the union was dissolved. He committed suicide in 1925, writing her a goodbye note in his own blood.

Following that diversion, Isadora danced whenever she could, whenever friends could manage to scrape together the money for a hall and publicity. According to the testimony of those who saw her, she performed with great power and increasing depths of feeling. But her life had frayed out. She was trusted by no one, certainly by no professional managers. She was frequently out of control of her actions. She plunged from happy, spendthrift opulence to dire poverty, without giving thought to staving off the consequences of her spending. She still talked nobly. She still was a presence to be reckoned with. She still spoke out on all causes. But she was considered by many to be simply raddled. Yet they could not disregard her: there was too much power, and certainly too much vision, in all she said.

Isadora may have been seen by relatively few; she influenced unknown hordes. She opened the dance profession to serious artists; in fact, she opened it to all women. She believed that dancing was principally an expression of the vigor of living, that anyone at all could dance if she chose, and that everyone should so choose. What was chiefly wanted, she urged, was spiritual rather than physical preparation; no special technique to speak of was called for. Off with the shoes, down with self-criticism, and away to the strains of Schubert.

This was artistically a dangerous point of view, and one that led to unpleasant excesses, such as those bevies of gamboling young ladies in cheesecloth who were such a nuisance in our mothers' youth and who did more to confuse Duncan's issues than anything else. A whole generation of men grew up loathing dancing because of their sisters' nonsense. A whole generation of women believed they were artists when they were nothing of the sort. That Isadora herself spent years in preparation tended to be overlooked in the general fun, and in urging freedom Isadora did not stress this point—which is too bad, because it set the case back rather sharply for professionals and for dancing. But dancing is a practice that perforce corrects itself: similar eager young ladies are today at the ballet barre, where an older and more stringent technique provides a salutary winnowing. Isadora did not promise that others could readily be the artist she was. In fact, she did not imagine any other dancer could be. She thought the experience of dancing was an emotional tonic and therefore desirable.

Isadora was a moral anarchist. She vowed when very young never to submit to woman's usual fate, that is, never to put herself or her fortune into any man's keeping, to bear children if and when she pleased, to leave them or look after them at whim, to be absolutely free and to remain so. She wished to have the freedom of a pagan as she imagined it, for she recognized love as a transient ecstasy. The communion on which marriage is built she never envisaged, I believe, nor constancy, security, fruition, these being the rewards of the female life she scorned. She followed a dream: power without responsibility, release without cost.

She declared herself against marriage only after being jilted by two lovers, and some think she was putting a bold face on a sorry situation. She is reported to have said that she wanted a child by each of six of the greatest living men. She is supposed to have approached Bernard Shaw with the inducement that a child with her body and his brain would be a wonder. "But," Shaw is rumored to have replied, "suppose it has my body and your brain?"

She is reported to have put the same proposition to Maurice Maeterlinck. "I am honored, madame," replied the poet, "but you must consult my wife." Madame Maeterlinck (Georgette Leblanc) is credited with rising to the occasion: "You want a child? Well, so do I. But my dear, as you see, it is not possible, not with him."

The lack of modesty and humor in Isadora's quoted remarks and in her autobiography and the lack of moderation in her life have been from the first an easy source of ridicule to the unconvinced. But Isadora dealt in absolutes. She knew she was beating against congealed prejudice; any hesitation or diffidence, had she been capable of feeling it, would have been taken as a confession of weakness in the art itself. She admitted no weakness. Dancing was to her a spiritual communication, and before the lift of her head and the summoning of her arms, people—even the prim and the scoffing—one by one fell silent, as before the bold and vigorous life.

Isadora's life was heroically bold and daringly vigorous to the death. In many ways she was as controversial and arresting a figure as George Sand, but without the balance or intellectual power of that great woman. Her courage was as fierce, however, her spirit as independent, and her voice as clamorous. She spoke out on marriage laws, sex, the rearing of children, prenatal influence, astrology, reincarnation, fortunetelling, childbirth, clothes, diet, government, vaccination, education, and, of course, art in all manifestations. Her pronouncements were an impartial mixture of wisdom and poppycock, delivered with conviction and often viva voce from the stage in her unforgettably beautiful voice. They were calculated to attract attention. Only about a third of what she said made sense, but because of the range she covered and the violence with which she attempted to prove her beliefs, her influence is felt today in many fields besides dancing.

The trends she set may or may not have led, as Isadora hoped, to free love. They certainly did cause girls to abandon corsets and bulky underwear and to revolutionize dress, posture, and sports habits. The modern girl, free-walking, free-running, nearly naked in bathing, and brown in the sun, is Isadora's creation.

She revolutionized the theater in lighting and decor. Many of the innovations were introduced by Gordon Craig, but it was she who realized his ideas and made them known to an entire generation. She influenced costume, choosing Greek dress for herself and her dances not because her dances were authentically Greek, but because they were liberating and simple, revealing the body and suggesting classical sculpture and frescoes. This had a profound effect on the next three generations of performers.

She urged, she implored, all dancers, all people in the theater, to use the greatest music, not the cheapest, and she was instrumental in introducing into our theaters the work of many of the fine French modern composers. Rock music and sound systems contradict her good influences.

She affected the education and training of children, making a plea for healthy, natural children, barefoot and wearing simple, weightless clothes. She urged dancing in kindergarten and primary school. The result was calisthenics, but it was a step toward the better use of the body.

Within the trade, her innovations demonstrated what turned out to be a stimulating surprise: that there were several ways of dancing. Up to this point performers had held that there was only one art, that is, ballet, and there was non-art, which consisted of the vulgar forms of theatrical dancing — skirt, tap, comedy — always in shoes. Isadora, although barefoot, turned out most disturbingly to be art too; and the ballet strongholds rocked from Moscow to Milan. Isadora herself fell into the ancient vice, however, and proved as bigoted as the others. For her also there was only one way of dancing — her own. She believed that folk and social forms reflected the faults of the cultures that fostered them, and classic ballet she considered a depraved distortion. Any deviation or attempt at experimentation by her pupils was cut off short. She intended to be the definitive, final revolutionist.

Her recipe was simple. She believed that the basic movements of walking, running, skipping, jumping, and standing could be as meaningful as acrobatics, and that all other movements essentially derive from these. She added nothing whatever to dance vocabulary, but she peeled away and destroyed a monstrous accumulation of formalism, leaving gesture stripped where it had been artificial and corrupt.

Isadora's greatest contribution, however, tends to be forgotten, because it cannot be copied: her personal performance. She had the gift of revelation and worked on the audience spontaneously. The technique of improvisation has today all but disappeared, but in the past two centuries it was practiced extensively. Great orators and musicians used it; musical cadenzas were usually left to the discretion of the performer, and when the performer was also the composer, they were frequently invented on the spot, as always with Beethoven. A substantial part of the training of the great organists has always been improvisation. But now only certain old vaudevillians and comedians dare perform as the spirit moves them.

What a phrase — "as the spirit moves them"! Our concert

artists pound out their one-night performances from coast to coast, giving more or less identical programs everywhere. Our ballet dancers leap nightly, changing planes and doing laundry in between, while our commercial-theater performers — actors, dancers, singers, instrumentalists, and conductors — repeat identical actions eight times a week for three or four years. Performing becomes a feat of endurance and an effort, not to deepen or sensitize a relationship between audience and actor, but to reproduce by every device and discipline known a stencil long since set. The practice is stultifying — but it does earn money.

George Copeland, the pianist, once told how he was summoned by Isadora to accompany her Chopin interpretations. He accepted diffidently, and she invited him to her studio to watch a rehearsal so that he might acquaint himself with her method of work. When he arrived, he heard sounds of a piano and tiptoed in. It was in the evening, and the dimly lit studio, hung from floor to ceiling with Isadora's famous blue curtains, contained a score or more guests reclining on sofas. They smoked, chatted, made love, or watched, as they pleased. To the layman this may sound like what one might expect at any dance rehearsal, but to professionals today, accustomed to either the strenuous gloom of a modern studio or the disciplined enervation of a ballet session, it takes on all the aspects of a Gypsy wedding.

In the center of the strange congregation moved Isadora, paying her guests not the slightest mind and solving some of the lengthier problems of interpreting a Brahms symphony. Copeland sank surprised on the edge of a bench and watched. He seemed to be the only person giving her any attention. At the end of two hours, during which she continued to improvise without repetition, discussion, or halt, he rose to retreat. She then spoke to him: "There, you see how it is. You see how I work." He left the place thoroughly bemused.

Isadora did not telephone or send word of any rehearsal plans, and as the performance date approached, Copeland grew increasingly apprehensive. Four days before, he called her in a panic. She reassured him: "Play as though I were not there. Play as you would for yourself, out of your own heart. Forget me." (This is a practice followed by many accompanists and most conductors, but I have never before or since heard of a dancer requesting it.) "What about dynamics? Pauses? Tempi?" he mumbled. "Forget about me," she urged.

The next time he saw her they were walking side by side toward the stage. He played at white heat, as though she were not there. But she was. And the audience rose en masse, cheering.

After reading this story, Irma Duncan, one of Isadora's disciples and adopted daughters, wrote to me indignantly, claiming that Isadora planned very carefully, that she knew her music absolutely, and that she knew what she was going to do; her dance was plotted and rehearsed, and the story is nonsense. But I have to believe it, because it was told me by Copeland himself.

In Isadora's own telling, her dances to Strauss's "Blue Danube Waltzes," Chopin's "Funeral March," and the Schubert "Moment Musical" were also improvised, as encores, without any rehearsal whatever. One acute observer has told me that Isadora always appeared to be listening and to dance after, not on, the music. This would not be surprising, under the circumstances. It would also mean that she was often behind the beat.

But none of this mattered when she had an audience in flux, so to speak. Then she began to invent, using the shared rapture as intoxication. She knew her music, she knew what she wished to say, she could create on the moment, and the audience's response and mood were a part of her creation. There is the legend of her interpretation of a Beethoven symphony, in which she began by standing at the back of the stage against her blue curtains and used the entire first movement to advance forward, seemingly with no dancing at all. At the climax she was down at the footlights with her arms above her head. It was enough. The audience went mad. Women threw flowers and bits of clothing. In very strict parlance, Isadora's audiences were sent—not charmed, nor delighted, nor intrigued, but altered, profoundly shaken, moved out of and beyond themselves. They left the theater stretched in every dimension.

Perhaps the most authentic voice about Isadora is that of Ruth St. Denis, her coeval and colleague, the other American who made dance history in the early twentieth century. In her book, *Ruth St. Denis: An Unfinished Life*, she writes:

> It is difficult to find words with which to pay tribute to the indescribable genius of Isadora. I can only say in brief that she evoked in a pitifully small audience visions of the morning of the world. She was not only of the spirit of true grief in her effortless, exquisitely modulated rhythms, but she was the whole human race moving in joy and simplicity and childlike comedy that we associate with Fra Angelico's angels dancing 'The Dance of the Redeemed.' . . . It was some of this ecstatic quality of her soul that I received, never to lose as long as I live. In one arm's movement was all the grace of the world. In one backward flinging of the head was all the nobility. . . . Her successors could be no more than a faint echo of the pure spirit of the dance.

A correspondent quite unknown to me wrote in 1952, twenty-five years after Isadora's death:

> When I saw her in Berlin on her way back from Moscow after her tragic marriage to Sergei Yesenin, Isadora was stout and flabby. She could not very well keep balance in arabesque, and the twenty or thirty spectators who came to see her sneered and shouted, some because Isadora was known to be a pinko and others because she had been violently anti-German during the First World War. This was a pathetic evening, but Isadora outdid herself. That memorable night I understood that Isadora was as great as the frescoes of Michelangelo or the paintings of Leonardo. I was breathless after the performance. To the end of my life I shall remember

that evening in the empty theater, when this aging woman, fat and in sad form, revealed the ultimate truth.

Geraldine Farrar, the great opera star, who had seen Isadora at the time of her debut, told me she was considered foolish and extravagant in her public remarks. Her plans to adopt twenty or thirty children and to buy small beds and equipment by the dozen were of course pure publicity nonsense—"but I tell you, Agnes, when she stood on the stage in Berlin with her little pupils and her adopted daughters around her and they followed her across, they were creatures apart, blessed. It was something to make your heart stand still. It was something one could never, never forget."

And Francis Biddle, our attorney general from 1941 to 1945, said to me, "It is worth being old now to have been young when Isadora was and to have seen her."

Such godlike domination implies absolute confidence, something of the rapt inspiration of a hypnotist or priest, and presupposes a spirit in perfect health. Isadora made no allowance for illness, depression, grumpiness, or grief. Any blocking of vitality meant paralysis. The risk in either direction was total. All good professionals can perform broken, ill, or shocked, but to *create* under these circumstances is almost beyond human control. Isadora made this demand of herself—never anything less—and she sometimes failed. But this was rare, for she took care not to run the risk of performing when she was not ready and eager to perform. What a refreshing example to contemporaries! Imagine the luxury of not performing when one does not feel like it, or of altering the program as one alters a conversation to suit the response of a listener. But today we are bound into a matrix of organization, and any refusal to go on breaks all the rules in the gigantic tournament in which we seem to be engaged. Never mind if an artist has every reason to believe that he will give a bad performance and that his appearance under the circumstances will constitute a public swindle as well as real damage to his good reputation. "The show must go on." Why? Because the manager wishes to count the box office every single night, not just when it suits the performer.

Isadora's rhapsodic, spontaneous approach was possible only because she was a soloist and because she was endowed. She might do much for money—run away with rich gentlemen, leave bills unpaid, borrow, threaten, and extort—but she never made her dancing serve commerce. This was inviolate. She danced only as her spirit dictated, and did not concern herself with business practicalities. The bills would always be paid, or nearly always.

She accordingly allowed her irresponsibility considerable latitude. She ran out without one word of explanation on a series of Berlin performances when she met the beautiful young Gordon Craig, and hid for days in his studio while her manager and her mother, mad with anxiety, all but dragged the river in their terror. (It has been suggested that both her manager and her mother knew very well where she was, or guessed, and relished the publicity.) She was not read out of her union for unprofessional conduct; she was not even sued. "Die Göttliche, heilige Isadora" was a goddess and was permitted vagaries, and the aura of irresistible love made her all the more provocative. Her fees mounted; her tours lengthened.

Her two children she turned over to the care of friends and her sister for prolonged stretches whenever it suited her. She founded a school and invited parents to send their young children to her for rearing and training. She adopted six of the girls, gave them her name, and took all the legal responsibility— then turned them over to the patient sister, Elizabeth, while she went off again. Then she brought the six Isadorables (Anna, Irma, Lisa, Margot, Therese, and Erica) to America and shortly after departed for Russia, abandoning them to fend for themselves. They all but starved until George Copeland organized a concert group for their rescue. As far as Isadora was concerned, the only results of this episode were a memorable love affair and a baby.

Should she have done otherwise? Should she have been stead-fast and reliable? Hers seems to us like borderline behavior. In other spheres — politics, for instance — such behavior breeds fascism, and when there is no talent it generates crime. At the least it is selfish and impervious and hard. But Shakespeare ran off to make his fortune and left behind a wife and young children without help or support. Is Isadora to be more criti-cized for similar behavior because she was a woman?

Even when young, she made no attempt to discipline herself as to food or drink or exercise. When she was middle-aged, she grew fat and soft; she *looked* middle-aged, and saw no reason to try to retain a monstrously overlong adolescence. She became a mother figure, the earth-mother. "Before," said Carl van Vechten, "she had been a nymph from a temple. Now she was the Parthenon itself." She was no athlete. She was a vessel, and the flame illumined her body, whatever size or shape it might take.

This individual genius cannot be taught or imitated, but it should be remembered. We have grown muscularly pedantic and physically factual, and spiritually we have all but ceased to function. Neither should Isadora's life patterns be imitated, but they should be remembered. She lived a foolhardy, dare-devil, wild, bold, and gallant existence. She was an outlaw, a kind of emotional commando. She questioned every single tradition, artistic, social, religious, and moral, and she tested them out for us on her own bleeding spirit. She made us reevaluate all our concepts.

In the end the wildness, the delirium of her ways, and her loneliness destroyed her. She drank heavily. She was exhausted with melancholies and despairs. There were attempts at suicide. She was poor, and she squandered in daft compulsions the money raised by friends. Once in a time of real hunger and illness she was lent a considerable sum and straightaway bought out a flower shop. She must have beauty around her, she said. The donor was understandably taken aback.

Her death was just of this pattern. "Adieu, mes amis," she said as she climbed into an automobile on a fine afternoon in

Nice. "Je vais à la gloire." Her long scarf caught in the hub of the wheel, and the movement of the car suddenly tautened the silk and broke her neck. She was off on that afternoon with an employee of the Bugatti automobile dealer, who was going to show her how well the car took the steep curves of the Grande Corniche. "Je vais à la gloire." What a consummation! Like a bacchante, Isadora gave no thought for the morrow but threw herself upon the moment and counted exaltation return enough. She walked her own high path alone, and the wonder is that it burns still with a passion beyond ridicule, beyond censure, beyond time. She is a great legend. We live by our legends.

ALICIA MARKOVA

BECAUSE OF its evanescence, a characteristic that has been impossible to correct in thousands of years, the dancing art is classed as a minor one. Now, however, we have films and can preserve the beauties of its chief works and its finest performances. Unfortunately, films cost money, and the people with the money have not until recently been persuaded to spend it for anything so commercially unrewarding, with the tragic result that fine works have been lost and the memory of performances of legendary beauty have dimmed into obscurity. Fifty years ago Alicia Markova was acclaimed the greatest of her kind, but who remembers her vividly? Who can recall why she was so outstanding?

I can. I saw her repeatedly. I worked beside her—not with her, but beside her in the same studios, at the same barre, on the same stage. I can testify that she was indeed the stuff of immortality.

Why was she so extraordinary? First of all, her appearance. She had inordinately long arms and legs and a small head. Her body line therefore had the pure luxury of ease and melting continuity that made for delicious phrasing. Her arabesque (a ballet position in which one leg is raised against a strongly arched spine and the supporting leg is straight) was more fragile, aerial, and brilliant than anyone else's, possibly because of the almost double-jointedness of her hip and back. It invariably brought the shock of delight one experiences from the high E of a great coloratura. One old gentleman sitting beside me gasped, "It is not possible, but I see it with my eyes, so she must be doing it."

Her foot was long for her height, but very slender, strongly arched, and as delicate as a bird's claw. On the end of this delicate parenthesis she alighted and hung poised like the crescent moon, a stillness in the movement of time.

She was tiny, dark, compact, and as fragile as Venetian glass. Her legs and ankles seemed so remarkably slender, her hands so tapering, one felt they would snap off with the first jar; actually, a tennis champion's wrist, or a surgeon's, was probably a weaker instrument. In those delicate leg bones she had the kick of a stallion, and although she appeared not to have the virtuosity or durability of, say, a Baronova or a Toumanova, she could in fact do anything (except brilliant turns). Her technique was prodigious; her technique was bolts of lightning and steel. However, it took a professional eye to recognize this. She seemed to laymen to float in a mist, and they remained wonderstruck—even people who professed to hate dancing and who had been dragged to their initial evening of the experience.

In keeping with her unworldly effect, her expression was demure. The dark lashes rested tranquilly against the wax-pale cheek, a Mona Lisa smile was fixed on the noncommittal lips, until she suddenly glanced up in childlike wickedness and chuckled with a tiny sound like something very valuable breaking.

Always about her there was an aroma of sadness, a hint of death in the moment of consummated effort. This was her Jewish heritage, as it was Anna Pavlova's, who made her worldwide reputation with a dance of death, the "Dying Swan."

On reflection, I realize that Markova seemed, for all her delicate beauty, unphysical, even unsexed. Admittedly, no great ballet dancer is physically sensual—preferably, she is the instrument of sensuous release—but she, more than anyone else (with the possible exception of Margot Fonteyn), suggested romance while preserving always the chaste austerity of classic discipline. It could almost be said that the passion of her discipline, like all great restraints, was in itself a kind of sensuality.

Although English (born Lilian Alicia Marks), she was in face and body astonishingly like the Russian Pavlova—the same black-and-white beauty, the same serene brow, the dark, burning eyes, the precise, patient mouth, the swanlike neck. Indeed, Markova was well aware of the likeness and was often accused of modeling her style closely on her great predecessor's. She did not have Pavlova's gift of outright hypnotism, but she did have the same quality of dancing in an aura.

For quite a period she even claimed that the spirit of the Russian inhabited her body. Jerome Robbins, when a very young performer, invariably used to station himself in the wings to watch Markova's *Giselle*, which he felt, as we all did, was history-making and worth attention. But he was impious. As she came offstage with slightly heightened breathing, demanding powder and a towel, he asked pertly, "How's the spirit doing, Alicia? Are you in tune tonight?"

"Not bad, ducky, really not bad." She twinkled. "That last bit was pretty good." Then she was off on a pas de bourrée too rapid for the naked eye to follow. She minded his joking and his mocking not a bit. She simply disregarded it and rushed back onstage to rejoin her "spirit."

Markova's story is straightforward, even simple, a tale of chilling discipline and fanatic acceptance of the proofs, trials, mortifications, and final glories of perfection. Hers might be the history of a nun or a saint, as she was dedicated from youth by her parents to a calling, much in the style of a maiden given to temple service.

She was born in London in 1910, the daughter of a prosperous Jewish engineer named Marks and an Irishwoman who adopted Judaism in its most rigid and orthodox form, marrying in a synagogue. "Think of the strength of mind of that woman — think of the character," said Alicia soberly, fixing her great dark eyes on me as she spoke. "An Irish Catholic, yet she abandoned her entire background and family and accepted, for love of her husband, a way of living so strange and overwhelming."

There was no grand plan in the choice of Alicia's vocation; it came about almost by accident. The little girl was set to dancing simply because she seemed to have an aptitude for it and because her mother had been impressed by Adeline Genée and Anna Pavlova. Alicia herself at the beginning had no overwhelming desire to dance, nor ever expressed one, and correspondingly her family felt strongly neither one way nor the other. But they did all things meticulously in that household, so she applied herself to the job with cool precision, learning to move nicely just as she learned to keep her clothes neat and to speak politely when addressed. She remained always the excellently brought-up middle-class British child, dancing throughout her youth hard and correctly, if without expression of any sort.

Other ballerinas may have been more emotionally infectious, more adorable or communicative. Alicia's art, through sheer concentration and focusing of impulse, became transfigured gradually to the beauty and cold endurance of the star's. A young student, Sydney Francis Patrick Chippendall Healey-Kay, first saw her dancing at the Kensington Theatre in South London on December 27, 1920, and he was so struck with amazement that, in a gesture flashy enough for any Hollywood musical, he rushed out and bought a bunch of white chrysanthemums with the last of his allowance and sent them to her anonymously. Alicia at this point was ten years old and was performing the leading dance in a Christmas pantomime. Her solo, unusual for a child, was an Oriental slave number that ended with a stunning shriek and a stiff-backed fall onto her skull. Alicia remarked with characteristic slyness that she was gratified every night, as she lay panting on the floorboards, to hear gasps of concern and horror.

Her father had wanted a son, but he loved Alicia and shared with his first-born all the interests he had longed to develop in a boy. For many years the future Giselle, the epitome of fragile vulnerability, rushed off in spare moments to rugger matches and ice hockey.

Mr. Marks died when Alicia was thirteen, and Alicia took over the role of head of the family, including the male role at the weekly Sabbath ritual. At this young age she shouldered the support of her mother and three sisters.

Her early dance lessons, her first performances, and even her imminent seasons with the Diaghilev company (with which she danced from age fourteen to nineteen—there didn't seem to be any law about child performers) were policed by a governess-dragon named Guggy, who kept her from all easy contact with other children and colleagues and from all daily effort that was not included in the barre regimen. Alicia could do nothing for herself around the house. She had been appearing with the Ballet Russe for a year before she was forced by Guggy's illness to tie on her own slippers, apply her own makeup, and take her costume off a hanger. As for making a cup of tea, washing her stockings, or sewing on a button, she was helpless! Whenever Guggy had to go out shopping, she locked Alicia into her room with no playmates, not even her younger sisters. Alicia learned to love cats and talked only to them. "After removing my ballet slippers at each performance," she later wrote, "[Guggy] would take them to the strong electric light of the make-up mirror. If she found so much as a spot or a streak on the pink satin, I lost my chocolates, not only for that day, but for the entire week, and, in addition, our visit to the cinema was cancelled."

After the Guggy treatment, becoming first dancer in any company must have seemed a simple task. Is it any wonder this child grew up bewitched by ambition? From the time she was eight she was treated as someone apart, a conditioning usually reserved for young lamas or queen bees. Not even royalty is reared in this wise. It explains much in what dancers have come to recognize as Markova's aloofness. It explains much of the mystery and unworldliness of her art. It explains further her lack of creativity. The girl who did exactly as she was told for over twenty years, who remained as passive as a baby, as cherished, as self-absorbed, grew to be the perfect instrument for more aggressive forces—but herself initiated nothing. Choreographers always agreed that she was a delight to rehearse, as she did precisely what was asked and nothing else. But she knew what would suit her, and her suggestions were valuable. Her memory was legendary: she could remember not only everything she had done, but—much more unusual—what she had merely seen. She could compose nothing, not even a schoolroom series of steps. She had to see and to copy.

This passivity explains her life history, which constitutes an awful and impressive story that she told with the propriety of a Victorian children's tale. Reading her autobiography, one forgets that the chief characters were the mad and rascally bohemians who comprised the Ballet Russe. Diaghilev, the demon-genius who drove them to world renown, became in her version "Sergeypop," the "one whom Alicia considered the greatest man on earth," while the tainted and inflamed group he ruled with such sadistic vigor appeared as kindly folk suitable for any Charlotte M. Yonge novel. One might be reading about nursery teas and how little brother broke his cricket bat. But one is not.

Diaghilev first saw Alicia in the ballet classes conducted by Princess Astafieva in Chelsea and invited her to join his company at Monte Carlo. She was at this point a slight, thin fourteen-year-old with black hair cut in a Dutch bob; she wore white socks and middy blouses. Guggy took her to rehearsals and brought her back to her hotel room. On nights she did not perform she was in bed by seven-thirty.

She was given the lead role in *Le Chant du Rossignol*, Balanchine's first choreography for Diaghilev, in 1925. She made a notable première at the Lyrique in Paris, with Stravinsky conducting. Her success earned her the promise of better roles. I saw her in 1929, when she was eighteen or nineteen, dancing the "Blue Bird" variation and Papillon in Schumann's *Carnaval* at the Coliseum in London. She seemed like any string-bean adolescent in a diamante bandeau, like a little girl dressed up in her mother's party clothes. I think she must have weighed sixty pounds. She had all the voluptuousness of a grasshopper, but she hit the stage like a veteran. For all her youth, she *was* a veteran.

Unfortunately, Diaghilev died in that year. The immediate disbanding of his company brought Alicia's career to an abrupt stop. At that point the young choreographer Frederick Ashton introduced her to Marie Rambert's tiny Ballet Club theater in Notting Hill Gate in London, and there he devised ballets for her. The little auditorium seated only 125, but its stage was the only place where she was invited to perform. Her salary was ten shillings and sixpence—roughly $2.50—a performance, a sum worked out to cover the exact cost of new slippers and taxi fare. Rambert thought that Alicia could very well use buses and dance like the others for eight shillings, but the Number 52 bus did not run after 11:00 P.M., and Alicia won out. This was a good thing from a prestige point of view, because it ensured her and Ashton (who also got ten and six) the highest salaries at the Ballet Club.

Ashton was her artistic mentor and coach, but there was

also another, a protégé of Diaghilev's who had danced leads with the greatest and who believed in Alicia's fabulous promise. He was her first admirer, Sydney Francis Patrick Chippendall Healey-Kay, an Irish boy, now transformed into Anton Dolin. He had studied beside her in Astafieva's classes and watched her progress in the Diaghilev troupe, where he himself had starred, and he now became her partner and constant companion.

Dolin was internationally known but by no means in Alicia's class as an artist. He was athletic, flamboyant, and unbridled, and produced narcissistic displays of egotism matched by only a few. With her, however, he curbed his more aggressive instincts, and he served her truly and well. They made a remarkable couple, the unleashed vulgarity of the one offsetting the purity of the other. When she joined him he was busy making a commercial career in the music halls; he took her on as partner, and she obediently did the two and three performances a day with surprising zest. From time to time they made forays to the Continent with a more legitimate concert group. Alicia always returned to the Ballet Club in between trips.

In 1934 she was invited to join the newly founded Blum–de Basil Ballet Russe as a soloist, which promised international exposure, but she decided instead to throw in her lot with Ninette de Valois and the budding Sadler's Wells company, on the promise that they would mount all the great classics for her on a normal-size stage. This decision plunged her advisers into acute consternation; they implored her not to bury herself in a group of students in the suburbs. She followed her instinct, however, and in January 1934 starred in the first full-length English *Giselle*.

Marie Rambert took me to the première. People were very proud of Alicia. She was a hometown girl and doing nicely, but of course, they thought, was not to be compared to the Russians—to Toumanova, Baronova, or Danilova. Ninette de Valois and Rambert thought otherwise, de Valois for patriotic reasons and Rambert because she based her opinions not on current comment but on exactly what was before her eyes, and her eyes were among the sharpest in England. I was present when she took Alicia's head gently in her hands and kissed her. "You have come of age," she whispered.

Giselle was followed by *The Nutcracker* and the complete *Swan Lake*. Alicia now had the three great classic roles under her belt, something she never could have achieved in twelve months with any other company. She left the Wells to help form the Markova-Dolin Company (1935-38), with Bronislava Nijinska as chief choreographer. Then, in 1938, she joined Massine and the Ballet Russe and started touring the world, wishing to give herself serious competition and wider challenge. In the Russian company she was just one of an incredible group of soloists, which included Danilova, Toumanova, Youskevitch, Slavenska, Riabouchinska.

Markova's name was at this point practically unknown in America. She could not possibly consider herself a star until she danced *Giselle* in New York. That night everything she did provoked an ovation, an eventuality that her partner, Serge Lifar, had not foreseen. He became upset, and somehow, as Alicia was being set down from a high lift, her foot became broken. "However," Alicia told me later, "I continued the whole solo variation, little hops on pointe and all. Think of it: right across the stage on one toe on a fractured foot. In the mad scene I began to feel something was wrong, and it seems at the end I passed out cold."

"When finally Alicia stepped out in front of the curtain alone" — this was Lifar's rival, Pat Dolin, speaking straight from the heart — "she was greeted by a roar of applause that was almost terrifying. Just behind the curtain Lifar was being held back by two male dancers."

New York had witnessed enough to know what moved before its dazzled eyes, and the city and all its press were at Markova's feet, broken or sound. Backstage there was a good deal of explanation in Russian about what had happened, and some plain monosyllabic English.

When the Ballet Russe split into two sections after phenomenal quarrels, threats, and lawsuits, Markova joined the Massine faction and toured with them for some years. Then she moved to the American Ballet Theatre, in one of those swift coups that proceed so naturally and spontaneously from lunch at the Russian Tea Room.

Dolin had been a choreographer and star in the American Ballet Theatre since its inception in 1940, and had been anxious to install his great colleague and partner in the new fold. For her part, Markova was nothing loath to rejoin him, for he had proved over a long period more understanding than anyone else in setting dances for her. He was, moreover, a remarkable theatrical figure in his own right and was acknowledged generally as an unmatched partner for classic work. Markova was annexed as top star. Gollner, Baronova, and Stroganova, their noses just a touch out of joint, stepped obediently aside.

Dolin treated Markova in many ways like royalty. He insisted that the red carpet be spread. She always had the star dressing room, the best accommodations, the biggest billing, the longest orchestra rehearsals, and the largest salary — with one exception: his own. At the time she worked for Ballet Theatre, she got the largest salary of any woman in the business — four hundred dollars a week.

Madame Marks, as she used to be called at Ballet Club, knew her own wishes. She never shared her dressing room with another woman. She insisted that every costume be cleaned each time she wore it. (Costumes almost invariably belong to the company, not, as in opera, to the star performers, and two or three ballet stars have to share the same dresses.) Nora Kaye came offstage one night during *Romeo and Juliet* and held out her arms for the next costume, a cloth-of-gold robe. She was informed that Markova had visited the theater that afternoon and that on her instructions the overeager dresser had sent the costumes to the cleaners; there would be no further changes during the current performance. On hearing this news, Miss Kaye's face was, as they say, a study.

At that time Markova lived sparsely in unmodified hotel rooms, without a personal maid. She had instead a kind of acolyte—neither dresser nor maid, but a humble young professional who ran errands, stood by, listened, sympathized, handed things, and worshiped. This person was always present and silent. Besides her recompense she received instruction and coaching in ballet technique and the daily opportunity of watching genius. Markova always talked in front of her as though she were not there, with regal imperviousness to human criticism; two or three intimate attendants constituted for her complete privacy.

It goes without saying that her discipline about sleep, food, and drink was rigid, continuous, and lifelong. She did not smoke. Her only real expenditure was on ravishing clothes by name designers, but these did not include furs or jewels. She held herself to a severe budget, permitting herself a first mink coat only after the South African tour in 1949. About twenty-five years of dancing paid for this. She always supplied all her own tutus (to ensure their freshness), her own headpieces and accessories, and, of course, all slippers and tights—a very sizable expense. She rarely entertained.

Dolin seemed to live high and fancy, but he was doing public relations for both of them, and Markova paid for half. It was always Dolin who held court in his dressing room for columnists, civic functionaries, movie stars, and fans, talking his way through cold cream and towels. His dressing room had the air of a levee, but he usually remembered to point out the quiet little figure, already cleaned up and dressed impeccably, sitting in attentive silence.

He was very grand at these séances, lounging about in his expensive dressing gown. He was ducal, even royal, languidly receiving homage and never rising. At one interview I stood in his dressing room for ten minutes discussing problems about the current production (he was appearing in my *Tally-Ho*, and there was much about his performance that distressed me). Elsa Maxwell was in the other chair, but he didn't bother to introduce us. He also didn't bother to offer me a seat. At the end of the interview I said quietly, "You must excuse me for not removing my hat," and I left the room.

When the royal couple went out socially, it was Pat with his Irish wit who talked; Alicia, looking exquisite, sat in a nimbus of attention and chirped. She was not seen too often without him. Two of Pat's jobs as big brother and partner were to escort her to dinner and to see that she amused herself in her scarce leisure moments. I have known him, with this in mind, to take her out to watch him play bridge. Alicia did not play bridge. If by any maneuver you could sneak her away, get her feet up, her hair down (metaphorically, of course; not a hairpin was ever loosened, even by her speedy daily activities), a very small drink in her hands, you would find her reminiscences worth the effort. The fact that she rarely took time out to comment does not mean that such passed her unremarked.

Her fame grew. She received all the prizes, all the medals, the OBE being her crowning achievement. Alicia is a dame of the British Empire and can quite correctly be addressed as Dame Alicia, although I think she prefers her old Ballet Club sobriquet, Madame Marks.

In the summer of 1941, Dolin organized a school and concert series at Jacob's Pillow, Ted Shawn's farm near Lee, Massachusetts, using the personnel of American Ballet Theatre spiced with visiting guest soloists. I was to be a weekend spice. I arrived on a rainy night to find matters in considerable turmoil. There were tales of Markova hurrying from several classes in tears. Baronova was crying down the road in a neighboring farmhouse. Everyone rushed around, very busy with housekeeping and rehearsal chores, stopping only to snarl at one another. I was assigned to a dormitory with Lucia Chase, who wasn't crying that summer; Nina Stroganova, who was; and Nana Gollner, who moved through all with good-natured untidiness.

When I arrived at Jacob's Pillow, Markova had been closeted

upstairs for two days and showed no signs of coming down, although the weekend performances were imminent. Passing across the upper hall, I peeped unkindly through the half-open door. She lay in Ted Shawn's great double bed, stretched like Rachel on her death couch, the dark silken locks unmoving against the waxen shoulders. The eyes, neither open or shut, stared in sealed misery.

Few changes had been made in the room. Beyond replacing photographs of Shawn and his young men naked in the wind with more maidenly symbols — the ballerina's tutus suspended as always inside out, a satin ribbon tossed on the dressing table and a silk robe over a chair — the great star had done nothing to transform any of her rooms. She was a transient everywhere except in the theater dressing room. In that room only was she at home, and half an hour after she took possession, all the implements of her trade and her working comforts were in place.

In the farm bedroom the little head remained unmoving against its pillow. I watched for some time in fascinated shame. Tears trickled down her cheeks in an unending stream. In an adjacent room another lady devotee of Dolin's lay ill and weeping. (Most great male dance stars, I have noticed, seem to have one or more of these dedicated followers trailing after them, asking, and getting, absolutely nothing except the privilege of attending to mail, shopping a little, keeping a list of the star's social engagements, and waiting hand and foot on the brilliant center of their attention. Sometimes they are paid as secretaries and sometimes they foot their own bills.)

Downstairs the new master of Jacob's Pillow sat at dinner. The hoi polloi — the corps de ballet and friends — ate in a kind of barracks, but I, as guest artist, was entitled to a place on the host's right.

"Rooms full of weeping women," he said, spooning up his soup vigorously. "I wish they'd either get well or . . ."

"Or what, Pat?" I asked.

"Or — well, now look here, ducky, the house is getting

positively soppy with tears. What good does it do them to go on like this? I must say I think they enjoy it, I really do, but *I* certainly don't. For one thing, the weather's too damp."

"I think Alicia is not enjoying herself."

"Then why doesn't she stop? Women are too preposterously silly." He called to the cook, "Send a tray up to Madame Markova."

This was promptly returned untouched.

"Pat, what is the matter with her?"

Parenthetically, I wish to remark that for all his naughtiness, capriciousness, and flamboyance, Anton Dolin was one of the kindest-hearted men in the dance world. When there was genuine trouble he was the first to help. He labored for years to get the insane Nijinsky asylum in America. He succored Olga Spessivtzeva in her lamentable madness. He helped innumerable young artists with money. In the case of Markova, he shared an alliance of friendship and ambition. He was devoted to her, even dependent on her, but he could never resist wicked Irish mockery.

Alicia continued crying until it was nearly performance time and active measures had to be taken. An old friend and balletomane, a father and head of a household and thus someone used to family tantrums, advanced into her chamber of melancholy, pulled her from the bed, and shook her until her teeth rattled. "Alicia," he said, "if you don't start getting ready for this afternoon's performance, I'm going to turn you over my knee."

She whimpered and started to pick at her makeup. He left her to the care of assistants, who, scared to death and speechless, rushed to propel her through the preparations. She was supported across the yard to the theater. The porches still dripped with summer rain. There was the smell all about of wet pine and the green glitter that promised a brilliant sunset.

Alicia leaned in her dressing gown against a dank post. Her acolyte waited round-eyed beside her with the tray of powder, hairpins, and mirror. I was about to do a comedy dance and stopped to say that I hoped Alicia felt better. She gave me a graveyard smile and looked west to the Berkshires. Paddy Barker, her student assistant, shook her head with the air of a nurse who knows that the end is inevitable but hopes it will be quick.

When I left the stage, Alicia was in her skirt and trying out the points of her slippers. Her breath still came unevenly from crying. Below stairs, while I changed, I listened to the music of the prelude from *Les Sylphides* and felt the slight jarring of the floor overhead from her great soft descents. At the conclusion, there was a full six seconds of silence and then tumult.

Several girls drifted below and stood dazed. "What happened?" I asked. They sat, unable to continue with their changes. It seemed Markova had never before approached the beauty of her performance that afternoon.

I hastened to offer my congratulations. Alicia was bouncing around upstairs in the farmhouse, clad in a darling dressing gown and as happy as Christmas morning, purged, delivered, vindicated. She had tied a bow in her hair. "It was rather good, you know," she said to me with brilliant eyes. "I can't say I was too displeased."

"The girls said it was transcendent."

She put her head on one side and considered. "It was all right," she said. Then she scampered off down the hall to visit the other invalid's room, whence presently came peals of girlish giggles. They sent down for enormous trays of food.

I do not know why she carried on this way. I do know that she had only one concern in life: to dance better and better and better. This was all she did. She did not interest herself in one other thing. She never married—never, as far as I know, was even engaged. She was given over from early childhood to a dedicated and exacting vocation. Outraged nature must have backed up on her from time to time and taken blackmail payments. The sacrifice she made was enormous. Whether or not it was necessary is a question she probably asked herself from time to time at lonely moments.

Alicia came to the theater as a rule before anyone else. For a gala she was in and out of the place all day, but for each routine appearance she was on hand at least three hours ahead of time. Her room seemed as businesslike and as prophylactic as a surgery. The dressing table had pristine, dainty skirts and spotless cloths laid over the makeup. On a white-covered table lay her shoes, pair by pair, long and exceedingly narrow (triple A). Markova's feet were flawless — white, supple, and unmarked. Most dancers' feet look like the ace of clubs: gnarled, jointed, skinned, bruised, and blackened, with horny nails and rubbings and scars that have bitten into the tissue. The feet of dancers who dance barefoot cannot be imagined; they are hoofs. But Markova gave her feet solicitous, almost medical, care, and they were dreams.

She took ten minutes to put on her shoes. She cleaned everything she owned every day. She puttered and fussed and mended, the acolyte sometimes helping her clean, sometimes watching her. But often Alicia was alone and wanted it so. She was like a young mother assembling her first layette, cutting off connections with the world. She was already beginning to connect with the audience. They did not know this. It was afternoon still; many of them were at their offices. It would be an hour yet before they got ready for dinner.

After some while of this meandering, Alicia put on practice clothes and her makeup base and went onstage for a lesson from her coach, Vincenzo Celli. Celli put her through an hour or two of everything he could think of. In lieu of a barre, she hung on to the wardrobe trunks or the tormentors. Other members of the company appeared and started practicing, but apart from her. When she left the stage to go to her dressing room, she was dripping. Her acolyte waited with a towel, for from now on she had to keep in a light sweat. (Her audience was probably now having cocktails.) She sponged off and finished her makeup. She gave half an hour to her hair.

Twenty minutes before curtain she stripped and got into her all-silk tights. I have seen Alicia stripped. She had no body at all. She had no bust, no stomach, no hips, no buttocks; she had two long supple arms and two long strong legs, joined by a device that contained in the most compact manner possible enough viscera to keep her locomotive. She was utterly feminine but as incorporeal as a dryad. Her slenderness, her lack of unneeded flesh, was a rebuke to everything gross in the world.

The tights were held taut by elastics and tapes that wrapped around her twenty-one-inch waist (this was long before the time of elasticized stockings and tights). Her toes were swathed very exactly in lamb's wool to prevent shoe friction, and the priceless little mummies were then inserted into the flawlessly clean satin boxes, which were glued to her heel. (Pavlova used spit in the heel of her shoe, in the old tradition; Alicia used LePage's glue — it is stronger.) Then the ribbons were sewn; she had to be cut out of her shoes after a performance. Five minutes before curtain she stepped into the tutu. As the orchestra started she walked onto the stage. It always took four men to help her with the flowers on the return journey.

Classification is silly. Many stars are flabbergasting artists, quite different and mostly blessedly contemporary. When performers reach this standard of excellence, choosing between them becomes a matter of personal taste. But John Martin of the *New York Times* dared to risk his very considerable reputation by writing, "[Markova] is not only the greatest ballet dancer in the world today, but very possibly the greatest that ever lived" — a claim impossible to substantiate, but eye-catching.

I happened to be backstage the day after Martin's incredible pronouncement was printed. In my minor way, I was going through the process of warming up, quieting down, and cutting off from daily life. I passed Alicia's room. She was standing alone, rubbing the toe of a slipper with a piece of gauze soaked in benzine.

"Alicia," I said, slipping onto her sofa, "tell me something. As one woman to another, how does it feel to read in a newspaper a statement like Martin's — 'the greatest ballet dancer of all time'?"

"That's very well and good," said Alicia, placing the slipper precisely beside its fellow, drawing her silk dressing gown up neatly, and sitting down with crossed ankles. "It's easy to write something like that, but it's I who have to live up to it. What am I to do the next day, I ask you? I said to Celli, I must work all the harder. I mean, ducky, the audience is going to expect something after reading that bit. It will be hard lines if I let them down. There's always the next performance to think of. That's what I said to Celli."

Alicia had at the time reached the age (not a great one) when in the days of Russia's Imperial Ballet the stars were forcibly retired and pensioned, but she was dancing better than ever, with virtuosity and an enormous brilliance of dynamics and power. Instead of slacking off with the years, she seemed to be attaining greater and greater physical and emotional strength and achieving subtler and more exquisite refinements of style.

Building her reputation had been hard; maintaining it was harder. When Pavlova danced, she was the only great ballet star most of us had seen, and she brought with her the excitement of revelation. The theaters of Markova's day bulged with dandy technicians, and the beady eyes out front were knowledgeable and blasé, while in the wings stood those ready and able to crowd the star off center spot. If Markova seemed at times mettlesome to the girls and boys who worked with her, she was only fighting for her position and her future. One mistaken step from an assistant, one hand on a wrong light lever, undid a hundred hours of practicing. Markova might have had the proverbial nervous temper of a ballerina; she also had the responsibility. She might have seemed fragile, childish, and gentle, but cross her will, or turn on the wrong light, or make a damaging mistake in tempo, and you would know why Britain had withstood the blitz and held Gibraltar and girdled the world, and lasted as long as any other country in recorded history.

After an ovation, this airy, fairy, feathery little thing was known to place an armful of white orchids deliberately on the floor, pass silently and exquisitely over to where the head electrician waited uncomfortably, and break him.

She was acclaimed the greatest ballet dancer for just one reason: she intended to be.

K A T H E R I N E
D U N H A M

WHEN KATHERINE DUNHAM started her career in the early thirties, there were only a half dozen black dancers in New York. There were tap dancers, it is true, there were eccentric dancers, and there were the lively members of the Cotton Club line, but there were no dancers outside the commercial media, and the commercial dances did not include any moderns, any ballet, any ethnic or folk—not one. There were no black students of dance, for the good reason that there were absolutely no opportunities for them to perform. There was accordingly no hope and little pride.

The first Broadway show to mix races was the Howard

Dietz–Arthur Schwartz 1932 musical *Flying Colors*, which I co-choreographed with Warren Leonard and which had a serious ballet called "Smokin' Reefers." When I say the races were mixed, I mean they were housed simultaneously in the same theater, but they were prophylactically separated, quite segregated, the one group moving onstage as the other left it; they never mingled in view of the audience. The same, of course, was true of the dressing room and backstage arrangements.

The black girls, in those days called "colored," were a heterogeneous bunch—physical education teachers, tap dancers from the Cotton Club, gymnasts, honky-tonk girls, and just plain flotsam and jetsam having nothing to qualify them except their color. A few were highly gifted; some were disciplined. Some were savages, literally. In those ugly days the black girls were not permitted to use the white girls' toilet, and the conveniences permitted them were generally unspeakably filthy. They were shut up twelve hours in the theater. They made do as they could. They were forced to. They were all or nearly all on the verge of hysteria, and the hysteria was not without cause. The show's designer, Norman Bel Geddes, did not let a concern for safety restrain his fantasy. The girls were asked to dance (not by me) in costumes that blocked their vision and bound their arms tightly to their bodies, so they were unable to get their hands free, even when they had to pass close to lights of such intensity that any contact could have set them aflame. They had to walk out on platforms thirty feet above the heads of the actors below and dance without a guard rail of any sort.

There were, as a matter of fact, dreadful accidents. One time they were all seated on tall ladders, the white girls on the bottom rungs, which were safe, and the black girls on the top rungs, which were unsafe. During the performance one ladder tipped and fell over against a second, and so they toppled like dominoes right around the stage. The black girls at the top of the last ladder, knowing for a full six seconds that they were going to fall before they actually did, were helpless to save themselves, and waited in frozen horror. By the time the last one was lifted off her prone ladder, her hands had become hysterically fixed in rigor to the wooden rungs; she had to be taken to the hospital.

There was another reason for emotion. One night at a dress rehearsal the black girls began screaming in the dressing room, twenty of them shrieking and out of control. We all worked on them—stars, chorus boys, chorus girls, members of the staff—with pitchers of cold water, wet towels, and slapping hands. Then I said, in a moment of vision, "Are you hungry?" I gave them, I remember, $10 of my own money to buy steak. (You could buy quite a lot of steak for $10 in 1932. The weekly rehearsal fee that year was $20.) They came back happy as lambs and danced beautifully.

I was fired from that show, and Albertina Rasch put her name on my work, but that is not this story. When I was given a chance to do a ballet for the Ballet Theater, in its opening season (1940) at the New York Center Theater, I premiered my first work, *Black Ritual*, a voodoo ceremony with an entirely black cast to the music of Darius Milhaud's *La Création du Monde*. This was not an authentic ritual, but my idea of what a voodoo celebration might likely be. I chose to do a Negro ballet not because I knew anything about the black heritage or black roots, but because I was shy of rehearsing my first work in the studios uptown, where the regular company worked out side by side with Michel Fokine, Anton Dolin, Adolph Bolm, Antony Tudor, and Eugene Loring.

I was given a studio down on Fifth Avenue near 14th Street, and we began gathering girls together again in the same haphazard way as we had done for *Flying Colors*—the same sorts of girls—and the rehearsal conditions were, as before, chaotic. We met at night after our regular jobs were over. It was very hard to hold the dancers together. They were late. They were absent. They went to funerals. They went to christenings. Any excuse would do. I never had the same group three nights running.

Finally one evening I gathered them together and confessed, "I can't go on. This is my first chance to do a ballet for a big company, but it's also your first chance as black girls"—"as colored girls," I said—"to appear in a major opera house with a major ballet company. The chance has never existed before. You must do yourselves proud and I hope you'll do me proud, because it's my chance." Then I dismissed rehearsal.

The next night when I went back, there on the piano was a bouquet of flowers from these starving girls. I said to them, "I'm touched to the heart, but you must keep regular hours and you must come or we can't get the work done. Now we will take half an hour off and have some hot soup, which has been prepared for us by a friend." Another dancer, white, had made marvelous mutton soup, and we all had a big bowlful and hot rolls, and then they were ready to work. We kept the dancers fed thereafter, and they turned in a beautiful job. Their main deficiency, it seemed, had not been race or poverty or lack of training; it was, in plain English, hunger.

At this point I was looking around for a leading lady. The girl I had chosen, Luane Kennard, although extraordinarily beautiful, proved to have no magnetism. My friend Mary Hunter suggested that I take into my group Katherine Dunham, who had just come east from Chicago. Dunham had made a success in her hometown and had built a good name for herself, chiefly at the University of Chicago, but she was still unknown in the East. She had recently been brought to New York by the head of the needle trades theater for her debut. So three times she sat in the anteroom of my rehearsals, waiting for me to interview and audition her—waiting long stretches of time with a sweetness and humility most extraordinary to remember.

In the end I chose not to use her. In a way this was a historic blunder, but in another I followed a very real instinct for self-protection: my work for the blacks, although quite sincere, was false. Dunham could not possibly have fitted in with the design I was fashioning, nor the technique. Whether or not she would have wished to is also questionable. I had a strong hunch that maybe she would evince more talent than I could absorb, and some apprehension prompted me not to expose myself to humiliation.

Indeed, she would have been difficult to assimilate, because shortly after the Ballet Theatre season (in which *Black Ritual* failed), she had her own opening and was an uproarious success. Her dancing—stimulating and effective, vigorous, full of life, immediately and adorably communicative—was perfectly irresistible. She was thereupon invited to give a series of Sunday nights. New York took her to its heart and made her a very big reputation. It is amusing to think of that near encounter and how patiently and sweetly Katherine submitted to my whims and nervous terrors. Forty days after the experience—literally about forty days—she was as well known as I was, if not better known.

She needed girls, and so she selected whom she liked from my group, now unemployed: Luane Kennard, whom she chose quite rightly to put into a minor chorus role, and Lavinia Williams (the mother of Sara Yarborough, later a star with Alvin Ailey), and some few others. It was out of very rough material, misfits mostly, that Dunham made her first group, with patient, antlike industry, day by day by day. It is hard enough for the rest of us to compose dances with trained students. Katherine had to do all the training herself, and she produced results that were astonishing. She asked of her group nothing they could not physically do, and do right away, without months of study (although she did set them to practicing very hard daily). She was able to produce with the simplest and most direct means a sense of spontaneity and exuberance, something that requires the highest skill, so that her dancers seemed right and comfortable in all they did. She simply set them dancing, and they seemed just to be having a good time. They were thus able to enjoy immediate results, and this was probably the main reason she was able to hold these tatterdemalion gypsies together.

Katherine always seemed natural, and her large scenes with many people always seemed spontaneous—totally deceptive impressions, both. Her large scenes were works of art and were organized with deft skill. It was her tragedy that she was the first of her kind. At the time her concerts were introduced to the American public, blacks had not been indoctrinated to concert work and did not buy tickets; their own theater was entirely given over to tap dancing and nightclub routines. Katherine's sophisticated studies of folk materials were new to them, and the experience of going to the downtown Broadway theaters and mixing with white audiences was unfamiliar. Change in this has come about very, very slowly. There has been by both races a great reluctance to mingle and share, not only in the cities of the South but in the cities of the North as well. Katherine had to plow ahead with largely white audiences, which, it is true, she conquered completely, as was her wont. But there were disadvantages.

She herself had a very simple technique: a rudiment of ballet, I suppose some small aspects of modern — Duncan perhaps — but no tap, none of the big virtuoso black forms. She never attempted what she could not do, and whatever she did was accomplished with great finish and deftness. The treasure she gave was her personality, and that was nothing short of magic, for she had the unusual combination of seductiveness — very real, compelling, and strong — and humor. There have been many great comic women dancers, but few who have been sexually alluring. Among these few (Raquel Meller, Renée Jeanmaire, Gwen Verdon), the combination of both talents signifies, of course, a really first-class mind. Katherine combined all of these qualities with the viewpoint of a scholar and a scientist. In this I think she was unique.

A good part of her success was due to the unfailing and delicious wit of John Pratt, her husband and collaborator, who had been a painter of promise in his young days in Chicago but had given it up to design costumes and scenery for Katherine. These had to be paid for entirely out of company funds, which Katherine for the most part earned. To keep costs down, Pratt employed an ingenuity that has rarely been matched, using all kinds of material, new designs, new fabrics, new devices. His problem was to create folk costumes that could be made, for the most part, by extremely poor people possessing a minimum of craft. He made use of all the good cotton prints he could find, from Japan, from Africa, from the West Indies (these were probably manufactured in Birmingham, England, but they were intended for the island trade), as well as straw from Cuba and South America and artificial flowers and hats from all over. Wherever the company traveled, it purchased whatever the troupe could lug along.

Pratt's daring and joyousness, his unexpected combinations, and the humor and the piquancy of his ideas as displayed on beautiful young black bodies were an unexpected delight. He made his wife one of the most attractive sirens in the western world. Her hats were outsized, her skirts had more flounces than seemed possible, the roses she put on were manifold, and the fake jewelry was extraordinary, but it all worked together. Pratt used rags and working materials like denim and corduroy, or the most wonderful hand-dyed goods, like the Haitian "Gros Blue" and "Carabella" and cheap Martinique prints, and the effect was merry and persuasive and humorous, while never, ever condescending. Blacks often have a flair for dress, which he indulged and accentuated.

Pratt worked for very few artists other than his wife, but that does not lessen in any way the impact of his style. Some of the notables for whom he did work were Alicia Markova, Harry Belafonte, Miriam Makeba, Jerome Robbins in *Look Ma, I'm Dancing*, and Hermione Gingold. In Chicago, he dressed the Balaban and Katz Chorus Line. He died on March 26, 1986, of cancer of the mouth. An inveterate smoker, he refused to curb his habit until it was too late to save his life. His death was a great loss to the theater, as there are few finer costume designers.

Katherine Dunham was a pioneer, very truly. She had to train her company, as a good many others have. But she also had to take care of them, shield them, protect them, and in a real sense maintain them. She had no money, but she had to see that these people were housed and fed despite every possible prejudice and barrier. It amounts to a historic achievement.

People forget. Now people can go anywhere, stay anywhere, but in the thirties and early forties it was terrible for blacks, particularly on tour. In 1930 I gave a midnight performance for managers and agents; I rented the tiny Little Theater for the purpose, closing off the balcony and filling only the orchestra seats. I wanted our beloved cook-housekeeper, Mildred, who was black, to see the show, and sent word that she must be admitted. The management would not seat her downstairs with the white audience. They opened the dark, empty balcony and ushered her in, absolutely alone, and she sat there, solitary, throughout the evening. I heard about this from the management, and she was very embarrassed that I had heard, because she knew the news would pain me. Mind you, this was not in the Deep South; this was in New York.

In 1944, fourteen years later, I met up with Katherine in Hollywood. She had gone from success to success, and quite wonderful things had happened to me. I was in the West with American Ballet Theatre rehearsing *Tally-Ho*. She was there with her troupe, rehearsing and performing. Every city she went to posed the same problem: How should she house and protect her girls and boys? She solved the Hollywood situation by renting an unfurnished house that had once belonged to Wallace Reid, the great silent film star, and by laying pallets side by side on the floor. There were cooking utensils and plastic or paper plates and cups, but I don't think they had anything else. She and John kept a room for themselves and a closet for her beautiful costumes, and John set up his sewing machine among the mattresses. There he stitched on the costumes that made theatrical history, and there the girls helped him sew. In this way Katherine was able to keep her dancers out of the dreadful rooming houses and filthy hotels to which they would otherwise have been relegated. The dimensions of this persistent problem and the amount of trouble it caused her have never been discussed, but they were significant.

While I was in Hollywood I wanted to take Katherine out

to lunch—but where? This was 1944. I went to Chasen's and asked for an upstairs banquet room, which they opened up for me. There Katherine could eat a simple restaurant lunch as my guest. She came with her elegant husband; Katherine, draped in stone martens, looked rather better than a movie star—say, Merle Oberon. We had a good lunch with some friends I thought Katherine would like to meet. I looked all around the room at the stacked tables and chairs, and I bowed my head before this young woman who was one of our major artists and who was leading her people and mine, my colleagues, to great things. Downstairs the restaurant was fairly full, but there were plenty of empty tables.

About a dozen years later I met her in Kingston, Jamaica. I had heard that she was dancing there, and my husband, who was her manager, had to talk about business. She was very dispirited. She had just concluded a triumphant tour of South America in which she had been quite literally the toast of every big city and had made a very great deal of money. Alas, her business manager had absconded with the lot; she had been plucked clean. She was as penniless as before she had begun the trip. Dear Katherine! It was careless of her. She should have safeguarded herself. She didn't. We sat in the garden of a broken-down Jamaican mansion, and she gave me a beautiful little basket that she had found in some Latin American country, to carry my powder compact and handkerchief in. "It's all I have at the moment," she said. She also gave me a very, very small emerald to take to Mae Frohman, Sol Hurok's assistant and her particular sponsor, explaining, "This has been a bad year, or the emerald would be a much bigger one." She and John Pratt then sat glumly in their tropical garden. The Jamaicans had not yet learned how to go to the theater and how to respond; anything as sophisticated as Katherine was quite beyond them.

Many years have passed, a lifetime of achievement, and Katherine has been through many experiences, glories and disasters. She has been a star in Broadway musicals, a *grande vedette* in Paris, a star in London. For the past twenty years she has spent a good part of the time in Port-au-Prince, Haiti, where she has a sizable property with a beautiful villa, in large part designed and built by John Pratt. The house centers on a swimming pool fed by rock springs and contains a big kitchen and enough bedrooms to rent out to paying guests. Katherine has her own wing, with a master bedroom containing a bed of some acreage—the largest I have ever seen—and a sunken bathtub. Since she has grown somewhat portly and arthritic (for years her knees have given her wicked trouble), she has been forced to resort to a wheelchair and always the arm of an assistant. I wondered about the sunken bath. "How does Katherine use her gorgeous Roman bath?" I asked. "With difficulty," replied her assistant.

Across the road from Katherine's living quarters lies her enormous estate, which once belonged to Pauline Bonaparte, Napoleon's sister, and her husband, General Leclerc. Only a few columns of the original mansion still stand, but many stone buildings have grown up since, as have formal gardens, and around and through all stands the great primeval jungle: mahogany trees, rubber trees, frangipani, every kind of tropical nut and fruit, dark, mysterious, superb, and unfamiliar. These trees themselves, let alone the historic remains, are of considerable worth. I think Katherine wishes to make a museum of the place, and the Haitian government would do well to listen to her.

Her present position on the island is extraordinary. She is a ranking personage in voodoo, having gone through the complete initiation. She is a known writer of delightful and beautifully composed books. She is a recognized anthropologist, and of course she is the best-known dancer the Haitians have ever sheltered. She is also a hostess with an international, interracial, world-famous circle of friends. She is Madame Dunham, decorated by the government and treated like royalty. Her position and property have remained undisturbed even through the recent political unrest.

There she is so treated, but not here. Part of every year she teaches at the University of Illinois in East St. Louis, a bleak spot with not a friendly tree nor a friendly bush, a neighborhood of decaying houses and obsolete businesses and cracked pavement, a neighborhood of sinister, eerie aspect like a dream: sinister to enter, dangerous to stay in. Indeed, Katherine's leading dancer was murdered there for the few dollars he had withdrawn from a bank in order to visit his mother. The place seems friendless and hopeless. But there Katherine is established, with her drums and her tape equipment and her many assistants. There she teaches, and the children, the young men and women, come to her by the dozens.

Nominally these students attend the University of Illinois, but in reality they come to Katherine, and they sit in the room while she beats drums and her assistants beat drums and she establishes the ancient rhythms. She talks to them about the way the Latins walk and the Indians walk and the Negroes walk and the mixtures of these, and then she says, in her little-girl, ever-fresh voice, "You see how it is." Then she shows them. Because of her weight, one would think she would waddle, but Katherine Dunham does not waddle. She walks like a princess, a lovely girl, still magic. "You see how it is. Now do it."

Of course they can't do it. She can't explain how she does it. This is living art; this is the thing that cannot be explained. But the compelling and imaginative alternatives she offers these troubled young people have persuaded several away from lives of crime and drugs and have even, according to police record, broken up gangs. She does it easily, as a matter of course. They cannot — but someone will. Someone will take fire. There will be a follower. The young keep coming.

Katherine Dunham's honors and medals are in many respects history-making. She has of course received the usual American tokens of esteem, culminating in the Kennedy Center Award and the recent President's National Award for the Arts. Very unusually, she has been given the Albert Schweitzer Award for her humanitarian work in fostering intercultural rapprochement. Through Brazil, she received the Gold Medal for the Dance from UNESCO's International Committee on Dance. In Brazil also she broke the color line, receiving the country's highest civilian distinction, the Order of the Southern Cross, and helping to win passage of laws forbidding discrimination on the basis of color, religion, or origin. In Haiti she holds (among many other distinctions) the Grand Cross of the Legion of Merit, that country's highest civilian award, and in France she is an Officer in the National Legion of Honor and Merit. These medals and ribbons are all very beautiful, and whenever Katherine is on display she wears them across her breast.

Dunham's contribution is like no other, and oddly enough, it is the one true historical contribution of her people to American dance. Alvin Ailey produced a vigorous and remarkable group, but the technique is entirely modern dancing and ballet, and the treatment of all the subjects is, from the dance point of view, totally modern. Arthur Mitchell's Dance Theatre of Harlem is splendid, but that company's technique is classic ballet, and in particular Balanchine's, and it performs only ballet works. Dunham alone has tried to reconstruct the dances of black people: American, African, Caribbean, South American, Latin American, all of them. She has done this with a remarkable eye for exactitude, not pedantically, but with deep feeling. For these reasons she has given us a panorama of black dancing in the West which is historically important and aesthetically beautiful and moving.

Dunham belongs in the great folk tradition of Uday Shankar and Igor Moiseyev, but she is less formal in design, less spectacular in technique, and infinitely more personalized. Her works consist of a series of genre studies, employing popular, that is, common or traditional, steps. Her use of the body and hands is always particular to a time and a people. It is not in any way generalized, and in that sense it is not classic. Dunham tells about the people that interest her, the people she has known. It is from the aggregate of their individualities that the truth emerges gradually, not as old worn-out formulas but as the old familiar, *ours*.

We owe much to the black theater, and whether we know it or not, we owe a great part of our individuality in the dance to the black theater. Jerome Robbins is in debt, as I am and as are Eliot Feld, certainly Twyla Tharp, and yes, even Balanchine. It is essential that the work of Katherine Dunham be preserved and continued. It is our link with black history. She alone has dealt with indigenous material and indigenous expression. We need it. In truth, we cannot develop without it.

I HAD HEARD about Maracci from many sources, but the first time I saw her was in 1935, when I went to take a class from her in Hollywood, on Highland Avenue. She was dressed in a little knitted bathing suit, and she sat upright on the edge of her chair, her insteps crossed precisely before her (she had the most beautiful feet in the ballet world). She was smoking. She had tiny hands with long quick fingers, the nails extravagantly long to facilitate castanet playing. She was very small, doll-like, and compact; she had the most attractive small figure I had ever seen. She had, in fact, the perfect dancer's body: a small torso with narrow, trim shoulders and a high chest, and long arms and legs for line. Her black hair was nailed, Spanish style, in a knot at the back of her head.

I have said she was doll-like, but there was no hint of prettiness in the face. Her large mouth peeled back from strong biting-teeth, and was held, not like Martha Graham's in patience against the world or open in ecstatic acceptance, but in wide aggression and abandonment to emotion. Maracci had the head of a rather precocious monkey, or of a wicked marionette. Under the bald, hard, round forehead, her eyes were large and flecked with yellow lights like an animal's. It was an angry little head, proud and passionate—the head of a Spanish gypsy. She always held it curbed in, as though she had a bit in her mouth, the cords of her neck jutting out in strong vertical lines. She always looked out under flickering lids, as though she were about to bolt.

She suggested comparison with Graham constantly: the masklike face, the fixed, aloof gaze, the sudden unleashing of energy. But whereas Graham seemed universal, and on stage even monumental, with the limitless power of the primitive, Maracci was quick, nervous, small, and explosive. The eyes flashed with amusement or scorn. The voice rang out in flat, broad southwestern speech. "Oh my goodness!" she said the day I met her, in washday Bakersfield impatience. "Show some gumption! You look like limp lettuce leaves. What do you think you're doing?" She threw down her cigarette and ground it out on the studio floor with the toe of her pink satin slipper. "Now, let's get going!" Up came the chest; the spine tautened. Her neck and head assumed the tension of accumulated force that is a dancer's preparation. The long arms moved to fourth position, her knees galvanized, and she was off on cold legs, without a plié or an excuse me, in a series of the most astonishing chaîné pirouettes one could ask for, revolving as fast as the eye could follow, as smooth as silk unwinding from a spool. Her lungs were filled with smoke, her thighs relaxed from sitting down. She stopped in arabesque, erect like a T-square, the straight supporting leg planted on its delicate point, the structure of her body balanced and counterbalanced, sinew against bone against height against sinew, hanging in the air, tension counterbalanced on tension. The lovely, tense foot, like the hoof of a deer, was adequate to all, attaching itself to the bare floor and permitting the body to branch and flower above. She posed there on pointe, in defiance of gravity, until her knee got tired, and then, and only then, she allowed her heel to touch ground. She had remained immobile, from full flight, for about fourteen seconds.

"Glory be to God!" I murmured. The girls just stood and looked. We gaped.

"Well!" said Carmelita with a throaty chuckle. "That was pretty good. I think I'll have another smoke on that one. Now, how about some of you trying?"

I'll tell you something extraordinary. We did not match her performance, because there were only four or five people in the world who could. But we did much better than we had ever done before.

One day Anton Dolin visited her class. Carmelita rose from her cigarette, winked at her girls, and unleashed a series of entrechats six, interspersed with entrechats huit. Dolin had not been capable of these since he was thirty, and Igor Youskevitch and André Eglevsky would have had to stretch their thighs a bit to duplicate it. Today I believe only Mikhail Baryshnikov could match it, and possibly some Soviet male stars, and only one woman in history, Adeline Genée. Carmelita sat down, breathing a bit hard, her nostrils flaring, and asked Dolin for a light. I dare say his hand shook a trifle as he offered it. "It nearly sprung me," said Carmelita later, "but I figured I had to do it. He'd heard I was a technician."

"Stretch your feet," she would yell suddenly, sitting on the floor at our ankles and taking the offending member in her strong, surgical fingers. "Isn't that a good pain? I like to feel pain like that. That kind of pain is accomplishment."

We left at the end of an hour and a half, not too tired. Her classes were designed for exhilaration, and she had the great pedagogic faculty of helping us each day to do one thing we had not done before. After her students left she would change her slippers and reenter the empty studio for a little practicing herself, alone—something very few ballet dancers will force themselves to do, it being too drearily exhausting. Carmelita was the only great dancer I ever knew who worked without a coach. She also practiced two hours of castanet and heel work daily. All this was in addition to her composing.

She always said she had been born in Montevideo, Uruguay, but her husband discovered after lengthy and arduous searching (when applying for Medicare) that she had been born in Gold-field, Nevada. Her mother had lied about this. Carmelita never mentioned her father, who was her mother's second husband. Although Carmelita was not an only child, she grew up like one, because her mother drove off an older stepsister and encouraged Carmelita's older brother to leave home.

Carmie was her mother's spoiled darling. Her mother owned a nine-foot Steinway on which she played very well, and it was to her music that Carmie danced, from the moment she could move—danced before she could walk. Her very early formal ballet training began when she came to New York from California and studied with Luigi Albertieri and Enrico Zanfretta. She also studied Spanish dancing with Hypolito Mora. She made her professional debut in California, with a small troupe headed by Alexis Koslov, then she started on her own in San Francisco. At the same time she began teaching, to earn money.

When I first knew her, she was living and working in a cottage that had been built out of one of the rooms in my old school, the Hollywood School for Girls. I hung about and tagged along whenever I could, because I found the atmosphere of the house comforting. There was always a group of radicals, malcontents, and indigent writers, intermingled with painters and dancers, waiting to be recharged by Carmelita's personality, for she was great fun to be with.

Carmie did all sorts of interesting extracurricular things. She was a superb cook. She drew well. She sewed exquisitely and could make her own costumes. Most especially, she showed me how to enjoy a city when one had no money at all; she took me to Chinatown, Japantown, Negro Baptist churches, Spanish services in the Old Mission Church (where in the 1850s my grandmother George had been schooled by Spanish nuns), night court, and dollar day on Hollywood Boulevard. There were alluring cities within our city, and as Carmie revealed them, they were irresistible. All these were to be had for nothing, and I'd grown up right there without knowing anything about them!

We practiced and talked and shopped together and went to parties and improvised outrageous dances. We fell into glooms and were encouraged by our hangers-on. She never seemed to have doubts about her work, as I had about mine. Shortly I found out why.

Up to this point I had not seen her dance. I had heard rumors, but these were so extravagant that I gave them little credence. The night before she entrained for a San Francisco concert, she asked me to watch a rehearsal, so after my work I snatched a peanutburger by the roadside and walked up the crunchy driveway to her studio. The fresh, moist night air fanned through the garden leaves as I went, along with the sound of the piano, alive and unnaturally distant as always when heard outside at night. Carmie seemed to be alone with her pianist and a large Spanish hat. I sat in a corner quietly. She pulled herself up from the floor and said she might just as well do the dances right off—so she did.

It is no ordinary experience to discover one evening that an intimate, a known, well-loved, daily companion, has genius and stands outside of the standards we set for ourselves. The person speaks with the usual voice, laughs with the ordinary expression, and then, without transition or warning, becomes a figure of magic. I have known this experience three times in my life, with Antony Tudor, with Sybil Shearer, and with Carmelita. It is a very humbling experience, involving as it does some of the fastest reorientation a person can be asked to make, and strong discretion, because one is brought up sharp against the knowledge that the other fellow has known the score all along.

That evening my jaw dropped. I sat in the studio where I had done a daily practice for six months, where we had had parties, Christmas and birthday celebrations, and long, long talks. The place smelled of wood and floor wax; the trumpet vines tapped at the windows. Carmelita walked on incredibly high heels to the center of the room and sat down on a kitchen chair. She said to the pianist in her plain western dancing-class voice, "I'm ready, I guess." And it began. The great experience.

Not in Covent Garden during a Ballet Russe gala, when Kchessinska, Sokolova, and Danilova stood on the same stage, not in Pavlova's presence, not in the Bolshoi nor the Kirov, not in Graham's concerts, not in the most dazzling opera houses of the world have I experienced more. This girl worked with thunder. The dance she showed me was her "Cante Jondo," or "Deep Song." These notes were made at the time and record exactly what I saw and thought that night.

She begins the dance as she begins so many — sitting, her head snapped forward, her arms hanging like ropes to the ground. In the maw of her spread knees, her torso waits, ready, until the ground becomes vital under her heels. A shudder of energy twitches through her feet, jerking her knees and spasmodically lifting her head. She is ready. The ground takes possession of her. Her insteps quiver; the heels ring out nervously. Long shudders pass up her body — the head rolls on its supporting shoulders. She rocks on her hams, the weight of her head, of her back, is carried on arms thrust square against the knees, braced square, of a piece, resisting.

Then, like the splitting of wood, the earth-anger erects her and throws her out into space. She wrecks herself against the surface of the world. Her knees double up, jackknife fashion. She spikes at the ground with her heels. Her head rears back, her chest lifts, as she drills and drums. Doubling and straight-ening, wrapping and slapping, she flays the air in naughty rage. See the clavicles close and open under the taut skin. The cage of her little ribs works like a bellows. Her fingers poke and stick. Flecks of foam are dashed from her teeth. Her sturdy legs trot and strike like the hooves of a pony. She can kick up the ground all right! She can slap the air again and again. She can lash out at the sky, a merry hard time, a tattoo from hell. Olé, Carmelita!

This is a punishment. This is the anger of the dust, the wrath of the grave. The weakening pulse shudders through her body. Her eyes roll back — her fear becomes audible. "Ay!" she cries, and her teeth cannot hold the quivering lips. "Ay!"

This was the year the civil war got well under way in Spain. Carmelita was brought up as Spanish. She felt an anger in her bones, in her tight young sinews. She raged at the stones and dirt, the waste and dirt of death. "Ay!" It is done.

After the dance I walked to her quietly and put my arms around her. "Carmie, I didn't know."

"I'm glad you like it," she said. "I think it's good, myself." Then she laughed with a matter-of-fact, throaty chuckle that seemed to cut through all hyberbole.

She didn't do this dance very often, because it took too much of her strength. There were others: "Live for the One Who Bore You," sitting on a revolving piano stool from which she never rose; "La Pasionaria," about the inspirational miner's wife, the voice of the Spanish revolution, which got audiences screaming; "Dance of Elegance," a savage satire, an animalistic, monstrous caricature of a ballet dancer preening; "The Night-ingale and the Maiden," from Enrique Granados's *Goyescas*, which Jerome Robbins described to me as the most beautiful solo dance he had ever seen. In this dance Carmie's castanets made the sounds of the bird's song, much as they became the sound of the surf curling on the long shore in another of Grana-dos's lyric pieces, "Shells of the Sea Wind."

Plainly and simply, Carmelita's best dances were the most passionate and powerfully devised solos I have ever seen. She worked in the spirit of great caricature, being more of a grotesque than a satirist. She played with cruelty in a manner suggesting Goya and Toulouse-Lautrec.

Her line was visually flawless.

She baffled criticism because her technique fell into two categories: ballet, which, although impeccably correct, was not classic in style, and Spanish, which was virtuoso in its range but highly unorthodox in form and flavor. She had no wish to perpetuate aesthetic traditions and used only those stock gestures so deeply imbued with emotion as to have become, under her manipulation, original. Like the internationally known Spanish dancer Argentina, she made tradition.

At the time I first knew Carmelita, John Martin of the *New York Times* predicted international glory. So why didn't everyone hear about her? Why did she miss her career? She presented one of the most tragic and interesting paradoxes in all of dancing.

When Raquel Meller, the greatest Spanish *diseuse*, came to America, I was told there were fifty Spanish café singers back home quite as good. I am bored with hearing about the pianists who play as well as Gieseking or Rubinstein. What if they do? Have they arranged their lives so that they can perform for me under auspicious circumstances at prearranged times? I want the core of their hearts, foaming and red, between eight-thirty and ten-thirty, in a comfortable place of assembly near my home. For this I am willing to pay a small sum and go out to the auditorium. Between the perfect performance achieved in privacy and the blinding happenstance produced at my convenience, on my terms, is a spiritual and psychological gap as great as that which lies between great talent and not much. Only the giants leap the chasm.

Carmelita had imagination, verve, energy, and fascination. What she did not have was the ability to cope with the practicalities of her career, nor did she get herself assistants who could. She was a fugue of neuroses. I never knew a person to have so many megrims and vapors — her various decays came and went like passing moods. I arrived for class one day to find her sitting in the sun, knitting and moaning. She had developed cancer of the stomach, she informed me. She didn't think, however, she would care to see a doctor. I made three different appointments, and went three separate times to fetch her in my sister's car, before I finally got her under a trained eye. She did not have cancer of the stomach.

She nearly always got laryngitis the day before a concert. She was usually prostrated afterward. She could not be made to keep an appointment. If it was social, you could bet she wouldn't show up. Many a dinner I watched cool on my table until at last her husband phoned to say that she had a headache, or felt she must put in one more hour of rehearsing, or was forced to interview a critic, or . . . but does it matter? If she was not the hostess, she would not show.

But she never once taught a bad class or, having reached the stage, failed to perform superbly and like no other contemporary. The tragedy was that these occasions were so few.

In the late thirties Erin O'Brien Moore, an actress-pupil growing impatient with the public's indifference to Carmelita, gave her $35,000 — in those days a tidy sum — to come to New York for two concerts. She also procured her a manager — not one of the best ones, but the best one to be persuaded to manage an unknown. He was, incidentally, Erin's lover. Before Carmelita reached New York, Erin broke with the lover, but she failed to notify Carmelita of the change in her personal affairs. Maracci took exception to the manager and to the treatment accorded her, including her modest hotel accommodations. She expected to be hailed as a world-famous celebrity, like Argentina. She was not Argentina, the manager pointed out, and he was not prepared to fulfill Erin's promises. Carmelita was abandoned. She tongue-lashed all concerned. She turned on Erin viciously. The manager was no longer emotionally obligated and was disinclined to do anything helpful. Carmelita left New York forlornly and went back to California. She did not, however, return Erin's money, that having been spent on rehearsals, preparations, and fares. She salved her conscience for the failure to repay the debt by never forgiving Erin. But Erin forgave Carmelita, and at her next public performance murmured, "More beautiful than ever" as she walked up the aisle.

Carmie later came back to New York and was scheduled to give a concert at the YMHA, but she developed a septic throat the night before and had to cancel. This was, of course, momentous news in her life, but not, as it turns out, in the public's, because on the very day of the cancellation, December 7, 1941, we returned home from the auditorium's closed doors to learn that Japan had just bombed Pearl Harbor.

After the war I suggested that Ballet Theatre produce a suite of Carmelita's dances. After months of remonstrating and arguing, she was prevailed upon to come east again and rehearse the Ballet Theatre corps de ballet, which she did assiduously. They were fascinated, as everyone always was. The painter Rico Lebrun designed sets and costumes that were outstandingly fine in themselves, but they did not help the dance movement. The music was orchestrated.

Alas, Carmelita's solo dances, although left unchanged in their pristine beauty, did not assimilate into a larger piece. At the first performance the audience was puzzled and not a little put off by Carmelita's austere, sardonic personality, and on the whole was tepid in its response.

I met Oliver Smith, the codirector of Ballet Theatre, in the foyer. "What shall I tell her? Whatever shall I say?"

"You'll go back," said Oliver, in his heartiest Broadway fighting manner, "and give her a pep talk, as you would on any opening night to any pro. She can pull this piece together. You know she can. The material is there. It just wants the doing. But she'll have to get at it and work very hard, very fast."

So I went back to her dressing room, where Carmelita sat wrapped in a huge dressing gown, enormous-eyed and shuddering with nerves, and gave her a pep talk, as I would to any professional, and produced in no time a collapse. She had to be carried out of the theater by Don Sadler, one of her dancers, while her faithful acolytes addressed me in terms of sorrow and rage: "What did you think you were doing?" She terminated the season and went back home. I don't think she wrote to me for several years.

Then, in the late forties, Sol Hurok, the great manager, came to her. Argentinita—not Argentina, but another popular Spanish dancer—had just died of cancer. Hurok offered Carmie all of her unfilled dates, and Carmie, I felt very unwisely, jumped at this opportunity. In effect, it was no opportunity. Argentinita had been a traditional dancer, splendidly fine but orthodox. Carmelita Maracci was bittersweet and very particular in her appeal. She was an acquired taste. The audiences didn't know what they were looking at.

In addition there was the Maracci point of view. Carmelita took up causes like a street fighter, and she used this tour to propagandize her latest interest, which was at the moment loyalist Spain (later it was ending the Vietnam War). As later, she went to exaggerated extremes. Lee Freeson, her husband, suddenly found he could not meet his payroll, because Carmie had secretly instructed her concert management to send half the box office receipts to the Spanish refugees. The transaction was kept secret because she was afraid Lee would not approve. He did not; he had bills to pay.

The performances on the Hurok tour were successful enough while Carmelita herself was onstage, but dull when she was off it and the assisting group of three girls and one boy were forced to carry the show. One night in St. Paul a lone drunk, losing interest like many others, rose and began to burlesque the dances, prancing up and down the aisles. The audience welcomed the diversion and started to call out encouragement and laugh. Carmelita was in her dressing room, changing for the next solo. Her three girls were left alone with the hubbub, fervently going through one of Carmie's irate, merciless, and deeply felt anti-Franco numbers, "Spain Cries Out." Carmie heard the uproar and rushed half-dressed to the wings.

"Pull down the curtain," she screamed.

"Don't do it," said Lee. "It's only one drunk. The ushers will take care of him."

Carmelita became hysterical. "Close the curtain! Close the curtain!" She clawed at the curtain man's arms.

The curtain descended, to the amazement of the dancers and audience. Carmelita returned fuming to her room, denouncing in loud tones the decriers of loyalist Spain, the savages who could not understand a serious statement of the passion of our times.

Her fulminations were cut short by the enraged entrance of one of the backers. "Where is this Maracci woman?"

Carmelita stood at bay. Then she let loose in gutter terms, viciously and brutally, the full extent of her primal rage. She attacked the man personally and all of the people of St. Paul, their intelligence, their lack of ideals. Forty years after the episode she still referred to "the drunken audience jeering at Spanish heroes."

Carmie manufactured this quarrel. She was determined on martyrdom; she sought it, she wished it, she needed it — immolation at all cost, no matter how unnecessary, no matter how ineffectual. She would have it. Well, she had it.

That concert was terminated then and there, and so was her entire career. The management phoned Hurok's New York office as soon as they could get through and refused flatly to pay her fee. They also canceled all the remaining Hurok concerts for the rest of the year and threatened to maintain the boycott indefinitely. Hurok, of course, was frantic, and immediately repudiated Carmelita Maracci's contract. She was sent home with very little money, and her name was placed at the head of a blacklist.

She had done for herself.

. . .

Managers say they want reliable clients. They also say they must give the public what it wants. One thing is certain, they want no trouble.

Yet I believe that anyone who prefers practical cooperation to genius is a fool. Back and forth across the country every year trek the girls and boys who will do what they're told, give what they're asked, comply, conform, and adapt. All they do is corrupt public taste, drive interested people from the theaters, and make shabby and flat a fierce and magic calling. Do any managers know what the public wants? A good part of the public really wants a public hanging or a ceremonial deflowering. The rest of the public could not possibly say what it wants. People simply want to be moved.

What goes toward the building of a great career? I should say sixty percent of the requirement is character, by which I do not mean a kind heart. Rather, I mean durability, steadfastness, and realism. Above all, realism — as well as talent. There is no substitute for talent. Talent, however, can lie moldering for lack of common sense. It takes realistic courage to wade into the welter of crossed ambitions, tastes, and greeds involved in the theater and distill from the ferment what one desires. The work involved is rough, and the perils of demoralization and cheapening arise daily. Very many great artists must by their nature work in private, but these should not choose theater as a medium.

All dancers have to use other people as collaborators. The conflict is therefore generated right in the moment of creation. Dancing must have collaboration and help; help is people, and people are trouble. The point where the great artist and the great careerist fuse is on the public stage at eight-thirty sharp.

Most creative artists are neurotic, as most people are neurotic; I believe that creative artists are no more neurotic than anyone else. But they are more noticeable. However, I think it is possible to make another generalization: those with a great gift generally have in their character a certain instinctive protection of the endowment, so that while it may be deflected, tortured, or delayed, it is seldom destroyed. Carmie was a tragic exception.

Repeated collapses are usually contrived to hide flaws, weaknesses in the talent, and their inevitable exposure. In Carmie's case there was no flaw. Her talent was immaculate. Why then did she insist on withdrawing? What was she terrified of?

Tantalizing, magical hazards provided her with a staunch excuse for not standing up to her test and being counted. Behind these perils, which she almost cherished and which she certainly supported, she could hide. She could not put the blame on others. She had evaluated herself as of unmatched worth; she did not ever have to diminish this appraisal, not while she could hide behind other circumstances and other people.

Carmelita sometimes failed to meet an obligation because she could not pay her taxi fare to the date. Several times Lee came to me for money, always at the last moment. But this was not the real reason for defaulting. We all knew it. Money alone could not answer her need. At the beginning I could give her none, because I had none. Later, when I had a little, I of course sent her some. But once she made the appeal herself. I went to Jerome Robbins for additional help, and he asked if this was to be a regular thing with her. I had to admit that it probably was, so with the money I finally sent Carmelita a letter. In effect I said that I thought she had one of the greatest gifts I knew, but that she had not enjoyed the success she certainly deserved. I, who had a much smaller gift—and I meant this quite sincerely—was getting the most out of it, I felt, because I had had a psychiatric analysis. I had Jerome Robbins's permission and Martha Graham's permission to say that they both had had analyses, and I suggested that Carmie try one for relief and clarification.

The letter I got back almost burned the paper, after which Carmelita didn't write a word to me for six years. She thought my suggestion was wickedly mocking. The fault obviously lay in the perverted taste of the public and the venality of the management.

After her St. Paul experience she retired to a studio and spent the rest of her life in raging against management, against American taste, against her colleagues, against whatever. She broke off with nearly all her friends because she scolded so bitterly about their politics, their way of life, their taste. Most of her students, including Cynthia Gregory, Christine Sarry, William Carter, and Paul Godkin, testified that the steel and brilliance in their own technique came from Carmelita, but after a while they did not dare go near her. Either she quarreled with them or she demanded their entire time and service, which none of them could afford. Carmelita rehearsed two or more years for every concert, and while her personal performance sharpened, her assistants were bled juiceless — she sucked them dry. She never forgave them when they left.

Over the years Carmelita wrote many letters, most bitter, some directly scolding, all eloquent. I submit a few random paragraphs.

I think that a technique should be subordinate to the idea, and of late the opposite is true. . . . I don't want to see a well-trained dancing army in government hire who leap without question.

I am tired of the dancing department store, where people come and go and buy leg secrets and a hint of how they can do a better fouetté soufflé — in other words, a length of this and a yard of that. . . . I am not a pedagogue trying to prepare fodder for the dancing machines.

No one speaks of content, and Martha Graham looks embalmed. The ballet polish she has used in the last ten years has completely ruined her awkward wonder of the early years. The photograph of her with Gerald Ford made me gag. And Baryshnikov is surely the Mrs. Miniver of the day, in disguise.

The terrain I traveled was not the studio floor, for my world led me into Goya's land of terror and blood-soaked pits. . . . The life I lived could not make me a dancer of fine dreams and graveyard decor . . . so I danced hard about what I saw and lived. I was not an absentee landlord. I was one of the dispossessed. I was a gypsy.

And years later:

I live in anonymity. I can barely remember that I once danced. Some photographs reassure me.

I was a rotten soldier, Agnes, and it is you who want people to be good ones. [I don't remember ever saying anything to this effect.] I am more of an anarchist than ever. I could never have danced as I did if I had been an obedient servant.

I am changing my profession in November. I am stopping teaching after forty-eight years. I'm going to write. I hope it isn't too late.

Thirty-five years after the St. Paul evening, she still alluded to the tragic event with all the venom in her soul:

I have not forgotten St. Paul, Minnesota, nor have I forgotten my cruel dismissal and mismanagement. . . . No one should be given the power that Hurok knew to ruin another person, but it is natural that people preferred silence, since they might have hurt their chances of being managed by the powerful one.

Whether or not Carmie wrote anything beyond letters and scraps I cannot say. There were other things she could do. She drew cartoons, extraordinarily pungent line drawings of ballet dancers. Rico Lebrun thought she had a future as a caricaturist. "I am a dancer," she said, closing the subject.

She cooked extremely well, making dishes for her studio parties that were legendary. Lee told me she used long needles to inject wine into meat, then let it marinate for two days. She contributed articles to *Gourmet* magazine and was offered an annual stipend to be on its staff. "I am a dancer," she said, turning the offer down.

But she didn't dance.

As the years went on, she developed bad arthritis, until she had to teach from a wheelchair (which she could do with wonderful effect). Terry Orr told of her later teaching:

> One of my first memories is doing pliés and making raindrops fall from the sky. She didn't show you how you had to create the rain. Twelve people in the class might have twelve different variations, which shocked me, because suddenly my arm wasn't going from second position to the first, and then opening to the second again. Another time I remember is when she opened up a book after we had done pliés and tendues and started talking about poetry. After an hour and fifteen minutes had gone she made us come into the center for grand battements and we then did turns for the next fifteen minutes and that was the end of the class.
>
> But that day was not about learning to do pirouettes. That day was learning about poetry.
>
> A time of being free with dance! In ballet you don't get that chance very often, but that was exactly how I learned to pirouette. She created different arm movements, such as putting our hands behind our backs. She was the first one who taught me how to control centrifugal force. It was the first time I could do six or seven pirouettes, while at first I was doing only doubles or triples. After that I started loving the sensation of turning much more. When I went back home to San Francisco, I could do nine turns. (Walter Terry wrote of me that I was the Rudolf Nureyev of the West because I was jumping and turning in a way that had not been seen often.) To the lay reader this may not designate any radical change, but to the dancer, to depart from orthodox controls is as frightening as the loss of the thumb in piano playing.

Riddled with pain, Carmelita was carried about her house in her husband's arms. Then, most sinister of all, she began to feel that she was distorted by her disease (and she was), that she was a mockery of what she had been. She became a recluse. People who really loved her took to dropping by without warning, trapping her into a meeting, and after their departure Carmie would have weeping fits. Through it all her faithful husband did the housework, maintained his own business (selling rare manuscripts), and took the brunt of her incredible angers and vagaries. One never knew what to expect with Carmelita. Up to the end she sent the most enchanting cards and little presents, made phone calls, offered gifts of home-made cookies or similar delicacies, but any definite plan to see her met with repeated frustration, in spite of her ardent protestations.

In 1987 Carmelita had a massive heart attack. She was taken to the cardiac department of Cedars of Lebanon Hospital, but she would not listen to the doctors or do as they said because, naturally, she distrusted them. They allowed her to go home, mainly, I suppose, because under the circumstances the hospital could do nothing for her.

There was a second attack. This time Lee was desperate. Once again she went to the hospital. Her doctor came back only on the condition that she would obey him. Being sufficiently terrified, she complied. On returning home she stopped eating, which is a solution for almost every problem. Then one night she said she would like some fish. Lee gave it to her, then watched the television news as she lay quietly dozing. After the news he went to her; failing to rouse her, he discovered that Carmie had left him. She had died.

At the mortuary he had to identify the body—a legal imperative. Reluctantly he looked, and there, he told me, lay a little girl, at the most thirteen or fourteen years old, absolutely pure, incorporeal, weightless, a spirit. He thought she would float from the room. He had seen nothing like it in his life. This was the essence of la Maracci, a born dancer, a great one who had concealed herself, hidden somehow until this moment in an ambuscade of deceit, trouble, disease, and ugliness. Now she had escaped.

· · ·

Carmelita Maracci is barely remembered today. She is given hardly a paragraph in the dance histories and memoirs. Nonetheless, there are those who saw her in the thirties and forties, and like the notes of the nightingale about which she danced with her singing ebonies, she sounds in our memory sweet and clear, pure and crystalline. *Olé*, lost lovely voice, *olé*, our Carmie.

ALICIA ALONSO

CUBA HAS THREE chief exports: cigars, sugar, and Alicia Alonso. Everyone in the world knows about Cuban cigars and sugar. Everyone in Cuba knows Alicia. She is hailed with "Viva Alicia!" on sight, and bands accompany her arrivals and departures. Her name is not a household word outside of Cuba only because her traveling is politically restricted. The knowledgeable, however, are aware of her, and her place in history is assured.

She is a dancer, one of the finest classic ballerinas living today. What makes her unique, what makes her different from all predecessors, all rivals, is one simple fact: Alicia is blind. It is highly unusual for any athlete to have impaired vision, but for an active dancer to continue working with such a disability has never before occurred. Alicia is famous, however, not because of her blindness but in her own right, compared to the sighted. As Richard Philp, the editor of *Dance Magazine*, says, "She makes illusion. She is illusion."

She has other distinctions. Unlike most stars, who are notoriously and by definition self-centered, she is public-spirited. As a matter of fact, she is a militant revolutionary and has contributed to the social history of her country. Finally, she has built a ballet company that is a national institution and has world prestige.

Alicia is a small woman, and very attractive. Her two outstanding characteristics are her enormous smile and her eyes —her great eyes, black and piercing, blind yet piercing, apprehending accurately what they cannot perceive, judging, choosing, dismissing, masking in their impenetrable depths the inflexible will. Barbara Barker, assistant to Igor Youskevitch, the classic star and former head of the dance department at the University of Texas, says, "I think what happens when she talks to you is that she stares as though she were trying to see you, or, more particularly, as if she didn't want you to know that she can't see you. She looks very intently at where she hears your voice coming from. The intensity of that look is startling, and very hard not to flinch from."

Reinforcing the eagerness of Alicia's eyes is her smile. Her wide, slightly undershot mouth is like a child's, voracious for experience, determined to taste all, to know all. It is quick to smile, quick to speak. Her soft, voluble tongue, waiting to taste, flicks between the half-parted lips, which roll out the lightning Spanish. Alicia seems like a lady lizard that one longs to tame but cannot.

Her nose is straight and large, with the sensitive, quivering nostrils of a doe, alert to any signal. Her neck is long and supple, bearing the elegant little head like a tropical flower on its tender stalk. Her body is small, beautifully formed, with small breasts and hips, long arms and legs, the feet and arches of a great dancer. They were not hers early in her career; she had to create them. Her fingers taper. Her nails are extravagantly long, protruding three quarters of an inch beyond her fingertips and rendering them useless, one would think, for anything beyond ornamentation. But Alicia sews and makes all her own headdresses. She also paints.

Alicia Ernestina de la Caridad del Cobre Martínez y del Hoyo was born with perfect vision and saw quite clearly and normally until she was nineteen years old. She was the youngest of the four children of Antonio and Ernestina Martínez, and was brought up in the fashionable Vedado section of Havana. Her father was an army veterinary surgeon, and fondly hoped to give Alicia the confined, proper, comfortable life of a nicely raised middle-class girl. She went to Spain when she was eight and learned the flamenco dances, but only in order to perform them for her grandfather, a Spaniard living in Havana. That was to be all the dancing she was ever to know, her father supposed, except what she needed for ballroom purposes. As she puts it, "He no want me to dance. He not like the frivolity of stage, especially dancing."

But Alicia did not have the personality of a confined middle-class girl. She was an exotic, and she expected to do strange things. Her nickname was Unga, "the Hungarian." A neighborhood playmate, Fernando Alonso, and his brother, Alberto, were the sons of Señora Laura Rayneri Alonso, who managed the Pro Arte concert series and school; they introduced Alicia at the school, and there, unknown to her father but with her mother's connivance, Alicia started dance classes. Fernando helped her, with increasing enthusiasm. When she was a teenager Alicia saw no reason to continue formal academic training and stopped. She could read and write, but she has had to pick up other knowledge as needed—not too difficult for her, as she has an avidly curious mind and a totally retentive memory.

Fortunately, the Pro Arte school of ballet boasted a real

Russian ballet teacher, Nikolai Yavorsky. However, there was not a pair of pointe shoes anywhere in Havana. Many of the pupils were forced to work in sneakers or bare feet.

It soon became apparent that Alicia was remarkably gifted for ballet dancing. It was equally clear that Fernando was falling in love with her, and his family, growing alarmed, hastily sent him to continue his studies in Florida, to put a safe amount of saltwater between him and temptation. However, Fernando persuaded Alicia to follow, which she did enthusiastically. He seduced her in quick order, and they lived happily and precariously together, dancing all day. She was possessed of an ambition that he had never before seen. Indeed, I believe it has never been surpassed in the theatrical world in this century. She also became pregnant. She was now a mature fifteen years old.

The couple proceeded to Spanish Harlem, where relatives took Alicia in. In a month, after giving birth, she was back on the dance floor, struggling to perfect her technique. Fernando now acted as her coach. Her baby, Laura, was turned over to whoever could be arranged for in the way of a nurse. Everyone helped, even Alicia's contemporaries. She spent all day practicing, taking time off only to feed the baby, to marry, and to cook for Fernando. Eventually it seemed practical to send Laura back to Havana, so she did.

Alicia got a job with Lincoln Kirstein's Ballet Caravan, where she followed Marie-Jeanne in the role of the sweetheart in Eugene Loring's *Billy the Kid* — a role in which she has never been surpassed. After the Ballet Caravan tour, Fernando and Alicia attended the School of American Ballet and the Vilzak-Shollar School and danced in the chorus lines of two musicals, *Great Lady* and *Stars in Your Eyes*, the latter choreographed by Balanchine. Jerome Robbins, Muriel Bentley, and Nora Kaye were also in that chorus. In 1941 all five joined the newly formed Ballet Theatre as corps de ballet dancers. Alicia performed in everything she could, attending daily classes given by Alexandra Fedorova and Enrico Zanfretta, the Italian ballet master who also trained Carmelita Maracci. It was Zanfretta who gave both Alicia and Carmelita their first knowledge of Enrico Cecchetti's style.

In short, Alicia's schedule consisted of unbroken training. At eleven o'clock every morning she did the company class. That was an hour and a half of really hard work. Then she would take class at another school, another hour and a half to two hours of exhausting exercise. Every night before the performance, in full makeup, she would do a warm-up coached by her husband, and then, dripping with sweat, she would go to her dressing room, dry off, get into her costume, and conclude with a full evening's performance. I never heard of any other dancer putting herself through such a regimen.

I said to her one night, "Alicia, you will be exhausted."

"I must do this, Ahnes [no Cuban can pronounce the *g* in my name], or I won't get strong," she replied. "I must get strong."

Alicia got strong. Gradually, she was given solos to do— not important ones, but noticeable ones. She always distinguished herself. When Mrs. Martínez in Cuba first read the notices of these appearances, she burst into tears, not because the reviews were bad but because they were very good. Alicia also appeared in a double-page spread of pictures in *Life* magazine. When her mother hesitantly showed them to her father, the long-suffering lieutenant, he shrugged, then smiled broadly; he later displayed them proudly to his fellow officers. Alicia believes that he bought out the entire Cuban allotment of the magazine for that week.

Alicia's energy was inexhaustible. After the long and punishing hours of practice and rehearsal, she would give up her dinnertime to costume fittings, arguing over each seam, each tuck, the color and weight of the material, as though she were a pilot readying a new airplane. She knew her reputation would be modified by those seams.

Her feet began to change. They were not beautiful; "more like spoons," said a contemporary. She made them beautiful.

They became remarkable even among great dancers. They grew strong, of course, as well as flexible, agile, correctly schooled. But those qualities do not begin to describe the flashing, flickering dazzle of Alicia's footwork — what dancers call brio, which means bravura technique. I think her feet moved more rapidly than anyone else's, and always correctly in line. They were strong as steel but seemed soft and caressing. She stroked and touched the floor as a musician touches his instrument. She melted into the floor or she ricocheted from it like hail bouncing. At times she seemed not to have anything to do with the floor but simply to pass above it. "Her feet were not just doing a required step, they were expressions on their own," said her favorite partner, Igor Youskevitch.

Alicia was nineteen and succeeding splendidly when she began to notice that she was bumping into furniture, that she could not see her partner when he was at her side but only when he was slightly in front of her. Instead of seeing in a semicircle, as most people do, she seemed to see only in a triangle. Nor could she focus in a straight line; she had to turn and run in a little circle, which made lifting harder for the boys. In short, she had no peripheral vision.

She and Fernando played games to test the exact limits of her sight. In March 1941, Lucia Chase, the head of Ballet Theatre, arranged for her to go to New York Hospital to have her vision tested definitively. "Detachment of the retina" was the verdict, and she was ordered to have an operation. She lay in bed with her eyes bandaged for three months. Fernando stayed right beside her — "the inspiration of my life," she called him. She became the mascot of the hospital ward, where everyone referred to her as "our girl."

Leon Danielian, a fellow student at the Mordkin Ballet, went to see her at what is now the Columbia Presbyterian Medical Center. Although her eyes were bandaged and she lay motionless, her feet were moving under the coverlet. She was doing battements tendues, pointing and stretching her toes without moving her body. According to Danielian, "I said, 'Don't move,' but she said, 'I have to keep my feet alive.' It was extraordinary to see her. She was heroic about it."

At length the bandages were removed. Alicia could see better, but certain troubles persisted. A second operation, a very serious one, was recommended. It too was only partially successful. The third operation was in Havana. Her doctor told her she had only one chance to see: she would have to lie completely still for a year with her eyes in bandages.

The orders were brutal. She could not move her head one sixth of an inch for twelve months, nor laugh, nor cry, nor chew hard, nor play with her child or her dog. Every day and every evening Fernando sat with her and helped her learn the great roles with her fingers — *Giselle, Swan Lake, Aurora.* She would show him the dance she was practicing and he would correct her. "It was torture for me to lie still, feeling my body gain weight and become flabby," she recalled. "I saw all the steps I had done and how often I had done them wrong. I danced in my mind. Blinded, motionless, lying flat on my back, I taught myself to dance *Giselle.*"

After a year of bed rest she was allowed to lead a modified life, but not to dance. She took walks with the Martínezes' Great Dane, and stealthily visited the ballet studio two blocks from her home, where she practiced every day. No one told on her. Then a sudden tornado visited the island. Alicia went outdoors to help her dog, who had just given birth, and the glass door of the porch shattered, showering all over her head and face. She fell. Her screams brought Fernando rushing; he picked her up, but found her miraculously unhurt except for minor cuts.

After the hurricane accident, the doctor told Alicia she could dance again, if she did so discreetly. He probably reasoned that if she could come unscathed through flying glass, torrential downpour, mud, and a bad fall, she could weather the exigencies of an ordinary ballet performance. She notified Ballet Theatre immediately by cable and returned to the United States, leaving Laura and Fernando in Cuba. When she arrived in New York, her head was still in bandages from the broken glass. Suddenly she was asked to go on in place of Markova, who was ill, in *Giselle*. Anton Dolin, who had always believed in Alicia, was her partner and régisseur and shepherded her through this extraordinary and terrifying comeback. She was instantly acclaimed. We now had a new ballerina.

That was gratifying, but Alicia faced a great challenge. She had partial sight in one eye but no peripheral vision. Her first task was to learn how to move independently on an open stage. She arranged to have two very strong spotlights in different colors focused on the front of the stage, a safe distance from the edge. These she could sense. She was aware that if she stepped in front of their glow, she was in danger, for beyond the lights she was in immediate peril of plunging into the orchestra pit. Of course, any fall would have been broken by the wire that is always stretched at waist height across her footlights, but I don't think the wire could have prevented Alicia from hurling herself full force into the danger zone.

For the most part, she danced within the cage of her partner's arms. Her partners were very carefully trained in how to guide, how to lead, without seeming to do so. As long as she was encircled and supported, she had their protection, as though by a trained nurse. All the time she was onstage with a partner, his voice guided her: "Come back," or "You have room to move forward," or "Go more to the side." Sometimes Youskevitch clicked his tongue. But when no partner was there, when she was alone, what guided her? There were always flashlights in the wings, but this does not explain the miracle of a blind girl rushing, racing, leaping, throwing herself rapidly in dazzling light against a wall of black emptiness — without falling.

Reader, try this experiment. Tape your eyes closed. Now walk around your bedroom, with which you are familiar, without using your hands. Walk beautifully, proudly, grandly. Now imagine that the fourth wall has been removed and in its place is a yawning pit, ten feet deep. Now run the course. Take to the air. There is no help, no safety. There is freedom to fly in beauty or to plunge to destruction. Alicia's stage was a minefield, and this was her nightly testing. She has been quoted as saying, "The dancer enters a bullring at every performance. At every performance he faces death."

Alicia was known for her balance, her rapid dancing, and her turns. Her balance was so exaggeratedly good that sometimes her partner confessed to pushing her off balance in order to force her to follow the musical phrase. As for her speed, she had the fastest feet in the business. They flashed and folded into the boxlike fifth position, and opened and arched out and shut like knives, with the rapidity of someone flicking a wrist. Her pas de bourrée, a tiny traveling step on full pointes, was of a gossamer, shimmering perfection unapproached by anyone within my memory (I especially remember the pas de bourrée in the final waltz in Fokine's *Les Sylphides*).

Her turns were unmatched. The secret of the balletic turn is the use of the head and the eyes: by snapping around as your body revolves, you maintain your focus on one fixed spot so it never deviates, except for the merest fraction of a second. This is called spotting, and it is indispensable to preventing vertigo. When a dancer does the turns and pirouettes in one place, the head motion is easily discernible, for she moves her head to focus each time she makes a revolution. When she does the turns in a chain or line (chaîné pirouettes) across or around the stage, her vision is fixed on the corner toward which she progresses. On reaching the corner, she spots the next corner, until the circle is completed. But what if her vision is obscured, so she cannot find a point to fix on? How then does she make the revolutions? What keeps her from losing direction? Alicia Alonso could see only points of light, but she did the turns serenely, beautifully, and rapidly and ended just where she intended to end, with her arms out to the audience and a slow smile spreading on her wide, mobile lips.

Alicia was saved by artificial arrangements and also by a

sixth sense, an extrasensory instinct. I was helping her along a passageway once. There were stairs ahead leading down. Suddenly she stopped, six feet in advance of the well: "There is a change of level ahead, a descent. I feel it." She anticipated my warning.

One time she did not anticipate danger, however. During a rehearsal of my *Fall River Legend* she was completing a ferocious pirouette, one foot held straight out in front of her, waist high, cutting the air like a scythe. My two-year-old son suddenly left my side and ran toward her. She stopped with a scream, her hands to her head. "Was he there? Was he there all the time? I can't see." I quickly reassured her: "He wasn't there, Alicia. He ran out suddenly. He was naughty." We were completely undone. The baby thought it all extremely funny. If her foot had caught him on the side of the head, she would probably have killed him.

Alicia's condition has fluctuated over the years, but she has never regained clear sight. She has had three operations on her retina and two for cataracts. "I had cataracts in both eyes," she explains, "like a veil covering my eyes all the time, and each time thicker." The morning after one operation, in Barcelona, she almost saw clearly for a moment: "I was so happy I could see again, I said without thinking, 'Oh doctor, you didn't shave this morning.' " When she reads, watches TV, or attends auditions, she uses high-powered binoculars like a naval commander's.

Having solved the problems peculiar to her own agonizing condition, Alicia must tackle the problem all star dancers face: maintaining the great and fragile technique. The discipline for this must continue until she ceases to dance. Now an acknowledged ballerina of world renown and the most famous woman in her own country, she must still walk into class, place her hands on the barre, and sweat.

Whenever Alicia takes class, she is driven to the school. "Are we there?" she must ask, turning her unseeing eyes to the building before which the car has stopped. "We are there," answers whoever has brought her, opening the car door and lending her a supporting hand to guide her up the front steps. In the classroom, however, she walks unhesitatingly and authoritatively right across the open floor to her place at the barre, where she executes her moves on order and on count. When she leaves the barre, she is surrounded by an unhelpful and unsupportive space in which other bodies approach and recede. Naturally the other dancers are careful of her, but she asks no favors. She can hold her own.

For an hour and a half daily she goes through the full routine, under the discipline of Fernando or, often today, of their daughter, Laura. Why does one of the ranking dancers of history submit to this? Nay, demand it? The pianist can hear what he does. The singer too can hear. But the dancer lives within the instrument and cannot see, so there must be an outside caretaker. The work for any star, as for any beginner, is unremitting and painfully hard, so there must be a disciplinarian to goad her on to the effort. The spirit and the flesh flag and droop, even with the indomitable Alicia.

Triumph by triumph Alicia mastered all the great roles. She became known as a phenomenally quick study. She learned Antony Tudor's *Lilac Garden* with three hours' preparation; she opened the bill with a Balanchine work, as programmed, then proceeded directly upstairs to the rehearsal hall during the following ballet. Four hours after the first frantic phone call she stepped out in the Tudor role and completed it without fault.

When Nora Kaye fell ill and was unable to open *Fall River Legend*, Alicia learned the ballet, a fifty-minute work, in two weeks. It was in a dramatic style that she had never before attempted and to a modern score of a kind quite unfamiliar to her.

In 1947 Balanchine created her signature piece, Tchaikovsky's *Theme and Variations*, which she and Igor Youskevitch performed for years. It was instantly recognizable that theirs was a union made in heaven. When Igor first danced with Alicia, he didn't know the partnership would be the smoothest of his career, and the most rewarding; as he later put it, "When we danced, we'd flow together." He was a great Old World cavalier, the star of the Ballet Russe de Monte Carlo, and she was a magic girl from a southern island: it was a collaboration that became a legend.

Most ballerinas have a coolness and an impersonality, a disembodied effect that comes from total intent and total concentration. Alicia adds to this the warmth of an extremely passionate woman. She is a Latin, and even her stage relationship with her partner is that of a woman who favors and is excited by the man. Whoever he may be, she does him the homage of recognizing him as a man. When there is also real personal feeling, as in the case of Youskevitch, the union becomes electric. They were both tender, caring, and proud. As Youskevitch said, "We felt pretty together. It was the best partnership I ever shared. We felt we were important."

Other dancers go through the schooled positions and transitions with varying degrees of expertise. Alicia murmurs, sighs, seems to be talking. There are no positions, no transitions, only yieldings, bestowings, yearnings, gestures that are serenely loving and of a continuing, living breath. She moves in life. Her feet, her torso, her arms, neck, and eyes, are one continuing action, taking their dynamics from her meaning. She talks. Her heart is open. Here is the essence of a dancer. It is her core she gives us; it is our core.

It goes without saying that her partner must be sensitive in order to further these inclinations. Of Jorge Esquivel, her pupil-partner, she says, "He respond at any movement what I do. He's like an echo, like a conversation." And he says, "With every position, every balance, she transmits to me all her expertise." And Youskevitch says, "We felt pretty together."

Oh, and they were! They danced in an aura of enchantment.

Everyone believed they were in love. It was the common understanding for years. James Mitchell, the former dancer and film actor who is now a star of the TV show *All My Children*, tells about it: "I remember when she and Igor would do *Black Swan*. The entire company lined up in the wings on one another's shoulders to see her do her balances, her turns. The excitement . . . they were in love, and you could sure tell it. . . . The interplay between them, always without interference to the context or style, was absolutely breathtaking. She had that gigantic smile, and her tongue was just slightly extended. We all enjoyed watching." He goes on to say, "I partnered her in *Fall River*. I remember her being very soft and light, not like the others, who were solid. She was like gauze."

Barbara Barker, Youskevitch's assistant, says, "What I sensed in her — and I'm sure that a lot of other people have sensed it in her too — was the passion for her partner. She is just such an enormous flirt, and an enormously intent performer. But Youskevitch was always the important one. Their emotional bond was obvious."

"Why doesn't she marry him?" I once asked Lucia Chase.

"She is going back to Cuba later. She wants Fernando for her old age," Chase replied.

Alonso and Youskevitch danced together until 1959.

James Mitchell continued:

When Alicia was programmed to do a pas de deux, Nora Kaye might follow it with *Fall River* or *Pillar of Fire*. Alicia would finish to screams, flowers, applause, and repeated curtain calls. The stagehands then would set up whatever ballet was due to follow Alicia, and the new cast would assemble. But Alicia would not go to her dressing room; she would stay right on stage and rehearse anything she had missed — a few pirouettes, balances that did not last all of ten seconds. Nora might be on that same stage trying to get herself into the proper kind of emotional state for her own performance, and she would literally have to kick Alicia out of her way, because Alicia just wouldn't leave. It was her stage.

Every individual who achieves prominence must have iron in his soul. Iron? Glue, rather. Every other person, every situation, is twisted, bent, used toward the one purpose of the one will. The supreme artist or statesman may seem on occasion harsh, and invariably oblivious and selfish. What matter, as long as the unique quality is achieved? That is the sublime goal.

Walter Terry wrote in the *Saturday Review*: "Alicia Alonso is that rarest of dancing creatures, a prima ballerina assoluta. The vast public sees only a great artist, a remarkable virtuoso who can do multiple pirouettes. As an American ballerina she brought us international luster for more than three decades, a vision of enduring dance beauty."

Alicia went back to Cuba in 1948, at the height of her popularity and fame in the United States — "Because," she now explains, "I am a revolutionary. Because to me, the most important thing is the human being. Human beings are more important than my own art, than my own life. My life, my art, would have little value if human beings did not have the right to go to the theater, to have an education, to have a high standard of living, and other fundamental rights. The human being is worth more than any dollar bills that you could place in front of me. I want to feel I have given my life knowledge back to the people. I want to feel I have a little place permanently in life itself."

In fact Alicia returned to Cuba because at that time both Ballet Theatre and Ballet Russe de Monte Carlo had stopped functioning, for financial reasons. She suddenly found she had no American stage to dance on. It suits her now, however, to believe in the greater humanitarian and patriotic reason — which was present also.

Alicia Alonso began dancing in Havana without capital or backers. The Pro Arte lent her costumes, and she bought transportation with money from the advance sale of seats. Eventually Fernando, president of her new ballet company, and his brother Alberto, the artistic director, won subsidies from the

Cuban Ministry of Education. They didn't receive much. This company had to be built out of their own unceasing labor. There were no trained dancers, no choreographers, no composers, and no designers. All of these had to be found. Furthermore, initially there was no audience.

The will that kept Alicia dancing in spite of sightlessness worked all the time in her behalf. She had been known in the Ballet Russe de Monte Carlo as the "Black Cobra" because of her relentless drive toward what she wanted. What she wanted always was preeminence. Today her heart bleeds for the woes of others, for the poor of her country, for the hungry and the miserable, she says. It is very true that she feels deeply about these things, and she says she thought about them for years. She used to talk at great length of doing something to help the deprived people of the world, in particular the Cuban people. While she talked, Fernando did something: he joined the Communist party. He and Alberto were active in all the Communist agitation, even under Fulgencio Batista, before the advent of Fidel Castro. When Castro finally entered Havana as a young militant, taking up the course of injustice and righting the popular wrongs, there were the two Alonsos in the front rows of meetings, plainly visible in all the old newsreels. They threw their entire enthusiasm into the cause of the new hero. This was unusual, because on the whole dancers are too egocentric to be interested in anything except their own careers.

In a few years, Alicia followed suit and became one of the most vocal advocates of the new order. In Cuba there was now only one way of thinking—Castro's—and this pertained to everything everywhere on the island, out to the ten-mile fishing limit. Castro is a Stalinist. He does not hold truck with any newfangled, pantywaist, democracy-spoiled Russians. Alicia falls right into step. She can address any group at any time, and is eager to do so. In all Iron Curtain countries, Alicia is considered a dear little rabble-rouser. She flows like an uncorked bottle.

She repeatedly tours South America, Russia, China, the

eastern bloc countries—never England, seldom Germany or France, and only occasionally the United States. In Washington she once held a committee of senators and representatives spellbound for thirty-five minutes while she addressed them (not about Castro). Her English is faulty but forceful. She loves holding crowds in abeyance and then stirring them to enthusiasm with pyrotechnics of exhortation, just as she loves holding them in silent awe with her exquisite dancing. Alicia does not persuade, she performs, and she is no more democratic than the czarina. One thing is certain, though: she is one of Cuba's best advertisements.

These days Alicia seldom comes to her old stomping grounds. The relationship between the United States and Cuba is so ticklish and her presence in this country is achieved with such difficulty as to enjoin caution. When she does come, it is as a model of discretion. Her friends and close intimates understand that she will talk about anything except politics.

Alicia has received every high honor the profession can bestow, as well as many national medals, particularly from Eastern European countries. Perhaps her most noteworthy awards are the Cuban Carlos Manuel de Céspedes and the Gold Medal of the Gran Teatro Liceo de Barcelona. She was voted a National Hero of Labor by the Cuban Workers Union and holds membership in the advisory council to the Ministry of Culture and in the national committee of the Writers and Artists Union of Cuba.

On a return visit to Washington, D.C., with Ballet Theatre, her old friends flocked to pay homage, particularly the members of the company who had known and loved her. Enrique Martínez, a fellow Cuban, came from seeing her awestruck. "She is beyond time. There is no time for her. She has no age," he said to me. "And Ahnes, she has a new husband, much younger, very nice—a writer." It was true. Alicia, who had been away from home a great deal, found that Fernando had been incautious. Of course fidelity was not required of anyone in Havana, but decorum was. Fernando had been rather too public, particularly considering that his wife was a national idol. He was sent away, and Alicia divorced him and married the editor of a dance publication.

In the spring of 1977, after an absence of seventeen years, Alicia Alonso came back to American Ballet Theatre for an unforgettable *Giselle*. There was muttering among the Cuban refugees, who did not like to see Castro's darling returning. But a great many other people did, and every seat in the Metropolitan Opera House was sold out, to an audience in full evening dress. The crowd assembled in good time and found the auditorium doors locked. The police were busy searching for bombs. For an hour and a quarter the audience waited, standing in the lobby. Then the all-clear sounded, the doors opened, and the people streamed in.

But what of Alicia, waiting backstage, preparing to make a comeback after seventeen years before the most exacting audience in the world? She was preparing to dance the most demanding role in all of dance repertory, and she had to keep trigger-ready for a full hour and a quarter and at the same time face the threat of death! Well, her nerve held. She kept her muscles warm and prepared, and when she jumped lightly from Giselle's doorsill, she was greeted with a roar such as I have heard only in a football stadium. It was topped by the continuing clamor that broke over her at the close of the work. Alicia was back. Never mind bombs.

Alicia came to Austin, Texas, during the week of March 22, 1982, for the jubilee organized in honor of Igor Youskevitch's farewell. For some time Youskevitch had been head of the dance department at the University of Texas. Now having reached the age of seventy, he was retiring, leaving Texas, and going back to New York to live. Dancers from all the world over gathered to do him honor, and the university managed to get permission from our State Department and the Cuban government to have Alicia come. She arrived from Havana with her new husband and four hefty bodyguards, who were dressed in ordinary suits that bulged with what looked like very effective hardware and who followed her closely everywhere.

She had promised to do a pas de deux with her present partner, Jorge Esquivel, and if she liked the looks of Youskevitch, a pas de deux with him. When they had danced together in the 1940s, she had proclaimed that he was the best partner she had ever had. But that was forty years previously, and they had not danced together in all that while. Time works cruel changes: loss of balance, loss of elevation, loss of muscle tone, loss of breath control; all of these can eat away a great technique. But Igor's old *Giselle* costume was brought by his former costume mistress, and he stepped into it as if it had been fitted for him the night before. He was still the most beautiful man in the business, and he was still a danseur noble, a true one.

Alicia came to the rehearsal studio with her bodyguards to judge him. Barbara Barker peeped through the door, and later reported:

> She was in there with Igor, giving herself a barre, and Igor was doing what he always seemed to be doing, which was smoking a cigarette and looking out the window while waiting for her to finish. Just watching her give herself a truly killer barre was an amazing experience, because she has ear-high grands battements and effortless balances. Then I watched Igor try some supported pirouettes, some lifts. I don't know whose judgment she was relying on, because Jorge Esquivel and the bodyguards and Anatole Vilzak, her old teacher, and Walter Terry, the dance critic, were with them. She couldn't see what Igor was doing, but she decided that she would perform with him. On the day of performance the stagehands were finally notified what was going to happen.

Walter Terry devised their appearance. It was Alicia's second appearance of the evening. First she performed with Jorge Es-

quivel in *White Swan*. At the end of the program Terry announced that there would be a surprise. The whole proscenium
of the theater was then filled with a giant movie screen, on
which was projected a home film that Tina, Igor's wife, had
shot of *Giselle* at the Hollywood Bowl in 1945, with Igor and
Alicia doing the pas de deux from the second act. It was a
silent film, and the orchestra accompanied it softly in the background. At a given moment the image on the screen was frozen
and all the lights came up slowly on Alicia and Igor, standing
in the identical pose in the same costumes. As they were revealed you could hear an enormous gasp, as four thousand
people caught their breath simultaneously. This woman and
this man on stage! The audience's beloveds, the immortals, the
legendary lovers, now grown old and honored, Igor with silver
hair and Alicia very nearly transparent. His gallantry, tender-
ness, and care, her kindness and gratitude to him, were beyond
wonder. Their lifts were like mist, like caresses.

At the end, as Igor led Alicia forward for bows, carefully
avoiding the flowers at her feet, Alicia clung to his hand and
turned her sightless eyes up and around the balconies. Then
she stepped back and apart from him and made a royal obei-
sance to the floor, laying her head in the dust at his feet. There
followed absolute silence. People were heard to sob. The silence was shattered and pandemonium broke as Igor gathered
her up.

Barbara Barker shared in the wonder of that evening, but
she was also responsible for all the housekeeping details sur-
rounding the performance. She reported:

During the whole series of events prior to this—classes,
lectures, seminars—Alicia had come in and out with her
bodyguards. On Saturday, the day before the performance,
she came to me with her honorarium check, which was for
$6,000, and she said, "Cash, please." So I called the president
of the university, and he called the president of a local bank,
and the local banker opened up the vaults and cashed her

check. All day Sunday she and her bodyguards shopped, and when they boarded their flight to Cuba on Monday, they were loaded down with VCRs, tape-recording equipment, slide projectors, and every conceivable thing you could imagine for filmmaking. It was all for her school and company.

Alicia's life is now dedicated to her school, which has become a national ballet school subsidized by the Cuban government. This institution, which holds auditions around the island, furnishes complete academic schooling as well as dance training. "In the last few years," says Alicia, "our prima ballerinas have won numerous international prizes, in the Soviet Union, in Bulgaria, and in France. Of course, since the revolution we have been able to train men from an early age, and now also men are recognized. We have developed the Cuban Ballet School according to our own physical characteristics, our own taste, within the boundaries imposed by international techniques and standards. We are doing a great deal of work with children, and at the same time we give educational talks in widespread centers."

Jorge Esquivel is one of the school's stars. He was a foundling in the Casa de Beneficencia Maternidad de Habana, an institution for children whose parents had no means of support. Alicia and the Cuban revolution gave him opportunities he would never otherwise have had.

Alicia continues: "We also have another company, the Ballet of Camagüey, and also the Folkloric Ballet, and a third company that dances at the opera, and a fourth that dances for television. All dancers say they have broken down the prejudices against dancing as a homosexual activity. We have always kept in contact with the working masses — always. We are members of the military work brigades, because we are also working, not a separate class of artists who consider themselves superior to the working class. We have our own mass organization, like the Communist Youth Union and our labor union. We are totally politically integrated and we do voluntary work. Often we harvest tomatoes, grapefruit, coffee, and oranges. We used to harvest sugarcane, but that was too strenuous, and after studying the situation the government agreed to assign us work more in line with our profession."

Jorge Esquivel adds: "Whenever there is a mobilization, all our people go; there is a high level of revolutionary consciousness. We work together in labor unions. We keep in touch with the managers in order to plan political and ideological work for our fellow workers. We have cultural activities such as museum visits, expositions, book discussions, and movie debates. There are weekly group meetings about administration and governance. Staff, stars, and pupils eat, dress, and play communally."

Cuba is a small country, and in a sense Alicia is a prisoner of its political position. She uses the island as a springboard, however, a jumping-off place for repeated trips to South America and all the Communist countries. Further, she is happy there. In Cuba she is treated like a queen, and she deeply loves the land. "I can only stay away from Havana three, four months at the most," she says. "I need come back. I need how blue the sky. And most of all I need the sea." Above all, the building of a company is a fascinating necessity to her. Hers is a good company, worthy to be a national company. Unfortunately, it is not quite of that stature, because it has only one central figure, one star, one set of capabilities and achievements. It is the vehicle for a single woman. There have been several people in the history of dancing who have made their own troupes their tools, but those troupes have not endured beyond the performing of the central figure, and they cannot possibly grow or perpetuate themselves.

Alicia says repeatedly that she believes in the people and the people's rights and the people's expression, but in translation it is her rights and her best interests that she serves. The marked limitations of her disability are ever present. No dancer is allowed to surpass these limits or to outdance her, and the choreography must adapt to this peculiar Olympian restraint. She keeps younger dancers straitjacketed beside her, refusing to let them advance to bigger roles, which could allow them to rival her or replace her. To possible rivals she can be deadly. She believes in equal sharing, but not in the theater and not truly in political situations. Does any Communist? She invites great men to dance with her, but never great women. Maya Pliset-skaya's brother, Agary Plisetsky, has been her partner for years, but Maya, a very great Russian star, has not been asked to stand on the same stage. No great choreographers have been developed by Alicia's company; Alberto did the chore for many years, and now there are others, who don't rank because they have to serve Alicia's purposes and also because this theater has the quaint habit of not paying choreographers. This rather dampens the enthusiasm of visiting creators.

Now, at sixty-nine, an unheard-of age for a classical ballet dancer (in the mid-nineteenth century, ballet stars retired willingly when they reached the age of forty), Alicia still practices every day and still performs. Occasionally her grandsons partner her. She performs excerpts from *Swan Lake* and *Giselle* — seldom the long, body-wringing roles, but she performs. The excerpts she chooses are those bits requiring the most rapid and brilliant footwork. "When will be my last performance?" she says. "Just do not miss any of my performances, because you don't know exact if that's going to be the last performance."

Alicia has accomplished many great things. She has served dancing beautifully and she has served her country. Will she have the nobility of spirit to accept the fact that she is mortal? Will she be able to make the enormous gesture of yielding to history and bowing aside so that the Ballet de Cuba can develop and progress? She has done so much in her life, this fragile, nervous girl. Can she do this? To step aside requires the creative vision of a prophet, the humility of a saint. This may prove to be a crueler, more insupportable challenge than her blindness.

II

IMPRESARIOS

THE BROTHERS SHUBERT were a legend while they lived. They were also a power and a point of view. During their ascendancy, from 1902 to 1963, they booked over a thousand theaters in the United States, of which they owned outright or leased on a long-term basis 110. This aggregation amounted to the largest theater management holding in the history of the world, state and royal theaters excepted. In fact, after defeating Marc Klaw and Abe Erlanger's theatrical syndicate in a struggle for supreme power, the Shuberts maintained what virtually amounted to a monopoly. They manipulated these theaters at their pleasure until the antitrust forces curtailed the vast majority of everything.

The Shuberts were concerned with the theater for financial reasons and would present anything the law permitted if they thought there was cash in the project, and in the course of sixty years they sponsored almost everything, including some shows that were good. It was difficult to approach them with a new idea, because they bought only what had been proven salable; this usually turned out to be sex. But they accomplished one noteworthy triumph: they kept in operation the only theaters that withstood the overwhelming onslaught of movies in the twenties, thirties, and forties. The living American theater owes them this debt. The Shubert estate still operates fifteen theaters in New York, Chicago, Boston, Philadelphia, and California.

The brothers Shubert were originally three: Lee, Jake, and Sam (Levi, Jacob, and Samuel S. Szemanski). There are disagreements about their birthplace, but it is likely they were born in Shervient, Lithuania. It is known that they grew up in Syracuse, New York. They experienced extreme poverty when young, and the memory of these hard days dominated their point of view always. An older sister was said to have died of malnutrition.

Sam, the handsomest and seemingly the most promising, died young, killed in a railway accident, and the remaining two, Lee and Jake, mourned publicly and long. Whether they felt real fraternal grief may be questioned, but they created a tragic legend, a mystique of a young man cut off in the flower of promise. They hung Sam's picture, a rather big one that depicted him as good-looking, serious, glossy, and urbane, with a large cowlick swept over his forehead, in the place of honor —that is, adjacent to the box office, where he could keep a watchful eye and where, no doubt, he would have preferred above all places to be. After 1905, the year of his death, for as long as the other two brothers lived this picture hung in the lobby of every one of the Shubert theaters.

Lee and Jake prospered steadily and enormously, so that in the thirties, when most people were starving and most businesses were going broke, they found themselves accumulating property interests. They specialized in acquiring legitimate, not movie, theaters, in building them and in keeping them. Nearly all the theaters of America were being converted into or replaced by movie palaces, the more ornate of which displayed levitating orchestras, entrance pools, emerging Wurlitzers, light displays, and remarkably opulent powder rooms. Certain towns that were traditional stops in the road-show business shortly became devoid of any legitimate theaters whatsoever. Accordingly, there were large expanses of America that could no longer house a single play with living actors. Those few that lasted, one could be sure, were Shubert houses. Certainly the Shuberts persisted in this practice not for the love of the theater or from any great sense of altruism, which was an emotion unknown to them, but from the sure instinct that theaters occupied land, that theaters stood on central land and therefore were accruing in value every year. The Shuberts were pre-Trump in era, but their ideas and predatory appetites were equally grandiose.

There was a nephew, Lawrence, who made his own tradition. He built the Forrest Theater in Philadelphia, which turned out to be a charming and handsome house but was found after completion to have one drawback, something Lawrence had forgotten: it had no dressing rooms. Lawrence hadn't noticed, and none of the craftsmen engaged on the enterprise had brought the omission to his attention. This turned out to be an important oversight. A building across the back alley had to be hastily purchased and a communicating underground passage constructed. The performers were required to do a lot of walking, and Lawrence's uncles had a lot to say about his oversight. I believe Lawrence was not encouraged to build again.

Jake, I never to my knowledge saw, for although his office was next door to Lee's and their business interests were inextricably intertwined, the brothers had not been on speaking terms for decades — or so they wished to appear. There were those who thought that neither took a deep breath without the other noting the exact metabolic change. Therefore, although Lee was my boss, it did not follow in the natural order of things that when I worked for him I would be introduced to his brother. No doubt Jake and his henchmen came to every one of our big rehearsals to case the project, but if so, their presence with great delicacy passed unremarked.

Mr. Lee looked old, which in 1937 he was not, being only sixty-four, but his appearance defeated time. His hair was black, shiny, and flat. He was sunburned to a somber mahogany and so embalmed with unguents and oils that his skin had lost mobility and texture. Indeed, I never saw an expression of any sort cross his face. To further the effect of mystery he had cultivated the habit of speaking without moving his lips. When he did this his voice was an old man's, high and querulous, which came oddly from that dark, foreboding, gummy skull. His eyes were black and brilliant and burned with watchful steadiness. He seemed not to hear or recognize or take any notice.

Mr. Lee knew everything that happened in theatrical New York, every click of every cash register in every box office, every complaint of every chorus girl about salary or dressing-room plumbing. He didn't know about music or manuscript, but that was of no consequence. He could buy taste. He could not buy watchfulness, not of his sort. This was the dark, primal, digestive instinct that means survival. This was the eye in the jungle, the shellfish opening and closing in Jurassic waters. There are animals that can sit unmoving in this fashion, with unblinking eyes, apparently lost in thought, until something edible passes. I think Mr. Lee would rather have lost a leg than a bargain . . . and he was rather more likely to.

The sad memory of his deprived youth and his forlorn family probably haunted him always and kept him conscious of the need for money, but I think besides his psychological terrors, which were largely apocryphal and unrealistic, he possessed a genuine talent for greed. He was a rapacious man (as was Jake) through natural instinct. Where money was concerned, he knew no mercy and he knew no generosity. There was an evil magic about him. Like any witch doctor, he knew just where the lifeblood trickled, and the young and helpless gazed on him as on a fetish or powerful taboo. There was magic, too, about the great maroon car and its liveried chauffeur that waited in Shubert Alley. When that awful receptacle blocked the passage, the taboo was inside working, and little girls sweated through their mascara as they passed by.

I was throughout my youth a consistent flop as a choreographer, so I was not privileged to work for Mr. Lee until 1937. However, nothing succeeds like failure, as Rebecca West once said to me, and sure enough, after my last disaster I was given a chance to work on a stage show called *Hooray for What!*, produced by Lee Shubert. It was to be written by Howard Lindsay and Russel Crouse, to be directed by Vincente Minnelli, then a scenery and costume designer, and to have a score by Harold Arlen and lyrics by E. Y. Harburg. Ed Wynn was to be the star; the leading ladies were to be Kay Thompson, the choral director and singer and later the creator of Eloise, and Hannah Williams (Mrs. Jack Dempsey). This was a notable group of names, and one would think they might ensure a high degree of professionalism. That turned out not to be the case, although the project began decently enough, with a telegram from Vincente Minnelli mentioning a small but adequate salary. I accepted gladly.

The business manager, since deceased, I did not care for. It is the custom to speak kindly of the dead, but having entertained nothing except loathing for him when he was alive, I see no reason now to veil my opinion. He it was who set the dancers' salaries: "thirty-five dollars a week, twenty dollars for rehearsal, and a little loving on the side." Plain and frank like that. He smiled, or he thought he smiled. His lips twitched; his eyes changed not a whit. I insisted on having two girls I knew, Mary Meyer and Dorothy Bird. He thought they were hideous. Mary had done a part for Irving Thalberg and George

Cukor and had modeled for Honigan-Huner for *Harper's Bazaar*, and Dorothy was one of Martha Graham's chief soloists and in body looked like something off the Parthenon, in face like one of Romney's milkmaids. But they were not the business manager's type (he had been in the cloak and suit business), and he did not want them around. Fortunately, Arlen, Harburg, and Crouse disagreed.

The business manager's type, or the type of the men who put up the money, or their lawyers' type, I was to learn well as time passed. They did not assemble all at once; they drifted in day by day, faded, jaded, raddled with drink, hawk-eyed, hardmouthed, and insolent, as rehearsals progressed. For every one of these chorus girls I had to let a trained dancer go. I had to take them, and I couldn't fire them, not if they fell down dead drunk at my feet, not if they were three hours late. They wore fine furs over their bathing suits, and diamonds, and platinum slave bracelets, and they talked about how they wished they were Barbara Hutton. Great limousines with liveried chauffeurs fetched them at the stage door. They didn't know their left knee from their hair dye. One astonishing girl, freshly back from Australia or South Africa, allowed as how she always got a job whenever she blew into town. It didn't matter how far along rehearsals were; people didn't dare not hire her. She didn't specify why. She thought I was nuts, but she liked me. They all thought I was nuts, but Girlie was the only one who liked me.

I committed the indiscretion of making the girls bend their backs the first day. The next rehearsal none of them could walk, and they complained to the management. I was asked to be reasonable. I also haughtily refused to give the favorites special things to do, although I knew very well what powers stood behind them. I might have played ball just a little, but I scorned to and worked my own ruin. I knew it, but I would not change.

Right off I got into trouble. The management, i.e. Mr. Lee and lawyers, wanted the girls exposed as much as possible:

face front always, bosom bared, legs just visible to the waist. Minnelli had planned all sorts of trick costumes that almost totally concealed their bodies—gas masks on their faces, barbed wire wrapped around their torsos (these were made of rubber, $45 a yard—at today's prices, $250). He was stressing irony. Business Manager was more interested in sex. Neither gave way. I took my instructions from Minnelli, since he had hired me.

During this entire time, during the rehearsal weeks and the ensuing out-of-town runthrough, Mr. Lee Shubert spoke to me only once. Cornering me backstage at a rehearsal and looking at me with opaque eyes, he whimpered, "In five weeks, couldn't you do better?" His high little voice was plaintive. "Those gorgeous, beautiful girls! Those gorgeous, beautiful girls!" He shook his head. "In their lovely, gorgeous dresses!"

I went once more to Minnelli. He was terse. "Keep the gas masks on them and the whole apparatus on their bodies." I had been trained to obey my director; I kept the gas masks covering their faces.

Rehearsals were a horror, and we never had ten minutes of privacy or quiet. When I sat onstage, I knew that the bosses had sneaked in and were prowling the aisles, whispering. I developed a tic from snapping my head to see who was spying behind me. When I sat out front, I knew by the sudden inattention and heightened chattering and giggling that you-know-who had entered through the stage door and was sitting just out of sight in the wings, teasing and snooping. I pleaded for privacy. I denounced. I warned. No use. The evening rehearsal was the after-dinner fun of all the bosses and their lawyers and their lawyers' guests, and all visiting bigwigs from Hollywood, and all backers and backers' wives. My little adventuresses primped and giggled and studied the guests with experienced eyes and paid me not the slightest mind.

Naturally—I was on the way out already, only I didn't know it. The management had never wanted me. They didn't like what they saw. It was Minnelli who had forced me on them, along with his damned gas masks and rubber wire. They got along busily with their plans at the back of the orchestra while I sat onstage and tried to compose something good and tried to see who was walking out there and why. Very soon the great dance director of musicals, Robert Alton, made his appearance, and I was told that he would divide the work with me. I had no agent. I accepted this without a word, but I was chilled to the last nerve. Thereafter I got the troupe for rehearsal only now and then.

We went to Boston. The dress rehearsal lasted, without break, three days and two nights. That is, we went into the theater on a Tuesday and came out on Thursday at noon. Minnelli had altered the sets for his own reasons without telling me. I had been given to understand that there would be exits at the four corners and had worked out the dance patterns accordingly; I now found there was one exit, directly center. Short of breaking up the dances, there was no way to get the dancers offstage. Also, the stage was not square but pie-shaped. The dancers were handed trains, hats, and swords they had not counted on. Several numbers became disasters.

Now the henchmen arrived in a body, together with the backers and agents, and walked up and down the aisles selecting what girls they wanted and giving advice indiscriminately to everyone about whom to fire and what to cut. They were a very handsome, upright group of men, as helpful in this time of stress as they were entertaining and refreshing.

Things weren't going too well, and we were all treated to the spectacle of our chiefs screaming at and reviling one another across the theater. Harburg, who had just gotten out of a hospital, denounced Minnelli; Minnelli, his eyes bulging from his head with fixed fury, turned on Wynn; Wynn took his time; Business Manager harassed and chivied Crouse and Lindsay. Hannah Williams was in tears; Jack Dempsey wanted to poke someone but did not rightly know whom; Kay Thompson was grim-lipped and sardonic. The chorus boys began to fall over like ninepins. (Hugh Martin was one of them. A few years later he made an international hit with his trolley song for Minnelli's wife, a young girl named Judy Garland. *Life* magazine published a picture of Hugh in Boston fainting against Mary Meyer's shoulder.) The girls, of course, were indestructible, but they were not happy.

Vincente Minnelli took to his bed, as did Harold Arlen, who was too miserable to show his face in the theater. Yipper Harburg went back to the hospital with stomach ulcers. The Shubert lawyers flew around like bats near a burning belfry. With Minnelli in bed, there was no one to take charge. Bob Alton steadily redirected the dances I hadn't finished. I knew I was licked; I hoped only to save something of my work.

We opened. Most of the show was lousy, some was good. That night, after the six-hour performance, my girls were called on the hotel phone and ordered upstairs to a party. Mary and Dorothy refused to go; Mary was fired two days later. Two of the singers they were rooming with did go and very soon came back weeping: the hospitality upstairs was of the real old-fashioned kind.

The next morning I was fired, as were, the following day, Hannah Williams and the leading man. B.M. fired me in the middle of the Touraine lobby, but added the ameliorating sentence, "We'll pay you through last night, all we owe you, and we'll give you your fare back to New York, but you must be out of your hotel room by noon today." Then he forbade me to re-enter the theater or speak to my dancers. I disobeyed and did talk to my leading dancer, Paul Haakon, a Dane. He had been a most sympathetic worker, but B.M. came hurrying over to call him aside, and Paul slunk away to the other side of the house.

Minnelli stayed in his bed and seemed unwilling and unable to cope. I went to say goodbye to him. He had no comment to make. I said goodbye to Harold Arlen, who smiled weakly from his pillow. "Does this make you feel bad?" Yes, Mr. Arlen, it did. The others were busy in the theater, tearing one another's throats open. Someone had given me red roses, and I said goodbye debonairly at the stage door, handing them out to whoever was still brave enough to risk a nod and a smile. I went alone to the railroad station. A few dancers broke from duress and stole away, Haakon among them, and just as the train was leaving came my Mary, her face streaming with tears. "They're tearing your work to pieces, every lovely thing you did," she said. "I couldn't save one thing. It's all wasted and destroyed. They wouldn't wait until you got out of town." I said something terse and four-lettered, kissed them all, and climbed aboard. I was free of it.

The next night, at two-thirty in the morning, my New York phone rang. It was Kay Thompson, and she said, "I have good news for you. B.M. has just fallen off the stage and broken his back."

"This isn't true," I said. "You're just saying this to make me feel good."

But it was true. His back was broken, all right. It had happened during a rehearsal that began at midnight. He had been scrabbling up over the footlights to tear the pretty dress I had allotted to Dorothy Bird from her back, in order to give it to one of his harpies. His face was distorted with hate, his fingers were clutching for the hooks, when his foot slipped. Not one person on the stage moved to help him for appreciable seconds. In fact, they screamed with laughter until they realized he had been badly hurt. Then they stood circumspectly but grinning in real satisfaction. Even from the hospital, though, he wove his spell. Kay Thompson was fired, just tapped on the shoulder and told as she went from the stage, "That will be your last performance, Miss T."

The show wandered around out of town for three and a half months before it dared come to New York.

Equity has since made most such abuses impossible. I am sure a great deal of the reform stemmed directly from this unseemly and disreputable production. The 1990 union fee check for a chorus dancer was a minimum of $815 a week, and there are all kinds of stringent rules about firing for just cause and not for whim. Firing for whim is accompanied by dire penalties.

That was how it was, however, in the thirties and in the days when the Shuberts reigned supreme. The theater was full of vigor and life and challenge—the challenge of whether you would be able to eat the next day, or whether in fact you would be able to draw the next breath. Such an atmosphere kept one on one's toes all right.

The theater is not like that anymore. Young actors today are protected, armored, cosseted by the crutches, braces, and plaster casts of Actors Equity. Then they were totally exposed and had to fend for themselves. In a way, I am glad I knew that theater, because it taught me much about human nature and human ambition, and about myself too. Looking back, I realize there are worse ways of earning one's living. There is, for instance, prostitution, which I have heard spoken of very poorly, and there is combing in the garbage heaps for scraps of food, and there is working on a treadmill, or in a poorhouse, or in a prison. But in the latter cases one is guaranteed shelter and some sort of food.

Now the Shuberts are dead, the ones we knew, the originals. They have left a vast fortune, which is entrusted to the guardianship of very shrewd businessmen, and they have left a foundation that helps young artists—really helps them, all kinds—and they have left a remarkable library and research collection housed in the Lyceum Theatre, with whole floors of documents and pictures. They are becoming known as benevolent sponsors of the arts.

But my memory of Mr. Lee is of his sad, mournful voice in the only direct remark he ever vouchsafed me—"Those gorgeous, beautiful girls! Those gorgeous, beautiful girls!"— and his sad headshake. Inasmuch as all my shows since *Oklahoma!* except *Brigadoon* played in Shubert theaters, we had occasion quite often to meet; we bowed with silent ceremony and passed on.

One of the chorus girls in *Hooray for What!*—a blonde, Ecky

—married Lee Shubert secretly, and on his death she unexpectedly inherited a very great deal of money, to the evident distress of other family members. In her gentle, insistent way she hung on to it, for keeps. Never mind the lawyers, or the lawyers' henchmen. She got it. Good for Ecky!

B I L L Y   R O S E

FOR FIFTEEN YEARS I gave auditions constantly, hoping vainly for a job. Fifteen years is a tidy stretch, particularly when it extends from twenty to thirty-five years old, and during that interval I never got a single job from the effort. Then I did get a job, a good one, without an audition, and I was a success. Was everything different? Nope. Oh, other people acted differently, but I was the same, just as good as I had been, and just as flawed. I was not surprised. Now, however, I paid income tax, which was a step up. It was droll to see how the others behaved.

During this time I auditioned for Billy Rose (William Samuel

Rosenberg), the manager of a circus and several nightclubs, including the Diamond Horseshoe restaurant, as well as of several outstanding theatrical extravaganzas. He had begun his career as a songwriter and composed the lyrics of several dozen hits, among them "A Cup of Coffee, a Sandwich, and You," which Gertrude Lawrence sang so adorably in *Charlot's Revue of 1926.*

My audition for Rose took place in the afternoon, at three o'clock, in the empty Diamond Horseshoe, which was very elegant and cozy. He was accompanied by his wife, Fanny Brice, the great comedienne and star of the Ziegfeld Follies, but there were no assistants or advisers. After the first two dances, which I performed in full costume and full makeup, warming up as though I were going to dance on the Metropolitan Opera stage, I asked him if he would like to see any more. He said yes, indeed he would, it was fine, very interesting, and Miss Brice was eager also. So I did another, and another. By five o'clock I had performed eight different dances in full costume, changing shoes from pointe to heels and back to barefoot, with partner, without partner. The backstage was littered with my wigs and skirts. I was exhausted.

Rose came back and told me that it had all been extremely delightful and that he was immensely gratified to have seen it, and his wife added her intelligent and gracious praise. He concluded by saying that he would think about employing me, although he didn't see at the moment how he could. But he would think about it. That closed the episode — two hours of grueling effort, with a paid dresser, a paid accompanist, a partner, taxis to take, my big skirts tied up in sheets, and the packing and unpacking and storing, which I had to take charge of myself. Actually it was two days' labor. I had no money for incidental expenses; I had to borrow. Nothing came of it.

A few years later, on October 16, 1942, I premiered my ballet *Rodeo* at the Metropolitan Opera House with the Ballet Russe de Monte Carlo. The ballet was a smash and had a historic opening. Not only the auditorium but the lobby of the theater buzzed with excitement. Billy Rose was among the loudest. "Where has she been?" he cried, waving his arms. "Who discovered her? She can't have just sprung to this eminence from nowhere. She must have been somewhere. Where did she hide herself?" In all my subsequent experience with Rose, I never reminded him of the afternoon of the audition.

He would have sent for me after the *Rodeo* opening, but I was engaged immediately by the New York Theatre Guild and Rodgers and Hammerstein to do a show which came into New York under the title *Oklahoma!* This was followed by two more big hits and by my marriage to a soldier who stood in line to go overseas (he did indeed go, in November 1943).

In the summer of 1944 Billy Rose bought the Ziegfeld Theatre, a jewel of a theater designed by the great Viennese architect Joseph Urban. He aimed to transform it into a music hall, leaving the beautiful multicolored frescos intact. In the meantime he had divorced Fanny Brice and married Eleanor Holm, a lush and extremely beautiful swimmer who had been thrown off our national Olympic team for drinking while training. Billy cared not a whit for her loss of athletic status; he married her and starred her in his aquacade at the 1939 World's Fair, held in Flushing Meadow, Long Island. There she swam in an open-air pool with Buster Crabbe, and they were a gorgeous sight to behold.

So in 1944 Rose was planning a revue for a later date. He sent for me, and I was taken to his house in Sutton Place— the house that figured so picturesquely in his divorce proceedings against Eleanor Holm. I was ushered in to meet him in the beautiful drawing room, which was hung with Memlings and Rembrandts and lit by full-length windows that gave a magnificent view of the passing traffic on the East River. He was lounging in slacks and an open shirt on a superb Queen Anne settee done in seventeenth-century needlepoint. After installing me in a winged chair that should have been in a museum and offering me cigarettes and chocolates, which were lying about in receptacles of Georgian silver, he broached his plan. He waved his hands a good deal and spoke slowly and very softly, as though to stun me with the surprise of his ideas alone. He made a practice of throwing each idea away as though it were nothing special, only one of dozens he was stocked with. I sat quietly on the edge of my embroidered seat and listened. He did not watch for reactions; he took them for granted.

Briefly, he intended to make his new acquisition into an extraordinarily deluxe music hall. He was handing his other businesses over to his assistants. They could cheat him or not; if they did, he did not care to know about it, as he was going to devote his time to creative work. What he had in mind was a revue of just the kind that had never been attempted—the best of each sort of thing in the entire entertainment world. The dancing was to be by Alicia Markova and like *Sylphides*, but better and new, not something everyone had seen, contrived probably by Anton Dolin or possibly Frederick Ashton or someone better, if possible. The scenery was to be by everyone good, likewise the costumes; the comedy sketches would be by the greatest living writers, or better. As for the music, the absolute best in the whole world, the Philadelphia Orchestra—or if it was not available that season, as many men and just as good and conducted by Leopold Stokowski himself.

"What would you think?" he asked me in his languid soft voice, shifting his feet up onto a petit-point scene of stags and maidens and putting a piece of ecclesiastical velvet under his elbow. "What would you think if you went into a theater and sat down expecting to see just an ordinary funny revue, and the curtain went up and there instead of the usual opening number was a full symphony orchestra? And out came Stokowski in full evening dress and he raised his baton and started conducting Deboossy's 'Claire de Loon'? What would you think?"

"I should be astonished."

"I should think you would be!" He sat straight up.

"And I should think Mr. Stokowski would be too," I murmured, adding very softly, "It was written for solo piano."

"No problem. No problem."

I glanced around the walls. A Canaletto, a Memling, a Rembrandt, a Hals. In the hall, some eighteenth-century Venetian pen-and-wash gems. The breakfront with the irreplaceable Georgian collection. Maybe, on second thought, Mr. Stokowski would not be surprised.

"Now, from you," he continued, "we want a ballet — anything you like. A dream ballet, if you wish."

"No, please God, not a dream ballet, Mr. Rose! Everyone asks for that, and everyone has one whether I do it or not."

"Anything you wish."

"I can't commit myself until I have a really good idea."

"But you have those."

"Very rarely — and I can never count on having them."

"Oh, I have dozens. I'll give you some of mine. 'Alice in Funnyland'? Comics, you know. No? I would have thought so. Well, then, girls and boys saying goodbye during the war. That could be full of comedy bits, and very human. I tell you, if you want to see humanity" — he gave the velvet a stout thump for emphasis — "just go down to Pennsylvania Station and watch the soldiers and sailors with their women. There's more drama there in ten minutes than in a whole Broadway season. I've stood there for hours."

"I've stood there too, Mr. Rose, to say goodbye."

He lowered his gaze from the carved wainscoting and looked at me levelly, then put out his cigarette and reached across to pat my shoulder. "I suppose you have. Yes, of course, my dear. Where's your man now?"

"Overseas."

So the conversation shifted off the possible ballets, which was just as well.

Rose graciously asked me to go out to dinner with him and Eleanor. For some reason I can't recall, perhaps to get a coat or a script, he invited me to accompany him to his room. There was not the slightest hint of impropriety or self-consciousness in this. Billy Rose dramatized himself wonderfully well, but the role he affected best was that of the casual and absolutely natural genius against a background of splendor. One rarely saw his secretaries or helpers. Later, when he had installed himself in the Ziegfeld Theatre, he frequently wandered about the upper halls and rehearsal rooms in his pajamas and silk robe, and even went downstairs so attired to the next-door Chinese restaurant for a snack. One could often find him there, conversing with friends in evening dress, Billy in his comfortable silk dressing gown, his little feet sockless in Moroccan slippers.

Being frankly curious to see as much of the house as possible, I went with him gladly. His room was decorated like a tent, with red-and-white-striped material hung from a ridge pole. The bed was single, simple, and Napoleonic (Billy Rose was small in stature too), of fine Empire mahogany. The other furniture was equally chaste but priceless. There was a small table, I recall, in the guise of a drum, and on the walls were maps of reassuring spots like Wagram and Austerlitz. It was a room of memories.

We waited downstairs by the elevator for his wife, and when Eleanor appeared, svelt in impeccable black crepe, we were studying the ink Guardi in the hall. She peered over our shoulders.

"I should think his wrist would have got tired making all those wiggly lines for waves, line after line."

"No, he loved it," said Billy.

"Well, I don't see why," said Eleanor. "I couldn't stand doing it, I must say." She sighed and slipped into a box-pleated mink that had purple tones in the deeper folds. "A good many of these pictures leave me cold. You should see the one Billy hung opposite my bed." Her beautiful lean hand brushed back a lock of sun-touched hair that kept falling over her cheek.

I had seen Miss Holm's bedroom only in the newspapers. Apparently it contained a bed approximately half an acre in size, covered with white satin and swan's-down. In the photo Eleanor lay across it with the taut neatness of a champion, the discipline of her body a tantalizing contrast to the lush background.

"Opposite my bed, where I can see it every day when I wake up or go to sleep, he hung a drunk," she explained.

"Toulouse-Lautrec's *Absinthe Drinker*," murmured the donor.

"The lithograph?" I asked.

"Heavens, no! The painting. It's very large," he said.

"Well, I said to him," continued Eleanor, settling in the taxi in cerements of mink and an aura of perfume, "I said, 'Take that drunken hoor out of here or you won't find me one of these days.' "

"Did you take it away?" I asked my host.

He hummed a little tune. We drew up to Toots Shor's.

All the Georgian silver and Queen Anne stitching and uncheerful painting had taken Eleanor by surprise, but it did not abash her. She cared for it well and ran a house — what am I saying? She ran *three* houses flawlessly and was a considerate and gracious hostess. But she never pretended for one moment to be anything she was not.

We had a very pleasant dinner. Billy was a good talker, and his wife had a plain, outspoken way of stating her opinion that was extremely appealing.

"Excuse me," I said, "I do not wish to be vulgar, but that is the largest gem I have ever seen — outside the Tower of London, of course." My eyes were fixed on the topaz in Eleanor's bracelet, which was the size and shape of an old-fashioned reading glass. The stone was easily as big as the palm of my hand.

Billy chuckled. "They made a picture called *Diamond Horseshoe*. It didn't cost me a moment's effort and it brought in thousands. I had to do something for Eleanor."

"It's too heavy!" Mrs. Rose dropped her arm on the table with a clank that caused the glasses to ring. I got the impression not that she was dissatisfied with her presents so much as that she would have liked to have had a voice in their choosing.

"How do you manage to do so much?" I asked Billy. "All your business, and the out-of-town aquacades, and *Carmen*

Jones, and a new show every few weeks at the Horseshoe, and your daily newspaper column, and every now and then a new song . . ."

"Oh, it's all fun," he said. "I never worry—and I have lots of ideas. I'm always thinking of things. You know," he said, taking a forkful of the extravagantly mellow and suave graham-cracker pie that was the specialty of Toots Shor's, "if they could make Oscar Hammerstein into a pie, he would taste like this." He ate a generous mouthful.

Several of my later hits played in Billy Rose's lovely theater, and I got used to seeing him at all hours of the day and night, creeping about in pajamas and slippers. He would frequently go next door to the bar and have a corned beef sandwich and a whiskey, and then he would expound like a senior critic on the merits of the work in progress. Nobody asked him to, but he told us anyway. Sometimes it was heartening and sometimes not. He knew what we were doing because the top balcony of the theater gave onto his private office suite, and he would steal in to see what was happening.

During the rehearsals of *Gentlemen Prefer Blondes* he was extremely active in his counseling, although he was not a member of the staff. At one memorable meeting after rehearsal, our chairs were drawn up in a circle on the stage around the center table, where the directors, authors, and producer gathered. It was a meeting of awful consequence for me, and I knew beforehand it would be. It was a court martial, an auto-da-fé. A scene I had written, with the authors' permission but without their approval, was going to be deleted, together with the dance that illustrated it, and the star dancer whom I had teased from Ballet Theatre and persuaded to try her luck on Broadway. The bosses didn't like her, and she was going to be fired without ceremony, most brutally. Oliver Smith, one of the producers, did not make matters easy for me, by advising me that he expected her to commit suicide.

I sat at the table silent and tense, waiting for the axes and knives. I drew close to John C. Wilson, the director, who had always been friendly and understanding. Wilson was a handsome man, with snow-white hair, heavy black brows, and a sweet smile. He had been Noël Coward's close friend and was something of a wit. He was a good producer, although not a good director. He was however, directing this show.

Suddenly there appeared Billy Rose, who drew a chair up and joined our circle. I turned to Wilson in great consternation and whispered, "Did you invite him?"

"Certainly not," said Wilson. "Did you?"

"God, no."

Through his column in the *New York Post*, Rose was one of the best-known gossips in the trade. Whatever went on in our meeting would shortly be broadcast. Not choosing to have the court martial publicized, I signaled to Wilson to play for time. We tried to outwait Rose with banal and trivial conversation. He waited also.

I whispered to Wilson, "I will not speak in front of that man, nor will I listen to anyone else."

"Quite right," Wilson said. "Let's go to one side." So we took ourselves to the side of the stage and stood among the ropes and pulleys of the wings. Wilson had a long glass of milk of a dark brown color, his invariable comfort. It was milk and brandy, and he lived on it. "We might as well talk business while we're waiting," he said, and he started in on matters that concerned us.

After about eight minutes Rose sauntered over. "Well," he said amiably, rocking on his toes, "would you like to hear what an old pro thinks of your show?"

Wilson raised his eyebrows and turned around. "Oh!" he said.

Rose continued. "I thought you'd like to hear what I think."

"Are you speaking as a real estate operator or as a columnist? Or perhaps as a nightclub or circus producer?"

Rose went dead white and drew in his breath sharply. "I'm speaking as someone who's taken many, many thousands of dollars out of this little old trade and is very grateful. You have too," he said, staring at Wilson, "and you should be grateful, and I'm very, very hurt at what you've said." With that he walked away.

Wilson and I returned to the counsel table quietly. "Now," said Wilson, "let's get to work."

Rose was with us once more. "I consider I've been insulted," he said, "and I'm very hurt. I'm very hurt."

"I couldn't be sorrier," said Wilson. Then he murmured, "Most regrettable. I'm sorry, Mr. Rose, the meeting is closed." He bit the words off. "Private." He flicked the ashes off his cigarette.

Without a word Rose turned on his heel and walked slowly away.

"Well!" said one of the producers. "Whatever brought that on? Why was he here, I wonder?" This was a curious remark, because this very producer had secretly invited Rose in.

The meeting continued. The scene and dance I had written were eliminated, and the girl was fired. She did not commit suicide, but she did leave the profession.

Eleanor Holm subsequently divorced Billy Rose with a good deal of publicity. As I recall, she nailed the door of their Sutton Place house shut and took the paintings hostage, even the despised Toulouse-Lautrec *Absinthe Drinker*; she fastened a Memling across the inside locks. Rose was distraught, but he finally paid up and got his freedom and his treasures. There were three subsequent divorces, two from the same lady. Thereafter he all but lived in the Ziegfeld Theatre.

The last time I encountered him I went to raise money for American Ballet Theatre, which was badly in need of financial help. (It always was, and it is now — a condition true of nearly every American ballet company.) I went by appointment up to Rose's golden office at the top of the Ziegfeld Theatre, with its beautiful Urban frescoes and the 1920 art deco Viennese chairs — oh, so elegant! Billy sat behind a kidney-shaped Sheraton desk, his Moroccan slippers lost in a rug with a three-inch pile. I pushed across the floor to him, sat down, and stated my case. All the time he talked he was toying with two drum-headed pistols of great worth, probably of eighteenth-century workmanship. He knew I recognized their value and was pleased. He preferred not to trouble with his valuable toys unless he had an appreciative audience.

He heard me out, then he said softly, "But you see, dear, I don't like dancing. I can't bear it."

"But you do like the progressive theater, don't you?"

"I sure as hell don't," he said.

"Well," I said, "that closes the matter," and I rose.

On an easel nearby was an enormous painting of some biblical subject. It was roughly eight feet by four feet, and it was by Rembrandt. "This," he said, with a flourish of his beautifully manicured hand, "is what I like."

"Well, that's safe," I said. "Congratulations. Rembrandt doesn't need the money. We do." I tried to walk out promptly, which was difficult on that carpet.

"Wait!" he said. "Wait, Agnes. Come back. I can't let you leave my office empty-handed. You can't go away like that. I'll give you a check." With that he wrote out a check and handed it to me. It was for $150—not even enough to buy one tutu.

The interesting part of this story, if any, is that Billy had been in the theater the whole of his life. He knew what everything cost, and he knew that $150 would not buy a tutu. It would hardly buy one pair of chorus shoes. I imagine he thought it would keep my mouth shut.

He wasn't always mean about contemporary art. He gave the city of Jerusalem a sculpture garden designed by Isamu Noguchi. It must have cost considerably more than a million. Maybe he was telling the exact truth: he didn't like dancing, and he hoped this small check would put an end to my whining. Sculpture lasts and will be remembered. Is it possible that Billy Rose is going down in history as an important art patron? It is.

THE MARQUIS DE CUEVAS was a man of vast wealth and unlimited enthusiasm for the ballet, a combination to set local impresarios' pulses racing and manners tripping. Like a tropical hummingbird, however, he buzzed about teasingly, only to elude all efforts at capture. Why he chose to build a ballet company we can only guess, but he did.

His entry in Anatole Chujoy and P. W. Manchester's *The Dance Encyclopedia* reads:

De Cuevas, Marquis George (eighth Marquis de Piedrablanca de Guana de Cuevas), American patron of the arts, b. 1886,

Chile, of a Spanish father and Danish mother (American citizen since 1940), d. Feb. 22, 1961, Cannes, France; m. Margaret Strong, granddaughter of the late John D. Rockefeller; sponsor of the Masterpieces of Art exhibition at the N.Y. World's Fair (1939–40); founder and director of Ballet Institute (1943) and Ballet International which made its N.Y. debut in 1944.

Suddenly and most unnecessarily in October 1943 the Marquis announced his very own new company, a large, permanent company with unlimited financing. He decided to waste no time in slow developments. He bought the old but lovely Columbus Circle Theatre and completely renovated it, including the prettiest crystal chandelier in New York. It was a wonderful gala theater, white and gold with crimson velvet. The stage was a bit small, but the company took a pleat in *Sylphides* and squashed it into view, although the corps de ballet lines came out rumpled. Nijinska was hired for new works, Salvador Dali did the scenery, and Gian Carlo Menotti contributed his first fine big score, *Sebastian*.

Oh, how had de Cuevas managed to escape the baits and snares set by so many suave tongues? People had appealed to his artistic instincts, to his ambition for fame, to his concern for young artists, to his zest for creating, to the paltry arithmetic of possible financial developments. All to no avail. He wanted to have his own company all to himself, his own way, one that would bear his name. There followed on the instant a gnashing of teeth and the prediction of doom and bankruptcy. Dancers stood to gain, of course, but they had no voice in any of these matters. They just quietly rushed to sign up.

The Marquis soon had dancers enough. What he needed was choreographers, and in a dragnet operation, he approached all of us, every one. His emissary was a young Greek named Yolas who had been the dancing partner of Theodora Roosevelt. After several years of touring with moderate success, Roosevelt had given up dancing, married the young painter Tom Keogh, and started her brilliant career as a novelist (*Meg, The Double Door*). Yolas cast about for other activities and found the Marquis.

Rehearsals were held daily at Studio 61 Ballet Arts in Carnegie Hall. The Marquis arrived to supervise, frequently took charge, and on occasion, growing remarkably exorcised over points of discipline, jumped onto the floor to act. Diana Adams once told me with goggle eyes of the morning when the Marquis discovered that the star, Viola Essen, had absented herself without explanation. He flew into a passion and backed Yolas right across the room, denouncing him in French for failing to keep order. The dancers stood by, astounded. Finally the Marquis, who was considerably shorter than the large Greek athlete, grabbed Yolas by the earlobes and banged his head against the wall several emphatic times.

"Marquis, Marquis," groaned Yolas. "Pas de scandal!"

"Don't be an ass," said the Marquis tartly, punishing his skull once more. "The dancers don't know I'm scolding you. They can't understand what's going on. I'm talking French."

Yolas, no doubt chastened, came to me with a royal summons. I begged off time and again, but finally the great black Hispano-Suiza with the crest on the doors waited for me in 57th Street. I was led into it directly out of a morning class, at the outlandish hour I had deliberately and uncivilly designated as convenient for my lunch. Yolas and I progressed on feathers to the East Sixties, where a butler flung open the house door. I was led up hushing rugs to the first or drawing-room floor and left in a long narrow salon, where I sat gingerly on the edge of a baby-blue satin chair. Yolas went to fetch his master while I contemplated a naked amorous Bouguereau nine feet high. Suddenly there was a scream and the Marquis was with me.

"A *biche!* A *biche!* She has ankles like a *biche!*" he shrieked, and sat down opposite me, staring with satisfaction at my legs, which were decorously and nervously crossed. This was a flattering start, and I simpered prettily and rapidly recrossed my ankles several times.

The Marquis himself had very neat ankles, and his slender, delicate feet were shod in custom-made glove-kid boots. He was a trigger-tight little person, all black and white, and as he gazed at me with his agate eyes he seemed to be mentally biting his nails. Now and then a small flame winked in the opaque pupils. It gave promise of life but was no clue to emotion. He leaned forward or jerked with nervous excitement, and swung around and rotated on his blue satin chair as on a trapeze—and his voice was shrill. He wore the beautifully cut black alpaca trousers of a Spanish dancer and a shirt buttoned down the side of the neck like a Russian officer's but of the color chosen by Mussolini and Franco as suitable to their ideas. Since we were in the middle of the war and were battling most terribly with legions of fanatics in just this color, I didn't find his choice endearing. But I would guess that he had no personal convictions and found it merely teasing to be provocative.

With a series of yelps and shrieks he expatiated on his plans, which were in essence grandiose. At the moment he wanted me, and that I had other commitments and affiliations made no matter. He wanted me. He was, he informed me, going to have me. "But," he shouted with a giggle, "I am an autocrat. I am a true dictator. I tell the choreographers what to do."

"Which choreographers do you tell what to do?"

"All—all. Nijinska don't mind."

"Does she not? Well, now, who would have thought!"

"No. And when Romanov restages *Giselle*, he have no time for all details. He fixes the feet like so." The Marquis de Cuevas indicated the choreographer fixing the dancers' feet individually, a sight I have never been privileged to witness. "But he forgets the heads and I fix the heads. I run up and down the lines and fix heads like so, and so, and so . . ." He made a gesture of fixing heads reminiscent of the man who used to turn flapjacks in the window of Child's restaurant.

"Monsieur le Marquis," I said quietly, "I don't permit anyone to fix the heads in my rehearsals."

"No? You'll see what a help it is! I'm a dictator—absolute as to taste."

"I'm pretty sassy myself in my own rehearsals."

"Oh, we understand each other perfectly. We're going to get along."

This joyous conclusion was cut short by the entrance of the Marquise, a quiet, unobtrusive, brown-haired lady with very sad eyes and a gentle voice. I naturally presumed she would be our hostess, but after murmuring the amenities, she melted away. I never saw her again.

The Marquis had waved a hand and announced, "My wife." He then seemed to suspend all animation until she was gone.

"Now for lunch," he said, bounding up. Yolas, who had sat throughout unspeaking, jumped up on his strong legs and began to look interested. We were ushered into a long and superbly appointed dining room. At a table that could easily have accommodated forty, three places were laid—rather sparsely, I thought—at the entrance end, as though the butler had made sure that we could not get too firm a foothold in his domain.

We had hardly started on our cold sliced lamb and lettuce when angry voices were heard below. The butler whispered. The Marquis said, "Tch! Tch!" and "Pardon," threw down his napkin, and went to attend. Yolas attempted to make some sort of small talk and passed me cold lamb repeatedly. The shouting rose to the point of violence. There were several piercing screams.

I asked, "In God's name, what's going on?"

"Katya Gelesnova and her mother are suggesting a higher salary," explained Yolas.

"But I know Katya well. She is a gentle, kind, and quiet girl. She would never shout like that."

"That is not Katya. That is the Marquis—and her mother too, of course."

We finished lunch and then our host returned, smoothing down his hair and looking brisk. The butler had removed all traces of the meal. We sat facing a bare table. The forks and knives were assiduously taken away on a silver salver. The Marquis had not eaten a bite.

"Oh," he wailed, "I want something to eat."

The butler inclined punctiliously. "Too late," he said.

"Oh, Thomas," said the Marquis to his retreating back, "just anything, just something. I'm hungry."

Thomas barely turned. He stood with the implements for eating protectingly withdrawn in his far hand. "I have to set tea for thirty people, sir, and I'd better get at it." There was real rebuke in his tone. Both sentences were rebuking, in different ways.

"Anything," the Marquis begged. "On a tray, in my bedroom — anything. Some little tea, je vous en prie . . ."

Thomas looked exhausted and left.

I tried to understand what kind of ballet company the Marquis was planning and what his modern repertory was to consist of. He was distraught and unfocused, and he kept looking first at the door through which he had reappeared from his financial exercises and then at the door through which all hope of lunch had receded. Finally he said, "Ah!"

The tray had arrived — a small black tin tray such as is used in third-class cafeterias, presenting a kitchen cup and a small tin teapot with a teabag hanging out of it. Four saltines lay on a thick white crockery plate.

"And now, sir, if you please," said the butler, literally sweeping us out of the room. The doors snapped to behind us, and I got the impression of enormous activity suddenly released. Battalions of servants were swinging around that great table with Sèvres cups and crested plates.

The Marquis carried his own tray, although Yolas courteously offered to help. It weighed little enough, God knows. We made our way upstairs to the Marquis's bedroom. This was a surprise, a cross between a side chapel in a Latin American church and the corner of a nineteenth-century French museum. The *pièce de résistance* or center of focus was quite properly the bed, a narrow pallet with very high foot- and headboards of Spanish wrought iron entirely interlaced, festooned, and looped with stage jewelry — bracelets, necklaces, earrings, tiaras, and rings of diamonds and pearls, emeralds and rubies, as thickly massed as in the window of a junk shop. The effect was both grotesque and frightening. The pallet was quite simply and chastely covered with a zebra skin.

On the wall opposite the door was a splendid pen-and-wash drawing by Dali of a very naked young man. Facing the bed was an equally aggressive naked youth by Sandro Botticelli. When I took this in, my jaw dropped, or rather it would have if I'd thought to shut it after viewing the bed. I had just discovered that one could go on saying no without closing one's mouth. Every horizontal space supported a memento or objet d'art, either precious or peculiar but always extraordinary. Crucifixes and rosaries, fine snuffboxes, jeweled intaglios, goblets, madonnas, superb little missiles, phallic symbols, were scattered everywhere. This was a room straight out of Gautier's lushest daydreams.

Under a large glass bell in the corner, reposing on a velvet cushion, was what I thought I heard the Marquis designate as his wedding wreath. He may have said it was his wife's, but I thought he said it was his, and by this time I was bewildered enough to accept any statement. The wreath was of exquisite wax orange blossoms, a little bent, a little dusty, and obviously quite old, like the wreath of a holy effigy. About the whole room there was the air of a crypt made cozy with superstition. At the side of the bed was a massive door, leading, rumor said, into the next house, which the Marquis had bought for guests and friends. This door figured in Theodora Keogh's *The Double Door*.

The Marquis perched on a little carved chair of fine seventeenth-century workmanship, drank his unappetizing tea, and tried to get a definite commitment from me. But I was not so far gone that I would make a promise, and the conversation frayed out while my eyes rolled round and round that extraordinary room. At some mysterious moment my host seemed to know that the audience was at an end, and he politely but firmly terminated the interview. I hastily agreed that I had a rehearsal I must hurry to.

As I made my way down alone, I saw Thomas through the dining room door, placing the thirty-fourth gold-painted porcelain dish on the lace cloth. He looked at me coldly as he laid a heavy embossed spoon at its side, and an egg-fragile cup. I hastened out. From the mistress and her apartments there had been neither signal nor sound.

That terminated my negotiations with the Marquis. I saw him next at the opening of his ballet company, which had a valorous and inauspicious season. The press was stringent and the audience paltry, adding up to losses that his rival managers hoped would be decisive but that, though great, proved to be nothing of the sort.

Thereafter there was a lull in his balletic activities, while the Rockefeller lawyers grappled with the chaos. But in 1946–47, like a phoenix rising from particularly wet ashes, the Marquis announced a new season in Monte Carlo. There was a sudden exodus of disgruntled professionals from our shore. That company survived for fourteen years, until 1961, and played all over Europe and the Mediterranean, the Marquis from time to time summoning world-famous artists for remarkable productions.

To quote Chujoy again: "The Marquis became one of the most popular figures in the European ballet world, and his personality was especially loved by his public. He combined the elegance of a 'grand seigneur' with a real simplicity of heart. . . . His apartment in Paris at 7, quai Voltaire, was known to all ballet lovers. He usually received his visitors lying in his bed surrounded by his Pekingese dogs." He was a generous host, I have been told, and he was also—although this stretches credence—a devoted father.

As a start in establishing his reputation in Europe, he threw a wingding in Biarritz on Lake Chibertan. This was in 1953, but it rocked Europe in the real pre-war style. The rumor was that nearly half a million dollars were spent. The guests came from every corner of the world, all in eighteenth-century costumes, many designed by Paris couturiers. There were cries of *à la lanterne* up and down the Cote d'Azur, and a few not-too-gracious examples of the invited said the champagne was only so-so and this was the profligate stuff of which revolutions were made. There were pictures of the Marquis in a wig of grapes and a Louis Quinze satin suit, tastefully embroidered with real diamonds. But the thunder of the evening and the cream of the publicity were stolen away by Renée Jeanmaire, star of Roland Petit's Ballets de Paris, who arrived uninvited on a camel, accompanied by an entire French country circus, also uninvited. They did not think the champagne was much either, and this may be a fair appraisal, since they gave it their most assiduous attention.

Although there were strict injunctions about costume, the gatekeeper had obviously been lax. Since Renée, or Zizi as she was known, was all but stark naked, it could be said that she was in designated dress, but the Marquis took a dim view of her. His guests did not. Tired of thirty years of private *Sylphides* at Monte Carlo garden parties, they flocked to examine Renée's approach to the eighteenth century, and so did the worldwide newsreels. It makes one wonder what her attitude would have been to the Marquis's *Giselle* correction, "like so and like so." But one will never know; he invited her into his company no more than to his party, and a professional rapprochement was never attempted.

Alas, the ballet world is different over here. That is, it has always been rather drab where I have worked or played. I do not have a flair for the grand entrance. When I leave, the butlers barely glance up, but go on setting out the gold spoons, like so and like so and like so.

THE LAST

IMPRESARIO

For forty-four years, from 1930 to 1974, Sol Hurok was the most famous concert manager in the Western Hemisphere, and since there are no managers of comparable scope and power in the Orient, I think we can safely say he was the most famous in the world. His name was the hallmark for all things excellent, all things top-grade.

My husband, Walter Prude, was Hurok's personal assistant and frequent representative for thirty-two years. He went to him right after the war, in 1945, having been hired promptly on demobilization. One Christmas Eve about ten years later he found Hurok moping alone at his desk. The old man was sitting disconsolately in the dusk, his heavy, strong hands stretched before him on the blotter. Obviously he had been sitting that way for quite some time. He didn't like to read and he never wrote a letter. (He had secretaries for that, didn't he?) He just sat and thought about his loneliness.

"Good night, Mr. Hurok. Merry Christmas! What will you be doing tomorrow?" Walter called cheerfully, buttoning up and wrapping.

"Nothing," said Hurok, with infinite pathos, shaking his head mournfully.

Walter lost his own head. He was seized with a bout of seasonal folly. "Come to us. Oh, do! Please come!"

Walter looked at me guiltily when he came home and confessed.

I went white and then red. "God help us!" I murmured. "But I will not rearrange our table! Dr. Harold Taylor sits on my right. Mr. Hurok must take potluck."

Potluck? Headwaiters unseated cabinet ministers to accommodate him. Duchesses forwent their favorite oysters and Scotch salmon to satisfy his palate. On 55th Street, in the greatest restaurant in New York City, the best table (except for Cole Porter's) was reserved permanently for him, and no one could sit there, not even the president, nor the mayor, without his permission. I had seen a royal Hapsburg, a descendant of Charles V, kiss him on both cheeks and hang a golden fleece around his neck. He had cornered the Queen of England in the royal enclosure at Ascot. "Ma'am," he had said, "I have no English honors yet. Don't you think it is about time I got one?" He received the OBE soon after. He was given the Croix de Guerre with Palms, on which occasion Emlyn Williams, the playwright and actor, commented, "Greasy palms, I trust."

Sol Hurok almost always spoke of himself in the third person. He never said "I" like an ordinary egomaniac, but "Hurok needs" or "Hurok has," in the manner of royalty. "Hurok" was his creation, his ideal, his bastion and protection. Behind this extraordinary image he could move and manipulate; because of it he could act and achieve. It was a grand image, and he obtained the best in its name. Whatever was acclaimed in any field Hurok tagged as his own. He decided to be the Tiffany of his trade, and he was. Hurok's seal was undisputed.

He was a great public figure — a fabrication maybe, flamboyant, in part spurious, but also in part genuinely powerful — and he demanded to be treated as such. He would tolerate no less. This was the man I was offering potluck! But Walter had said mildly, "He's a lonely old man. He has no friends, nowhere to go. This is Christmas, Button. He broke my heart. Mrs. Hurok has thrown him out again."

Actually, my history with Sol Hurok was longer than my husband's. It was by no means as cozy. In 1942 I choreographed *Rodeo* for the Ballet Russe de Monte Carlo, and it changed the course of ballet dancing. Hurok sent for me and said, "You should be Hurok artist. You deserve it." I declined, because I was about to do a Broadway show. He was amazed at my stupidity; no one turned Sol Hurok down.

The Broadway show was *Oklahoma!* After the press and hoopla of that production he sent for me again. "I want you should be Hurok attraction," he said. "You have earned the privilege." I declined again, because I believed I would like to stay on Broadway, and although Hurok was a great concert impresario, he knew nothing of Broadway. I explained this quietly, and I thought reasonably, to him. He was outraged; I had flouted him a second time.

After that our paths crossed only when I composed ballets for Ballet Theatre, which he managed for some years. He was bullying and tyrannical, and forced me to actions I thought ill-advised. The results were bad. He thereupon threw me away. Luckily, no one else followed suit.

It was during out-of-town touring rehearsals of Ballet Theatre that his chief assistant, Mae Frohman, saw a photograph of my young husband, who was then with the U.S. Army overseas. Walter was unforgettably handsome; she was struck, and she was very pleased to learn that he was a concert manager. That is why Walter had an interview with Hurok in November 1945, on his return and demobilization, and that is why he was promptly added to the office staff. Mae, freshly divorced, fell in love with him. But Walter loved his wife.

In 1953 Columbia Concerts, Hurok's only recognized rival, wanted me to form a concert program of my theater pieces. Walter was not happy. "You will lose money," he warned. "Columbia will make money."

Hurok heard of the goings-on and sent for Walter. He was furious. "What are you doing to me?" he demanded. "Why should Agnes work for Columbia? Why are they better than me? Tell her she should work for me."

When I heard about this, I patiently said, "Explain to Mr. Hurok, Walter, that I think it unwise to join an organization where my husband is in a key position."

"Nonsense!" replied Hurok when Walter relayed my message. "Tell her she should work for me." He nagged and bullied until negotiations began, but every time my lawyer tried to make a point, Hurok wheeled on my hapless husband and shrieked, "You're betraying me!"

The upshot of all the bother was that my lawyer asked to be removed from the proceedings. I was forced to give up my rights. So I became a Hurok attraction, and was entitled to all the splendid and imaginative treatment Hurok provided for his clients, except for fair returns in money. Mae Frohman hoped I would fail, and Hurok did not gainsay Mae. Notwithstanding this lack of support, I was a success, although I lost $45,000 of my savings. Hurok made a tidy sum in pure profit.

Walter, who had anguished over me, said, "If you go on with this, I'll leave you." So I left Hurok's fold. However, though I was no longer a Hurok attraction, I remained the cherished wife of part of the Hurok organization. I kept having successes, independent of Hurok's control. It was maddening to him. He could subdue neither Walter nor me.

That was why Walter's Christmas invitation was loaded with emotion and trouble. But at the time we kissed and shouldered the burden, and when Hurok stood on our threshold on Christmas day, we both smiled and welcomed him.

Hurok seemed shorter than he was because he was thick, with thick hands, thick wrists, thick fingers, thick head, thick neck, square jaw, and a square, baldish crown, so that he looked rather like an unjolly friar. He had ferret-sharp eyes and a wicked, gleeful smile. He was extraordinarily strong, as strong as a wrestler or a weight lifter. He had the back and arms and wrists of a boatman. The playful pinches he used to inflict on ladies all but cut off circulation. His hands and arms were real weapons. How he maintained their power I don't know, because he was never seen to take unnecessary exercise. He plodded in his walk, placing his silver-knobbed cane firmly down on the pavement before him as though he were staking a claim with each step. He was as impregnable as a field marshal.

Of all his distinguishing traits, his manner of speaking was his outstanding characteristic. "He spoke six languages," said Isaac Stern, "and they all turned out to be bad Yiddish." But his jargon was not Yiddish, it was Hurok. He could strangle phrases, savage syntax, and hang up shreds of grammar like dead chickens in a country market, yet his oral brutality added only pungency to his direct meaning. One never forgot what Hurok said. His humor was acrid and infectious even while his language remained beyond category. His ruling motto— "If people don't want to come, nothing will stop them"—has grammarians awestruck. He described a powerful critic by closing his fist in a sudden sharp movement and saying, "He has a mind like a claptrap."

He took pride in his displays of learning, which could be not only ludicrous but hurting and sometimes insulting. This happened when Mary Duke Biddle Trent and her husband, Dr. James Semans, two of the most generous art patrons in North Carolina, wanted to buy the services of the Greek pianist

Gina Bachauer for a series of filmed teaching demonstrations at Duke University. They came to Walter with the proposition. It was an important deal, as Hurok knew. He took the occasion for a display of his classical learning. Mary was a charming woman whose head was entirely covered with a mop of irrepressible curls. "Look! Look!" shrieked Hurok, pointing a fat finger, as she entered his office. "The Medusa!" Mary stared in dismay. Hurok looked smug and amused at his own wit, without the slightest idea of what he had said. It took a good deal of Walter's diplomacy to salvage the project.

Sol Hurok came to our Christmas party, but he did not participate. At the door he said, "I'm sorry, I couldn't bring roses. No flower shops were open. I tried. I know what a gentleman should do. I am a gentleman," he said again as he entered.

He refused our cocktails. When he discovered he was seated not in the place of honor but one over, he refused to eat. He was used to being treated as the most important guest at any gathering. He sat at the table idly turning over his dinner plate, which was early nineteenth-century Rockingham, and staring at the blue mark on the bottom.

"You shouldn't eat off these," he said.

"Not even on Christmas, Mr. Hurok? Surely on Christmas we may be permitted to."

Well, Mr. Hurok didn't eat off them. He didn't eat. He refused everything we served. It was the usual Christmas dinner, very well cooked.

"Wot's dot, mud on fire?"

"That's plum pudding, Mr. Hurok. It's traditional."

He grunted.

"Is there anything you would like? Some scrambled eggs?"

"Naw, I'm fine."

The party passed around him and over him. People ate a lot and drank and toasted one another, and the children at their little tables babbled and shrieked. Hurok was bored by the carols, bored by the charades, bored by the giving of presents.

Perhaps he felt uneasy. Artists he could cope with; artists he could buy or spurn. In either case he figured in their attention, but people whom he could not control, people of no obvious use to him—how could he handle these? He was lost. And we didn't treat him as all-important.

I, in my self-satisfied conceit, had not the humanity to recognize his predicament and help him. Not unnaturally, he was the first to leave.

"I go home," he said. "Tomorrow morning, early at the office, Wahlter. Meet me at half past eight."

"Boxing Day is usually a holiday," Walter protested.

"Not in America!" said Hurok triumphantly, and with that he got his Borsalino hat and went to the door. "Hurok will give party."

"I've been to your parties," I said as I stood on the sill. "They're marvelous, Mr. Hurok."

"Da," he said, smacking his lips. "They're very good. They're very good indeed, da. Fine parties!"

That was true. Hurok was the best host of the best parties I ever went to. I have been to state parties, which were lavish but in no way better. For the big bashes Hurok usually took over the St. Regis roof garden and produced an unmatched spread: bowls of Iranian caviar, the preferred gray kind; delicious hot Russian hors d'oeuvres and salads; vintage vodka. He threw parties for the Hamburg Opera, for Marian Anderson, for Arthur Rubinstein, for the Moiseyev, Bolshoi, and Kirov ballet companies, for the Royal and Stuttgart ballets and for all their friends and supporters and the diplomatic representatives involved. At the Royal Ballet's New York première, he even arranged for the company to be entertained not at the St. Regis but on the back lawn of Gracie Mansion. Mayor Fiorello La Guardia was gracious, but somehow Hurok appeared to be the host, taking over all the honors and privileges. It was not his house, certainly, but he preempted the major position.

At his home Hurok hosted New Year celebrations that al-

ways had the best food, the best entertainment, the most outstanding guests. During the times when she consented to live
with him, his dazzling second wife, the handsome Emma Ru-
nitch, attended in fine black lace, diamonds, and emeralds.
There were strolling Gypsy singers and balalaika players, world-
famous magicians, and Hurok himself, the boss, acting genial,
generous, thoughtful, attentive, kindly, humorous, princely.
Once when Walter inadvertently kicked over a small taboret,
spilling coffee, red wine, and ice cream on a brand-new white
rug, Hurok quietened his anguished offers of reparation by
saying gently, "I am only proud, my boy, dot you have honored me by coming here," and putting his arms around him.
Oh yes, he was princely! A deluxe, triple-A host in every high,
chivalrous sense! Walter loved him at this moment.

Hurok was also the worst possible guest. Since he could not
share power or be beholden, since he had to command, and
since being a host involves pride and only a modicum of generosity, it follows that he was neither humble nor trustful
enough to be a good guest. He saw self-seeking behind every
human action. Stars were to be cozened, that was obvious, but
employees were to be humiliated. How else keep them in line?
He maintained his essence through a constant show of power,
which could be at times cruel. In short, he had the characteristics of a member of a downtrodden class, and he was just
that. He had been born within the Pale. "All Hurok under-
stands is the knout," said Thornton Wilder to my husband and
me. "He reminds me of the Prussian general who said, 'Stamp
on their toes until they apologize.' "

Indeed, under Hurok's rough characteristics lay always—
and I believe this to be the keynote of his conduct—the fact
that he was a Jew born in czarist Russia and he had grown up
hemmed in by galling restraints. His father had been a small
hardware dealer in the provincial town of Pogar, near the
Ukraine, trading in tobacco (he owned several local planta-
tions) and in wholesale and retail iron, steel, paint, window
glass, and assorted hardware. Sol's schooling had been the basic

learning every Russian-born Jew received, plus some Hebrew and a smattering of Talmudic teaching. He developed a true love for Russian classic poetry and the great novels, but he never learned anything of the great literature of other countries, even those whose language he spoke constantly, like English. What he did learn was a soul-deep wariness. From birth Sol believed that every goy—that is, everyone who was not a believing Jew—was against him. He was not himself a believing Jew, and he never observed Jewish customs or went to synagogue, but just the same, he felt set apart from the people with whom he had to deal. Because his education was limited, he had no true pride of culture. He was forever on the run, and instinctively he hit out, as any hunted creature will.

Hurok's instant aggressiveness was so much a part of his nature he made a joke of it. "You're late!" he would begin a business conference by saying accusingly. "No," Isaac Stern would reply, "you're early. I'm on the button." Hurok always then giggled, recognizing a riposte. The preliminaries over, he could get down to basic matters. But non-Russians, like my husband, a fiery-tempered Texan, bridled. They did not find these sorties amusing. On the contrary, they found them often inflaming and always regrettable.

In Hurok's struggles to succeed he picked up a tremendous amount of worldly guile. It is curious—more than that, it is wonderful—that his chosen field was music in its highest forms, which required him to deal with masters, with the very people who presumably were beyond all the practices in which he engaged daily. He did not choose manufacturing, or real estate, or law or medicine (professions requiring long apprenticeships were closed to him for financial reasons); no, he chose fine art and high entertainment.

He emigrated from Russia, traveling in steerage, when he was under twenty, and arrived with two bundles containing all his worldly goods, including a goose-feather pillow and exactly three rubles (the equivalent of $1.50) in his pocket. By borrowing $1.25 from a Brooklyn relative who earned $3.50 a week, he was able to travel to Philadelphia, where he got his first job, as a streetcar conductor. After that he did anything that was offered. These jobs signified nothing. It was his ambition that was important.

The first concert he managed was for Mischa Elman, the great Russian violinist, in the huge, popular New York Hippodrome, for the benefit of a socialist organization in Brooklyn. Hurok's choice of the organization was not accidental; he was a believing Marxist of the purist type, that is, an avid anti-Communist. Throughout his life he was canny about politics and remained always an informed analyst and zestful critic. He was always valiant in his opposition to all forms of political oppression, intimidation, and harassment. In the days of the un-American activities fomentation and McCarthyism, when so many turned craven, he acted with unblemished courage on behalf of his artists. Threats and maledictions simply muted before his derision, and he proceeded exactly as he thought best.

Mischa Elman gave his services for Hurok's first venture, so both the organization and Hurok netted a few dollars. With this success he found his calling. His career thereafter was like a roller coaster, full of large successes and plunging catastrophes, up and down, up and down. Along the way he married a Russian and they produced a daughter, Ruth. Then somehow he dropped off the Russian wife, and she was heard of no more by the outside world.

He went on scrambling for artists. He managed his boyhood hero, Feodor Chaliapin, whom he had worshiped in Russia. He managed Anna Pavlova and did very well by her. How did he get to these two dazzling immortals, let alone persuade them to put their affairs in his keeping? He made chutzpah into a high calling; when it achieves this level it takes on Napoleonic overtones. I think he was also in love with Anna. Indeed, she was a radiant personality and an overwhelming artist, and she liked men, and Sol Hurok was above all virile.

He managed Isadora Duncan in her last trying tour, not with very much success, nor any great joy, but with a great deal of publicity. He managed anyone who had a name and could be built to higher notoriety. He went bankrupt twice, and twice Mae Frohman bailed him out with her own savings and kept paying the office rent long enough for him to hire new artists and start over. For this service he gave her nothing beyond her weekly salary.

When Mae thought that the firm was doing well enough to afford to give her a raise, she decided to negotiate. She took Hurok out to lunch at a fine French restaurant, at her own expense, and leveled with him. He sat opposite her, white-faced. Hurok was a gourmet, but his appetite that day, I imagine, was limited. The upshot of the meeting was that he gave Mae twenty percent of Hurok Attractions, Inc., by which she stood to make some real money. However, she apparently held herself in moral debt to him, because at her untimely death she willed the money back to the organization, and none of her family benefited by it.

Mae Frohman was the only member of Hurok's staff ever to own any shares of stock. Nobody else even had a pension of any sort; no bonuses were ever given. His other employees, even vice presidents, were paid only their yearly salaries. The very big gains, and they were enormous, went into Hurok's pocket, minus, of course, the twenty percent that Mae received. I never heard of a comparable business that operated without some sort of pension plan or guarantee for its employees.

After the second bankruptcy, Mae began to insist on honesty. It was hard work for her; honesty didn't really seem to matter to Sol. Still, Mae was stubborn, and gradually she persuaded him to get in the way of telling the truth and making his books balance, a habit by no means native to him. Gradually he began to find that general good behavior caused a pleasant feeling and did his business no harm.

It would have been logical and economic if Mae and Sol had

fallen in love and married, but they did nothing of the kind. She was his staunch companion-in-arms, that's all. When I knew him, he was married to a strikingly beautiful singer who was the lead soprano in the musical revue *The Bluebird*, an imitation of Nikita Balieff's *Chauve-Souris*. Emma was a dark Russian beauty of few English words and expensive tastes. She dressed richly and wore her dazzling jewels with fine effect. These jewels, however, were evidently not from Hurok; I remember her being introduced at one of his big parties to the consul from Bulgaria, glancing at the huge emerald on her ring finger, and drawling languidly, "I was . . . Bulgaria once," and she rolled her enormous eyes in nostalgia.

Emma had been married to a Russian lawyer by whom she had three sons, Hurok's stepsons. After her marriage to Sol they were in and out of his office forever. In her indifferent way, Emma had Sol completely under her thumb, and she got whatever she wanted — always something for her boys, never something for him. She was useful, though. She used to lie in bed surrounded by lovely embroidered pillows and lace most of the day, watching TV and collecting gossip, which furnished Hurok with a great deal of information. She was one of his best spies.

He had others. It was at his daily lunches at the Russian Tea Room on West 57th Street that the White Russians gave their reports. At his special table he gathered the half-world of gossip, tattletale, and rumor in which the Russian ballet swam and which was fomented by its hangers-on. Here could be found the unscrupulous Anatole Chujoy, the editor of *Dance News*, displaying the special privileges of the court favorite and dispersing unchecked, unverified trade gossip and malice. This broth of scandal was to a balletomane's appetite what the next fix is to a dope addict, and it exceeded in wicked intensity anything I have ever known, including the vicious excitement of army wives bandying scuttlebutt. Hurok loved it. He also profited by it, and so did Mae Frohman. Whatever she could get from the ballet tittle-tattle that went to my disadvantage was straightaway and with bitter satisfaction relayed to Walter, who scolded me over evening cocktails for any sharp word I had let fly that morning in rehearsal. This was the Russian way. I had met it first in Serge Denham's Ballet Russe de Monte Carlo. To the Russians it was the salt of life.

Hurok worked at his job without stop, arriving at the office by eight or eight-thirty every morning and nursing anger because those employees with families refused to come so early. Every night of his life he was in one of his theaters, patrolling the back of the audience, listening to the comments in the lobbies, collecting evidence for success, near success, or failure. What he saw or heard of the performance was of secondary importance, because he could never make up his own mind, but his faculty for collating reports and drawing conclusions was unmatched.

Hurok had no real musical knowledge and no taste, but he did have a true instinct for life, an instinct for recognizing emotional force, that was almost animal in its reliability and intensity. He knew that Arthur Rubinstein played best when he was "within his own skin"; he could not possibly have explained how he knew.

He also knew when to trust advice. Isaac Stern recommended the twelve-year-old Itzhak Perlman, a penniless youngster whose father worked in a laundry. The fact that the child was badly crippled by polio repulsed Hurok, who said, "He can never be a success on crutches." "If you risk it," Stern replied, "you'll pay for his lessons and his fiddle and give him five hundred dollars a week for two years. He will play six concerts a year, not more. He'll study. In two years you make a new contract, mutually agreeable. In five years he will be worth a fortune." Hurok took the gamble. In five years Perlman rivaled the best, even Jascha Heifetz.

So if Hurok could not always judge, he could listen. When an artist had achieved himself, he could recognize. And Hurok could be generous to colleagues—not to peers or rivals, but to dependent, lesser, smaller people, inferiors. When local managers fell on hard times and failed to meet obligations, on occasions he swallowed the loss (and so did the artists involved). He gained devoted and grateful friends, or rather slaves, this way. Few people knew of these appealing traits.

He conducted applause like a maestro. To see Hurok start up applause, augment applause, and then rush around to the critics and comment on the applause called for admiration. "You can't change a good critic's opinion by bribes," he said, "but you can soften the way he says you're lousy." He put his theory into active practice, not by anything so gross as gifts but by subtle favors, such as agreeing to manage the critic's favorites, people way beneath his ordinary standards.

My husband was frequently aghast. "Mr. Hurok," he protested, "this is unworthy of you. This is not Hurok caliber. This is dishonest."

"This is insurance," replied Hurok. "I need his help."

"This is undignified."

Hurok shrugged.

Hurok always made money on a deal, or nearly always. Occasionally he lost: "If people don't want to come, nothing will stop them." The performing artists or the ballet companies seldom profited — that is, in the beginning. Of course the seasoned stars made a great deal of money. Arthur Rubinstein, Gregor Piatigorsky, Isaac Stern, Gina Bachauer, Van Cliburn, Marian Anderson, Andrés Segovia, and Emanuel Ax did very well for themselves, but alas, the beginners or those not so well known in America, such as Uday Shankar, went home plucked.

Hurok made money, but for years he lost it as quickly as he earned it, because he never hesitated to risk it. I think overall he did not save very much. As he had no partners except Mae, it was always his own money he put on the line. He took chances, and they were real chances, because he simply had unreliable taste and did not know very much about what he was selling. However, he did have the instinct to find the people to serve his artists best, and the audacity to give them the scope to operate.

The exception to his general ignorance was late nineteenth-century Russian ballet. This he knew about and this he adored. For this love he was willing to lose money, lots of it. In 1933 he brought to New York the de Basil Ballet Russe de Monte Carlo, and after it its offspring, Serge Denham's Ballet Russe, both of which cost him thousands of dollars in their first season. He reaped a fortune on their later Metropolitan Opera appearances and tours, though, and made them known throughout the United States by his efforts.

In due time he had a falling out, not unexpectedly, with Serge Denham over money, and they parted abruptly. Denham claimed to have rid the ballet world of that "ok-ta-pus," and Hurok publicly swore great relief, saying, "Good riddance." Hurok straightaway kidnaped Denham's star, Leonide Massine, the choreographer and dancer, and moved him to Ballet Theatre. He then renamed the organization American Ballet Theatre, advertised it as "the greatest in Russian ballet," and began to Russify its personnel and its repertory.

It was at this juncture that my path first crossed Hurok's. Ballet Russe had hired me to do *Rodeo*, and Hurok's spies told him that it would probably be a stunning success and very valuable. This did not fit in with his plans at all. He was separating from the Ballet Russe after the Metropolitan season and naturally wished to leave the company in bad shape. He wanted no successes.

I quote from a letter I wrote to Walter on September 30, 1942:

> And now let me tell you the backstage story of de Mille and Hurok. You know he is trying to sabotage the Ballet Russe every way, so he sent for Libidins, our business manager, and Gerald Goode, his business manager, refused *Rodeo* for the Met season on the grounds that it was cheap, vulgar, poor, and unworthy. "How do you know?" roared Libidins. "We have seen the show rehearsal," said Goode. "It's goddamn lie," said Libidins. "No one from your office was

there." And he hit him in the face with a telephone book. And that, my friend, is the first time any male has struck a blow in my behalf, and I love him for it.

The story of why we didn't go to Canada makes nice telling. Twenty visas refused in a company of forty-two. [It was wartime, and a good percentage of the ballet personnel were *staatenlos*, with very unreliable passports.] Hurok is now suing for willful breaking of contract. All this is very important.

Sunday I stepped into the Russian Tea Room, the Ballet Bourse. Hurok and his henchmen were in congress. They hailed me and passed me from satellite to satellite until I confronted the great man himself. "You belong with us," he said, waving a fat jeweled hand and looking just like a Russian version of my uncle. "You should do American ballet for me immediately." (Start thinking, Walter, they're going to send for me immediately after the première and I want to have a story ready and I want your name on it.) "I love Americans. No gossip, no intrigue, no laziness, no dishonesty. These foreigners." He shuddered. "These foreigners make me sick. The American people will stand for so much — but all these foreigners dancing while my wife's sons are at war! It's disgusting!" [One of the sons, George Perper, was awarded the Croix de Guerre for valorous work in the French Underground.]

Ballet Theatre had always lost money. Indeed, all American ballet companies lose money all the time. (Most of the European ballet companies are state-supported and do not expect to pay their own way, any more than any other governmental agency expects to.) Hurok's problem was to keep a good part of the profits for himself and see that someone else underwrote the losses. This difficult feat he was nimbly successful at doing. Lucia Chase, the heiress, seemed ideal for the role of principal donor or mark. But when she found out the exact amounts Hurok was making in profit and the exact amounts she was paying in deficits, she understandably grew outraged.

Furthermore, Chase wanted Ballet Theatre to be known as an American company, and Hurok thought this idea a poor one. He was genuinely proud of being an American, but Russian dancing was box office, and he himself had made it so. He turned his full energies to making the American (it was wartime, wasn't it?) Ballet Theatre completely Russian. With American stubbornness and without warning, Chase broke her contract and took her company away. Hurok threatened suit but eventually did nothing. His chagrin was somewhat softened by watching her continue to lose money. She, however, just smiled like the Cheshire Cat; her losses were once more familiar and forgivable, and they were indisputably American.

Hurok transferred his excitement after the war to the Royal Ballet, which was English and not Russian at all, although it performed lots of Russian pieces beautifully. Most reassuringly, it had state backing and royal patronage. Then at last Hurok was able to have veritable Russians — oh, what joy! First the Moiseyev Folk Dance Ensemble, and then the Bolshoi company, and after it the Kirov company. When he ran out of Russians, he managed the Stuttgart Ballet, and then at last the mother of all companies, the Paris Opera Ballet.

Other managements produced ballet companies too, but Hurok always had the best known, the biggest, the most prestigious, and he made them the most successful. He became identified with great dancing of all kinds. He even managed Martha Graham for two years, but being American, she had no national sponsor, and Hurok lost money. He didn't like that one bit. Companies he would not lose money on were American companies.

In the meantime he was managing great musicians and introducing new names, and that meant taking risks all the time. In the mid-thirties he heard about a young American singer who had made a fine success in Scandinavia and was soon the toast of Copenhagen and Stockholm. When, in Finland, she had entered Sibelius's room, Sibelius had taken her in his arms and said, "My child, my roof is too low for you." She went on to Paris, and Paris succumbed. Nothing, however, had been heard of her in her own country, except in closed circles.

Hurok hastened to Paris and signed the new singer up. He brought her back to America, where he became perplexed as to what to do with her — because, you see, she was black, and launching a black's career was extremely limited as an undertaking, and he couldn't be sure, could he, that she was really good. She sounded fine to him, but he didn't know. And she was so black! He consulted his press staff. It was decided to present her in Town Hall, dressed in white, with a white piano, and carrying only white flowers.

The rest is history. It was not a very big chance he took; certainly he didn't have to guarantee her much, and her European reputation was splendid, but it was a chance. She got good press; in point of fact, Marian Anderson was hailed as one of the two or three great singers of her age, and she was the first black to crash through the racial barrier without reservation. She toured internationally, then nationally. When she played our segregated South, she insisted on vertical racial segregation in the seating, front to back, rather than horizontal separation, as had been the custom, which restricted blacks to the rear and the balcony. At her concerts, blacks could sit in the front row of their half of the house. This was an iron rule with her and never varied.

On April 9, 1939, Anderson was scheduled to give a concert in our capital, in Constitution Hall, the only big hall available in that city. It was owned by the Daughters of the American Revolution. Because she was black, the owners refused her the right to sing in their house. Eleanor Roosevelt, the most honored and prestigious Daughter, immediately handed in her resignation. Hurok held a council of war, and Gerald Goode, his business manager, came up with the inspired idea of getting permission from Harold Ickes, the secretary of the interior, for Anderson to sing in the open air, in front of the Lincoln Memorial. She did just that. A majestic and beautiful figure, her glorious voice ringing out over the Mall, she made international news. Outcry against the Daughters mounted, and they fell into a disfavor from which they have never recovered. Anderson became a universal figure.

Sol Hurok immediately claimed Marian Anderson as his own invention. Well, the idea of putting her in white with a white piano was his, wasn't it? No, it wasn't. The idea of putting her in front of the Lincoln Memorial? No, not his idea. But it was tactless to say so.

It is true that Hurok paid the members of his public relations department specifically to have good ideas. He therefore took for granted that any ideas they had on salary belonged to him. What else were they being paid for? All theater and concert managers operated similarly, but this contention opens a wide field of inquiry. Does the lessor own musical invention, as in the case of orchestrators and arrangers? Richard Rodgers, Irving Berlin, and George Gershwin supplied song melodies only and not one note of their scores beyond that. In the case of Rodgers, many minutes of music and of themes were not of his own devising. Was that dishonest? The entire show, the whole enterprise, depended on his melodies. No variations, no embroidery, would have been possible without them. Take the question further: in the case of scientific research, how many great discoveries have been made by employees working on fixed salaries for large corporations? Who has a right to the credit and the profit?

Hurok always kept a sheltering, fatherly arm around the Russian employees engaged in his productions, hiring them again and again. No matter what the nationality of the visiting attraction, if one looked into the pit, there would be the same assistant conductor, the same first strings, cello, bass, horns, and back strings. One also saw the same assistant wardrobe women, stage manager, and department heads (although in the latter case the unions kept strict watch). They were usually not the best of their kind, but they were Russian émigrés and needy, for the most part drawn from Hurok's *mishpocheh*. They

relied on him, and he was loyal. It goes without saying that
their salaries were paid by the visiting attraction, not by Sol.

Walter knew the boss probably better than anyone. He
worked with him, worked for him, protected him, supported
him, corrected him, and monitored him. He was well aware
of Hurok's sensitive vanity, so he never allowed his own name
to appear on any program, not once in the thirty-odd years he
worked for him. The rest of the staff had to be mentioned, by
union ruling. Walter belonged to no union and was therefore
privileged to remain anonymous. Mr. Hurok was well content
with this arrangement. Furthermore, Walter never got credit
for any business deals, even large ones that consumed great
portions of his time. For years he worked weekends and nights
on a pay television scheme, a plan that was ultimately defeated
by commercial advertisers. It broke the heart of the organizer,
Matty Fox, but Hurok was bought off handsomely, netting,
I believe, almost $1 million. Walter, who had done all the work,
received nothing, as a matter of course. Hurok argued that it was
his name they wanted, *his* artists. Walter was unknown. Hurok
was the *impresario*; as he said, "the last of the impresarios."

Hurok bought an able staff, and he had the flair to keep them
working in highly effective ways. Without the direction he
gave them, without his prodding, very possibly they would
not have obtained any of their results.

As Hurok's success mounted, he grew to believe in his self-
worth and self-importance. He had a full-page picture in each
of his programs, a photograph in which he appeared in his
opera cape, with his Borsalino tilted rakishly over one eye and
his hands clasped on his massive, silver-topped ebony stick.
He began to confuse his primal instincts, greed and vanity,
with discernment. His self-approval became akin to what most
people feel for the sublime.

"Wahlter," he would say as he portentously entered the
available air space in my husband's office, "write a lawyer
letter." He did not mean that Walter should take dictation,

because he could not compose a letter. He meant that Walter should compose the letter himself. Hurok knew that it would be done impeccably and also grammatically. "Tell him he should stop."

"I can't do that, Mr. Hurok," Walter would say. "He is within his legal rights."

"I want he should stop, tell him."

"Mr. Hurok," said Walter, coming into his office one day with a large stack of letters, "you must sign these. Read them over carefully first."

"Oh, why are you bothering me with these details?" Hurok cried in exasperation. "Don't I pay people to take care of these details?"

Walter looked at him coldly and dropped the lot on the floor. Three minutes later, the boss stood before him, smiling in his most winning way and holding out a bottle of his very best Scotch.

But these candid and endearing moments were rare. Tragically, his gruff, abrasive orders often meant pain. In my experience with Hurok, which covered a full forty years, I never heard him say anything laudatory about a production that was not his own, since he did not care to waste the benefit of his approval on something from which he did not derive income. About *Oklahoma!* he said not one word to me. About *Carousel* he said only that the costumes were dirty. The costumes were not dirty, but the production was not his, therefore it was of no account.

The fact that I no longer worked for him made our relationship tricky. Never mind that I was the wife of his close assistant; I was not his attraction, therefore I deserved no courtesy. In all the years of our association, much happened to me: I gave birth to Walter's son, who for years remained in a life-and-death situation; my mother died; Walter's father died; I produced ten major Broadway successes, eight books, and nine ballets. During that time, Sol Hurok sent not one telegram, not one bunch of flowers, not one personal inquiry. Yet all the while he used me, asking me repeatedly to serve as mistress of ceremonies at his galas, to present him with honors, to present his stars with honors, to make speeches for him. When Walter finally remonstrated, although mildly, pointing out that I generally got recompense for such services, Hurok smiled and said, "It does her no harm to appear with me." That closed the subject.

Hurok went on taking chances. He continued to have unlooked-for success. He astonished his staff. They could barely keep up with him. He came back from England once and announced that he had hired the Black Watch.

"That's part of the British Army," said Walter.

"You should see them march," said Hurok.

"I have," said Walter. "I fought beside them."

"We'll put them in Madison Square Garden."

"Doing what?"

"You fix," ordered Hurok.

"It's better in front of old castles and on royal lawns," said Walter.

"You fix," ordered Hurok.

So Walter arranged for the soldiers to march in full regalia up Pennsylvania Avenue for the first time since the British had burned the capital in 1812. On that occasion they had been highly unpopular. This time, Walter said with great gratification, the reaction was better. What he had not realized was that there were hundreds, even thousands, of Scotch, Irish, and English people in the audience who began weeping with the first skirl of the pipes and appearance of the kilted men.

Walter devised some very good effects, one of a lone piper high in the balcony playing "The Last Watch" as the lights dimmed to blackness. It goes without saying that Hurok thought he had invented this felicitous ending himself and took credit for it.

His confidence grew. He brought over the Royal Massed Pipers and the Royal Marching Bands. In the British Tournament and Tattoo performance, four marching bands, including the Royal Paratroopers, held a gala week at Madison Square Garden. The high point of this display was the astonishing stunt of a man sliding down a wire from the very top of Madison Square Garden to the very bottom, saved only by a parachute, which opened midway in his perilous trip and braked the descent. One night the parachute failed to open, and the young officer was shattered. Walter dashed from a dinner party to the Garden to take charge; he stood by the boy's side as he died, literally torn apart by the fall. Hurok later sent flowers.

Hurok was a difficult, unfriendly, unsympathetic, tyrannical old man. He often treated his employees nastily. Why did not Walter leave? For good reason. The pay with Hurok was excellent, the best in this harlequin business. Walter was given carte blanche to make decisions on all his trips abroad, to Brazil, Venezuela, Panama, Fiji, the Philippines, Hong Kong, Tokyo, Greece, and on a score of trips to England, Europe, and Scandinavia. He was also given a very generous expense account for these trips. Furthermore, the habits and character of rival managers were certainly no better than Hurok's. And, I think, Hurok was extremely fond of Walter. In the course of events, some of the staff did leave, but Walter stuck. Hurok accepted his loyalty with sardonic complaisance. Moreover, Walter's first loyalty went to quality, and the quality of Hurok's artists was the absolute best. Walter loved music; it was to him a necessity of life. In serving these men and women he achieved some part of the joy that had been denied him through lack of timely training. He was, as Isaac Stern said, a musician manqué.

At a great public dinner in honor of Hurok on May 15, 1967, I wrote:

How does one appraise his impact on American culture? He is first of all the Great Importer, and the treasures he has brought us from abroad have proved seminal. In a country which neglects its own artists, our need was great. Hurok saw the need and acted. "Hurok Attractions" means not just one thing, but a rich and surprising spanning of activities: the finest among instrumentalists, of course, and singers and conductors, but also, most gratefully and delightfully, booming calvary officers, chanting children, whirling Russians, bamboo-jumping Filipinos, neck-sliding Hindus, gourd-shaking Mexicans and flamencos kicking and swinging from the caves of Sacromonte, classic acting companies of the world, and his special pride, the greatest ballets. The one common denominator is superlative quality.

He has a mission that transcends business. Back and forth across oceans and continents speeds this indefatigable enthusiast, who travels approximately one hundred thousand miles annually, supervising, searching out, investigating, advising, and shepherding his chosen bands. Frontiers disappear before him; barricades tumble. After him stream the artists, the best voices of their countries, the truest and most lasting — the artists, bringing open eyes and ears, the vital compulsion to communicate.

Let artists pass freely, he says, let them see, let them hear, let them meet, and they will stop hating.

Here is a traffic such as never before was established. Here is hope.

Please note how polite I could be when the occasion called for politesse. And what I said was quite true, although there was much more to the story.

There was one occasion on which Hurok acted with valor and, yes, elegance. He had imported the Bolshoi Opera, the Bolshoi and Kirov ballets, the Don Cossack Choir, and such individual artists as the cellist and conductor Mstislav Rostropovich and the pianist Sviatoslav Richter. Hurok believed strongly that people who love and understand one another's art do not go to war, or, as he put it, "People who sing and dance together do not fight together." He believed sincerely that his imports strengthened the peace effort. Besides, they made money and made everybody happy. "The American people deserve the best," he said repeatedly. So he continued to import Russians, a practice that brought him under the sharp criticism of the terrorist organization the Jewish Defense League.

One morning at nine-thirty, when everyone in the Hurok office was busily at work, a strange young man entered and fiddled with the electric light in the outer office. There was a sudden flash. The youth ran out and down the fire stairs. Flames shot through the light stand. The office had been firebombed, and in seconds the outer office was ablaze. "In three minutes," said Michael Menzies, one of the chief accountants, "the entire lobby became a haystack of fire." The only escape stairs were alongside the elevators, which immediately stopped running. The office was twenty floors up.

As the hall filled with smoke and the flames from the lamp and sofa began to spread everywhere, the inhabitants of the offices scrambled for safety. Two vice presidents began fighting their way through the bewildered secretaries and making their own escape first. Walter, together with Scotty, the seventy-year-old mail clerk, struggled to get the fire hose working. They found it rotted through; it fell to pieces in their hands. Walter then tried to fight his way back to where Hurok was trapped, only to be halted by clouds of smoke and appalling heat. In one back room, four of the staff, two secretaries and two people from the business department, were cut off by a wall of fire. Unable to leave this room, they lay on the floor. The girls were praying, and one began to cry. The smoke thickened. Mercifully, they soon lost consciousness.

Hurok instructed his secretary to lie down beside him on the floor, first wetting towels and placing them over their mouths. But when he realized that no good was coming of this plan, he rose. Clutching a small silver cigarette box, he hurled it with his extraordinary right arm, with an almighty strength that must be imagined, smashing through the shatterproof glass of the windows. Fresh air came in; smoke poured out. Hurok and his secretary breathed.

The firemen got to them just in time. Hurok was carried

out on a stretcher, but he was conscious, and the girl beside him was all right except for a badly cut arm and extreme terror. From the other room two were found unharmed. Michael Menzies went to the hospital with a DOA tag on his toe, but was discovered on further examination to be breathing. (The *New York Times* labeled him as the "unknown woman on the left" in its photo; this brought him to such a pitch of indignation that he grew a moustache immediately after his release from the hospital.) The remaining girl, Iris Kour, the one who had been most frightened, was dead. Iris Kour was a devout Jew.

The police had been watching the arsonists for some time and had even bugged their office, but, alas, the police acted without proper permission, and owing to legal technicalities they were prevented in the end from prosecuting for one count of murder, three of arson, and many of assault, damage, and attempted murder. As a result of this carelessness the Jewish Defense League got off scot free.

The interior of the Hurok office was gutted, and what was not burned black was looted, possibly by the firemen. Walter lost many valuable objects from his desk. He had brushed all of the small items off the top into a wastebasket to keep them together, but the basket was empty when he found it.

Hurok seemed to show no dire effects from the experience, but he must have been damaged. He was in his very late eighties, and after these experiences he appeared frailer. He still gave parties, however, and as host he was effulgent, and benign, and magnanimous. And alive. But one can't always give parties. He had moved to Park Avenue, to a superb apartment befitting a prince of the theater. Emma, in a wifely manner, helped him decorate it. But after he moved in, she flatly refused to join him, so he found himself alone and abandoned in his brand-new, fabulously expensive apartment.

His weekends grew dreary. When he was not in the office, he was at his empty home. He used to send for Lillian Libman, one of the heads in his publicity department, to come sit with him. Once he asked her to read and witness his will, but she declined. Occasionally an out-of-town booker sat with him for an hour or two, or Joe Fingerman, the broken-nosed old Russian who sold illustrated programs in his lobbies. He also still saw his old crony Simon Simonieff, the character comedian of the Ballet Russe, whose flair for gossip approached the baroque in its intense variations. There was nothing truthful or straightforward about Simon, but he was entertaining, so Hurok kept him around. He had no real friends. He had nothing to do in his big, beautiful, empty white apartment with the white rugs and the spotless furniture—no books, no pictures, no games, only a tray with vodka and caviar, but no one to share the vodka with.

It seemed that the old man was going to go on forever. He reached the astonishing age of eighty-five, eighty-six. He was still buying and selling talent. He was still giving great galas. He was still having lunch with Rubinstein, Stern, Bachauer. Then one day in 1974 he had a magnificent lunch at the Côte Basque with Andrès Segovia and Walter. They dined well, but in deference to their age they dined moderately. Afterward Hurok went off alone to David Rockefeller's office. By some misadventure he was taken to the wrong office first, and he was standing at a desk waiting to be instructed when he suddenly fell forward, stone dead. There was no warning, no signal; he just died after a delicious lunch. That night in Carnegie Hall, Maria Callas, his old enemy (who had "aged him by ten years"), gave the last Hurok concert. It was of course sold out. She dedicated it to him—"not without," as Michael Menzies said, "a final air of triumph."

Hurok's staff went into consultation immediately. They had to plan a funeral, a super Hurok attraction that would be worthy of him, but this presented difficulties. The awkwardness was that no synagogue would house his obsequies because he had not gone to temple in sixty years. No rabbi would bury him. Jan Peerce, easily the most devout and orthodox Jew on the Hurok roster, thought of a happy solution: they would use Carnegie Hall and place the coffin on the stage.

So at eleven o'clock two days later, the house filled, with

standees against every wall. On the stage sat Marian Anderson, Jan Peerce, Isaac Stern, and a rabbi. (The family and staff found one at last.) Hurok's unadorned coffin held center stage. Marian Anderson could no longer sing, so she spoke: "His name was Solomon, a name for kings, and it is with kings he walked." Jan Peerce sang part of the burial service in Hebrew. Isaac Stern played unaccompanied Bach, facing the coffin. At the conclusion he put his hand on the undraped casket and remained for a minute in farewell to the Boss, his "Papa Hurok." The house in which Hurok had had so many performances that he surely could be considered a partial owner was hushed to the top balcony. Although people were not moved, because they did not care about him, they were impressed. An era of musical history had closed. It was a fine turnout. As Hurok had also said, "Give the people what they want and you cannot keep them away."

Then the rumors began. There had been much speculation about just how rich Sol Hurok really was. He liked people to think he was very rich, and I am sure he had $4 or $5 million. Naturally his only daughter, Ruth, expected the bulk of this money, and the people who had worked for him a long time expected suitable remembrances. But Hurok had never acknowledged the possibility of his own death. He had refused to imagine a world without him. He did not make a proper will, instinctively persuading himself instead that as long as it did not exist, there would be no need for it. Shortly before his death, however, Elias Lieberman, his lawyer, had insisted that he put his will in order and had suggested that he make substantial bequests to Adelphi College. Hurok had never heard of Adelphi College. He had never heard of any presents to colleges. He must have known that gifts were made to Harvard, but not by him.

Why did Hurok leave his hard-won money to a college of which he had never heard? Possibly because Elias Lieberman persuaded him to make his name remembered not only in the concert business but in the greater world of cultural influence, convincing him that he could leave an image that would be universally revered. Ruth got a sum, but nothing like what she had expected. A secretary Hurok had fired for dishonesty was given $35,000. Why? It was thought in order to keep her mouth shut. But other people knew more, my husband for one, and other people got nothing.

Walter had been with Mr. Hurok for thirty-two years and was his first assistant; he sat at his side on every occasion, did all his dirty work, took on all the office responsibilities and all the negotiating problems, presided on all arbitration teams (he was in fact known for his skill in arbitrating labor disputes, some of which were extraordinarily subtle; all the union men trusted him and abided by his decisions), wrote all his letters. To Walter Prude, Sol Hurok left not so much as a note, nor a photograph, nor a book, nor a memento from the top of his desk—nothing. Walter was sad but not surprised. No, that is not true. He was surprised, even from Mr. Hurok. There should have been some word.

Hurok was known wherever western culture was practiced, but I believe he was loved by no one, except possibly Joe Fingerman, the old Russian who sold the illustrated programs, and Isaac Stern, who understood him. Sol Hurok, the greatly acclaimed, worldly figure, was the loneliest man I ever knew.

III

THE DeMILLES

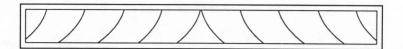

THEY WERE KNOWN on Broadway as William Churchill de Mille, the brilliant young playwright, and Cecil Blount, his not very gifted younger brother. In Hollywood, though, where Cecil ventured in 1913, followed doubtfully a year later by William, they were known as Cecil B. DeMille (he had capitalized the prefix to make his name—French or Dutch, depending on how you read the family history—easier to publicize), the director general of the rising Jesse L. Lasky Feature Play Company, and his scenario-writer brother, Bill. Thereafter, Father lived and worked in Cecil's shadow. By the time of his death, Father was generally forgotten; Cecil had become a world name.

The rivalry was profound and lasting, and through all phases of the brothers' relationship, the tragic awareness of the other persisted: Father, the thoughtful and subtle one; Cecil, the adventurer. The contest strengthened Cecil; I think in some ways it broke my father. Nevertheless, throughout their lives the emotional tie was strong.

Father died first. "I've saved a place for you and your wife in my cemetery plot," Cecil had promised, a touch pompously. "Thanks for the hospitality," Pop had replied. As Cecil stood weeping at his brother's bier—and they were genuine, heartbroken tears—he watched appraisingly the procession of old friends, university colleagues, assistants, students, and their children filing past the coffin and said to me, "How often have Bill and I stood together counting the house! It's a good one today." From Cecil DeMille, that was a tribute.

The publicity attending my father's funeral, in 1955, was minimal. When Cecil died on January 21, 1959, the news was carried on the front pages of very nearly every paper in the world, even the Russian ones, and on every radio station. The Los Angeles papers gave three full pages to his obituary. Cecil B. DeMille had been largely instrumental in building a world industry and founding a city; he had taken crucial steps in the shaping of a new art. He was a dramatist more widely known to his contemporaries than any other in history, and he was a religious propagandist with an appeal that, although superficial, was possibly the most popular of our time in terms of numbers reached within a short space of years. "When leaders of nations tell us," he is quoted as saying, "as the highest officials have told me, that as boys they derived their conception of the world, their ideas of right and wrong, from American motion pictures, they bring home to us our awe-inspiring responsibility." He was neither an economist nor a statesman, yet his labor and political pronouncements were given the publicity due a political leader. Labor disputes in his own business he somehow managed to publicize as national crusades for liberty. On more than one emotional level he held dominion over millions for upward of half a century. He lived the latter part of his life with the ostentation of a minor prince, but contrary to expectations (and precedent), Cecil was buried simply, with the ungarnished Episcopal service and only family and close friends present. He was laid to rest where his brother waited for him, in his cemetery plot.

Cecil was three years younger than William and ten years older than their sister, Agnes, who died in childhood. He therefore suffered all the buffeting of a middle child. Not enough attention has been paid, I believe, to the plight of the younger brother in our culture, which is dominated by the law of primogeniture. For nearly a thousand years England and England's colonies were ruled by an order in which the older brother took precedence by birthright in every choice, power, and opportunity the family had to offer, inheriting the name and rank, the lands and wealth, the place in government. These were his outright, with no thought of fairness to the younger children. The second son generally went into the army and received a small inheritance, but significantly less than the firstborn. The third son went into the church and was benefited by a still smaller bequest. After that all the children, male and female, took potluck and got along as best they could. They had to take their brothers' leavings, so when opportunity offered they took North America, and there, quite free from the supervision of their elders, they carved out empires and amassed names, positions, and fortunes. In this manner younger brother Cecil DeMille took Hollywood and the brandnew moving picture business.

The boys' father was a North Carolina Episcopal lay reader, their mother an English Jew. Cecil adored his mother, but for some reason regretted her contribution to his heritage and never once mentioned it publicly. "My English mother," he would say, and that was all. He respected his father for what he was — a gentle, honorable man of fastidious and brave conduct — but knew him only when a small child; Cecil was twelve when Henry de Mille died suddenly of typhoid, aged thirty-nine. The boys were brought up by their mother, a domineering and aggressive woman, with the clothes sense and some of the business scruples of a Gypsy.

On her husband's death, Beatrice Samuel de Mille became the second American female playbroker. She also opened a girls' boarding school in order to make a living. Henry de Mille had abandoned a small congregation to write plays with a message for a wider audience. He had been David Belasco's first collaborator, but although the two were successful, it was, unfortunately, before *The Wizard* starting earning big money. Nevertheless, the family mixed with the great and famous:

Edwin Booth when he was an old man, Belasco and his stars, Augustin Daly, Charles and Daniel Frohman, Charles Klein, the cast of the Lyceum Company, Edward Hugh Sothern and his wife, Julia Marlowe. Everyone in the American theater was their friend.

From early childhood, Cecil hankered for his own fame. He was reared to be a middle-class Christian gentleman, but the seeds of unrest bit into his soul. No one else in this family had such ambition, not his resourceful mother and certainly not his brother, who like royalty did not require ambition, since he believed he was already important, a theory reinforced by his mother and other female relatives. "William took so much for granted," said his very young aunt, Betty de Mille, "that he expected to be considered first in everything."

Indeed, William was brilliant. He was also handsome, with a long English skull, the coloring and dark, warm eyes of a Spaniard, and the high-bridged nose and open forehead of a Castilian aristocrat. "You look like a grandee," said Seymour Thomas, the portrait painter, who begged to get to work on Pop's fine and haughty physiognomy. Father deported himself with a sureness that approached nobility. He was witty of speech — everyone recognized this — but I think he had as well a certain wit of movement and demeanor. He was quick even in repose. His charm was quick, even sly, and above all intelligent. He made an impression through the content and rhythm of his speech, while Cecil made one through his manner, which was gallant and always a touch theatrical. Cecil too was handsome. His smile was dazzling, and his voice was moderate and well cadenced, lending his manner a nineteenth-century charm; in meticulous inflection he spoke as though John Luther Long had written his lines and he were still playing a part in *If I Were King*.

Father was like a swordsman. Cecil was like a young bull: dynamic, male, determined, and sassy. Wasting no time in subtlety, he went directly after what he wanted. He was without physical fear. "He had the courage of a lion," said Gloria

Swanson to me in later years. He had no patience with fear, within himself or anyone else. He demonstrated this a thousand times over throughout his career. The same was true of pain, for which he had an almost limitless tolerance — so why didn't others? I once heard him offer an extra playing a naked Aztec warrior forty dollars for sliding down a wall. The man's back was flayed, but he got his forty bucks. (I think Uncle Ce would not have accepted forty bucks for the same pain, nor four thousand. Possibly a hundred times that amount — possibly — but certainly he would have delivered for free, without question, if he had a guarantee that his pain would benefit the picture.)

When their father died, William became titular head of the family and was entrusted with opportunities and decisions that were denied the younger boy. It was William who was sent to the gymnasium in Freiburg and afterward to Columbia University. It was William who was the outstanding athlete, the tennis player and track star, and the hopeful pupil of the great Columbia teacher Brander Matthews. Cecil had to take what was left: a military high school in Pennsylvania. It was William who was a staff teacher at his mother's school, while Cecil was still a pupil. It was William who was thought to have creative genius. It was William who married Anna George, the beautiful red-haired daughter of the economist and philosopher Henry George, of Single Tax fame; who first got the chance to work with David Belasco; who wrote a Broadway hit (at the age of twenty-five); who obtained a staff position at the American Academy of Dramatic Arts; who was known by sight in every theatrical office and theater lobby.

Cecil had to content himself with minor acting parts in touring companies and with unrecognized collaboration on his brother's plays. Most bitter of all, his first independent drama, *The Return of Peter Grimm*, was confiscated after two years of Cecil's hard work by David Belasco, who claimed it was his own property. This was a wrong that, I feel, in spite of Cecil's repeated denials, he bitterly resented all his lifetime. He thereafter spent his life proving, first, that he was as smart as his older brother, second, that he was as smart as Belasco, and third, that he was smarter than anyone else.

Cecil despised my father for not making better use of his opportunities. "If I had Bill's brain!" he would remark with sardonic wistfulness, smiling to himself when someone commented that he had done right smartly as matters stood. He had a kind of affectionate contempt for Pop's loyalty and stead--fastness, for his directness of spirit, which forbade his taking advantage of position to bully or impose, and above all for his disinclination to fight. Cecil took nothing for granted. He was prepared to fight for whatever he wanted. To Cecil, who turned all experience to advertisement and subsequently to dollars, Pop's disinterestedness seemed childishly unrealistic, even lax and smug.

Cecil was a bit stock actor in the Sothern–Marlowe traveling repertory company when he met and courted Constance Adams, also a member of the company and the daughter of a judge of the Supreme Court of New Jersey. The choice of Miss Adams as a life partner was perhaps the most splendidly fortunate decision he ever made. Their early marriage was, however, financially stringent. At the time their daughter Cecilia was born, Aunt Constance told me, Cecil could scarcely afford a pram. It was at this point of desperation, in 1913, that he moved west and helped found the Lasky Feature Play Company with a borrowed $20,000, two known actors, and a pickup group of technicians. My father was asked to put up $5,000, but having lost money on Cecil's ventures before, he declined. Cecil never forgot that, nor did Pop. The investment would have guaranteed him one eighth of Paramount Pictures.

During his early Hollywood days, Cecil was as true a pioneer as any we have known, combating personal dangers, privations, discouragement, bankruptcy, chicanery, skullduggery, scorn, and slander to emerge with a fortune and his family intact. The blood races and the heart lifts just to hear the tale. After he had been in California two years he persuaded Father (who was at that time in an unproductive phase of his career) to follow him. That Cecil sent for William I find extraordinary. He hitherto had been crippled by his older brother's domination. Now he was free and on the way to being independently successful, and he immediately called for Bill. Did he feel so secure that he could afford the risk? Or did he need Big Brother? In any case, brotherly feelings still held. Cecil wanted to share his good fortune.

Of course, as director general of the Lasky Feature Play Company, Cecil was the dominant figure, and when Pop went to Hollywood he went as Cecil's subordinate, his writer. He was allotted one room in a wooden shack, where he hung a sign on the door: SCENARIO DEPARTMENT, the first such sign ever to appear in Hollywood. In the course of the next few years he not only wrote most of Cecil's scripts but evolved a good part of film technique. Father had been a superb amateur photographer, developing and printing his own pictures, and consequently invented several dozen technical devices, such as the closeup, lap dissolve, and intercutting, that are now taken for granted as the common language of the film medium. He was the first to show an individual leaving one place and arriving at another without a connecting shot of the man walking down the street.

At the beginning both men lived simply, walking to work in the morning and home in the afternoon, and they worked closely together. However, Cecil hankered for other ways of living, and their paths slowly began to diverge. He became almost fearsome in his growing power. Fortunately, his charm kept pace. Everyone recognized this—it was a charm full of energy, perception, and latent excitement. People adored him for it. He was invariably exciting to his own family, to his employees (he kept the core of his staff for thirty years), even to his enemies and mockers (and these he kept too). While in his presence, enemies were respectful. The most irreverent rushed to his summons and remained fascinated by his over-powering enthusiasm. And one must always bear in mind that an offer from DeMille was a guarantee of worldwide opportunity.

As long as Cecil stood by the camera, everyone's career was at stake. He could terminate all intermediate chances, and he could make an unknown famous; he had done both often. People might joke about him elsewhere, but on the set the air was electric with expectation. Here he took on the aspect and stature of a ruler. This tension of communication, this taking center stage, was with him all the time, and it gave his slightest remarks impact. The same sense of latent power is found in gambling casinos, at racetracks, and during parades — wherever events mount toward engagement with what really matters.

In our culture, what really matters is generally money. I believe money symbolized for Cecil an essential verity. He talked a great deal about God, but he kept a wary eye on the box office. I'm not sure he trusted God with the bottom line. But he was always reverential. He never forgot his manners; he was a nineteenth-century gentleman.

Early in the thirties he was invited by the Soviet government to make *War and Peace*, employing their army and navy and all the resources as needed. He asked as recompense his usual salary plus fifty percent of the gross, a sum that did not fit in with the Soviet plans. At least, this was the story he gave us. When he was going to produce his second and final version of *The Ten Commandments*, he arranged to film all the outdoor scenes in Egypt, using the Valley of the Kings and Queen Hatshepsut's tomb as one background and some 20,000 Egyptian civilians and a good portion of the king's cavalry as actors. "Are you negotiating through the State Department?" we asked. "Oh, no," he replied airily, "I don't bother with them. I make my own arrangements directly with the rulers of the countries."

Cecil always, even in routine circumstances, wished to make

his effect. If you went to him for a job in the old days, you would be ushered into his office after a very long wait; it might be early morning or after eight at night, but it would never be during shooting hours. The office would impress you, perhaps cow you: it had ecclesiastical windows, a vaulted ceiling with blackened beams (in emulation of Belasco's den), a baronial fireplace, a massive desk, deep couches, and various trophies from diverse triumphs. Cecil was not a sportsman, but he had hunted moose. There was a moosehead on the wall, and also a black and shrunken human head from the Matto Grosso—not, however, of his own catching. There were full suits of armor with velvet surcoats, medieval battle banners from *Joan the Woman*, highwaymen's silver-mounted pistols, huge white bearskin rugs, a silver bonbon dish in the shape of Madame Du Barry's bosom. No bust of Napoleon, as I recall. Du Barry's bosom did very well and was possibly more appropriate.

The boss might sit or he might stand during the interview, but he remained in a mystical twilight, while you were placed so that a spotlight shone full in your face, encouraging you to give the worst possible account of yourself. If your nerve held you were safe, but woe betide you if it didn't, for Cecil believed that shyness or reticence had no place in his business, and he wished to smoke out such qualities at the start, very much as the air force tries to expose and precipitate neurotic weakness during training periods. That these conditions would never be duplicated elsewhere he seemed not to consider. They constituted his obstacle race. They proved nothing about acting ability, of course. But as to this Cecil had odd ideas—for instance, that no lady could act, because a lady had learned self-control. Obviously he equated acting skill with lack of emotional stability.

Father thought all this ornate staging rather ridiculous and looked on it with amused indulgence. But occasionally he lost patience. Once, after he had been kept waiting, together with an important actor, in Cecil's outer office for over an hour, he left and sent this message: "Please tell God that after waiting an hour and a half, Moses and God's older brother grew tired." Father behaved as he felt, graciously pleasant and polite or surly and sharp-tempered. In that sense he was direct, not constantly striving for effect, and people loved him for his honesty. Then too, he was always, no matter what, amusing.

As Cecil grew older, he voluntarily moderated his behavior. If you paid him a call in the last twenty years of his career, you were admitted at Paramount through a special gate, the DeMille Gate, and taken to his "bungalow," a block of offices reserved entirely for his use. After a very long wait (still that) you saw him under urbane circumstances. The office had become domesticated, that is, it was no longer Byronic in its ungovernable romanticism. It was now the office of a vastly successful and suave businessman: normal expensive furniture, a great bowl of dark red roses on his desk, and set and costume designs stacked everywhere, against each chair. Not for him the Van Goghs, Rouaults, and Monets of his colleagues. He was far too honest or maybe too egocentric to pretend to taste he did not feel just because an expert told him he should. Any office conversation was interrupted every several minutes by business decisions of appalling magnitude. These had a rather more chastening effect than the spotlight or the armor, or even Du Barry's bosom.

If you passed muster or if you were an honored guest, you dined with him in the studio commissary at a special reserved table. The heads of companies and producers such as Louis B. Mayer, David Selznick, and Sam Goldwyn always ate in a private dining room, and they ate better. Cecil ate among the studio workers and shared their fare, but in full view, surrounded by his entire staff and distinguished guests. There were always fresh roses on his table—the only table to have them —and the table stood on a raised dais.

Afterward he would invite you onto the set. He reached his peak of energy before an audience. Cecil dressed immaculately for work and spent a lot on his wardrobe. His mother-in-law once told me she had counted 157 shirts on his shelves. (Father always wore good clothes but invariably seemed rumpled, and this appearance, I believe, he cultivated. His hat was very old; it became his signature piece. He refused to direct without it.) When working, Cecil wore riding breeches and boots. Since he was on his feet twelve hours a day, climbing all over the set, going up scaffolding, crawling around cameras, demonstrating, the boots and breeches were no affectation. The physical workout he gave himself was as strenuous as an orchestra conductor's. He was a vociferous, rhapsodic director who caused his actors to erupt in performance; he achieved effects not by innuendo but by command and tongue lashings and flights of baroque sarcasm.

In time he would call a halt, climb down off the camera platform, cross to you, and chat charmingly of politics, the weather, your personal plans, and family news. He might ask you suddenly for an opinion or professional advice, and he would expect an answer. This was both flattering and disconcerting, for on occasion he actually took your advice. He asked opinions of everyone. (Pop never did, until the picture was finished.) Cecil asked the electrician about a costume, the scene designer about dialogue, the sound man about the star's hair, a visitor about an actor's sex appeal. This habit certainly kept his staff on their toes, and it enabled him to get what he wanted most — a popular, average reaction. It was also, to the visitor at least, unforgettably flattering. You went home to Dubuque and told the Chamber of Commerce that the great DeMille had asked you about Lupe Velez's hairdo.

I don't recall his asking anyone about the direction of a scene, however. His questions in no way indicated doubt; he knew what he wanted and liked; he was seeking corroboration. In fact, he knew what was what on every subject, and when he had spoken he felt the matter was taken care of. It took a tremendously strong-willed, not to say bad-natured, egotist to disagree. Occasionally, I believe, his wife, Constance, demurred, but mildly and in private. Everyone else agreed. One longed to agree; one agreed through enthusiasm, excitement, and a kind of love. What he managed to instill in his staff and cast was the belief not only that the picture was the only work of art currently being realized, but that it somehow had to do with the continued well-being of the human race.

The effect Pop sought to make was quite different. Pop was regarded with loving respect by his cast and associates as a father figure. His directorial methods were sympathetic, as he sought always to call on the actors' instincts and intelligence, and actors generally responded sensitively. Large masses of people in emotional crisis and displays of architectural or scenic effect he avoided as none of his business. These were Cecil's specialties. The workings of the heart and head were Pop's domain.

It was in *Nice People* that Father devised a few bits of business in character revelation. A streetwalker is brought into a gentleman's house and, as a rebuke to his wife's companions, is seated at his dining table. Before she ventures to eat, she carefully cleans the forks and spoons with her table napkin. What a world of soiled eateries and sleazy hangouts this one gesture evokes! The implications were instantly recognized by every member of the audience. Similarly, in *Miss Lulu Bett* the camera travels around, noting each detail of a dining room. "If you want to know what a family is like, look at their dining room," says the caption. The camera stops at a wall clock, where Father stands comparing it with his pocket watch. He then deliberately advances the wall clock fifteen minutes and angrily rings the dinner gong. His ensuing remarks and glares as each startled member of the family arrives reveal him to be a testy tyrant eager to create a quarrel when none is justified. The exposition over, one can get on with the narration, which concerns the cruel persecution of the family drudge. Cecil would not have been capable of such deft, sure touches.

It is generally thought that William de Mille anticipated by fifty years the English and French schools of intimate comedy. He came to be the critics' choice. "I wish the critics would stop using me as the hammer with which to whack Cecil," said Pop.

Cecil quickly discovered he was an inspired businessman. He went to a business conference the way my father went to a tennis match. "Don't think of your opponents as people," he said to me. "You can't do that. They're your opponents in a game." He never drank during a business talk, of course, but he wouldn't smoke either. He wouldn't even permit himself a cup of tea or a stick of gum, lest some small part of his attention be distracted.

In these intricate competitions he began to forget affection, compassion, and family loyalty. I remember one night at dinner (I must have been fourteen of fifteen), Cecil said to Father, "Bill, remember those old lots we bought down near the oil wells?"

Father said, "Yes, Ce, I've been wondering how I could get rid of them."

"Well," Cecil said, "I'll take them off your hands."

"Done," said Father.

Then Cecil said, "I must tell you, I'm doing you. I know something about their coming potential."

Father said, "Take them. Take them. I don't want to pay taxes on them."

"Bill, you'd better hesitate," Cecil said. "I'm making a big thing out of this."

Father said, "Just get rid of them."

"All right," said Cecil, "that's agreed. Now I'll tell you. They're setting up a racetrack next door. Those lots will be worth hundreds of thousands."

In any other family I ever heard of, one brother would have said to the other, "At last, Bill, we can realize something together on those old lots." But Cecil thought of Father as his opponent, and he had to win.

However, except across a business table, stringent competition unmanned Cecil, so he either disregarded it or avoided

it. As a result, he was surrounded by people of abject, un-
questioning acquiescence. Name writers and musicians did not
collaborate with him for long. He made many stars; he never
discovered great actors or nurtured any true creative faculty.
He did not mingle socially where he could not dominate, and
so as time went on he could bring himself less and less to risk
the exposure that friendship demands. One must suppose,
therefore, that he was profoundly lonely, and his lifelong ob-
session with work would indicate as much. Indeed, at the end
of his life, as his daughter Cecilia explained wistfully, he had
"no friends, only associates." His adopted son Richard disagreed: "I do not for one minute believe Cecil was profoundly
or even slightly lonely. He simply denied himself the intimate
company of equals, feeling more at ease with wife, employees,
mistresses, and certain family members. He had lots of friends,
but they were not his equals. He was satisfied with that."

Sons and sons-in-law who could not readily disappear had
a rough time. The expanding personalities of growing individuals, if they were males, were not among the things Cecil
enjoyed cultivating; there was room for only one man in his
household. His sons- and daughters-in-law called him Mister
to the day of his death—never on any occasion Father, and
never C.B. So did his staff—Mister or Boss, never C.B. One
daughter-in-law, John's wife, called him Father, but she was
considered pushy by the other children.

Formality permeated most of Cecil's relations, although he
was a superb and gracious host and even a generous friend, as
long as he was dispensing largesse. I remember his enormous
appreciation of me when, as a child, I presented my small
Christmas gift—how he pushed aside the pile of splendor sur-
rounding him and gave my book of colored reproductions
(Vermeer, I think it was) his entire, lengthy, enthusiastic attention. I couldn't have been more flattered if I'd brought him
an original. He then handed me a $100 bill and commissioned
me to go buy every book of its type in the shop. This could
have been thought belittling. Certainly he intended it as reaf-

firmation, and I took it as such. He had the gift of making people, even children, seem important. "Do you remember how interesting and important he could make you feel?" Katherine Quinn, his adopted daughter, reminded me. Indeed, indeed I do. I remember his kindness and interest (way beyond my father's) in my childish dance experiments, my improvisations, and his interest in my appearance and my romances. His presents to us were always beautiful hand-sewn silk and lace French lingerie, or large bottles of French perfume. I once showed Father one of Uncle Ce's gifts; he took the cigar out of his mouth and remarked wryly, "Ever tried soap?" Pop gave us books.

Cecil's presents were always sexually helpful, but there were also roses, dozens of them, at graduations and galas and later at openings. He never missed (someone kept careful track for him). To discerning actresses he gave jewels, always suitably rich and beautiful—his rewards.

I received these gestures throughout my youth, except on one occasion, and this I believe was a deliberate rebuke for an open rebuff I had tendered him. Cecil had refused to help me when I needed help, so when I got married I did not ask him to the wedding. But Aunt Constance and Cecilia were asked and came. This was during the war; my Walter was in uniform. The guests were seven in number. Four nights later we went for Sunday night supper at the Big House; I thought Walter would like to see how the other half of my family lived. I did not expect a wedding present from Uncle Cecil, but I also did not expect a tantalizing tease.

After a courteous and warm welcome, Cecil asked if I had seen his wine cellar. I had not, so he did the honors. It was vast, built during Prohibition, dug out under the entire back lawn, and well stocked with everything, notably fine German wines. Remember, this was wartime; Walter was in uniform and about to go overseas. As we proceeded through the caverns, Walter began recalling all the great wines he had ever tasted. Yes, Cecil had them. We looked at one another. Maybe he would give us twelve bottles of something choice to start our own cellar! Maybe!

Then Walter thought of his favorite, a Vosnes-Romanée. Cecil had that too. Walter began drooling. "However," Cecil continued, "we keep a year-old whiskey in a charred keg, and we find that sufficiently potable. We will drink that." And that is exactly what he gave us to drink at our celebratory dinner. I must re-emphasize that no one knew better how to entertain than Cecil DeMille. No one. He knew exactly what he was doing, and he knew that I knew that I had asked for this treatment.

His feeling for paid employees was another matter. Once Cecil had hired someone, he tried to break his spirit, believing that whatever he paid for was his and he need only be careful of his inanimate belongings. This trait is not uncommon in power-driven men, who often are ungenerous to equals while always generous to the young or the abjectly dependent. The interest Cecil expressed, the gifts he made, satisfied his own ego; they never sought to strengthen the recipient's. Numerous elderly actresses and cripples may have relied on his private, unadvertised charity for the bulk of sustenance, but if any friend or relative went for business help, that person met with a calculation that was stunning. I never heard of Cecil's helping a young talent. He hired talent if it was useful and convenient; he never endowed it. He considered slow development a form of laziness. He could not forgive psychic disabilities. It follows that he thought Freud idiotic. The immature, although gifted, were not to be nursed. If you had guts you could get what you wanted; he had got his, without help.

Both Cecil and my father were extremely conscious of their possessions. One could say they were hoarders, but of quite different things. Cecil collected fine examples of master crafts-manship: Spanish shawls, books of prints, finely wrought gold and silver, real gems. If he wanted possessions for cash worth, he bought diamonds, rubies, or sapphires, and these he treated like royal jewels, bestowing on them proper names of his own devising: the Blue Lagoon, the Cornflower. They were not internationally known gems, but they were extremely valuable, and the family always spoke of them by name as though they were pets, a horse or a beloved dog.

Father's fancy was much more like a magpie's. He had some very fine bindings and nineteenth-century theater bills, but little else of value. The brothers shared a passion for guns. Father kept a small arsenal, which he maintained oiled and loaded and ready. Both men were dead shots, having practiced on rattlesnakes, and each went to bed at night with a loaded pistol beside him. As heads of families they could hardly do less.

Both men kept records, too. Father kept meticulous records of his gambling winnings and losses (they evened out at year's end), his tennis scores (they varied very little), his fishing expenses (each tuna cost between $2,000 and $3,000), his drinks (at that time moderate), but, alas, not his films. Unlike Cecil, who kept a complete, authentic record of everything he had done, which is now available to scholars, Father kept no record of his work, and neither did Paramount. Most of his films are lost, and this is tragic. Did Father begrudge the money it would have cost to preserve his films? Did he lack the money? Or was he so deeply embittered by the company's indifference to his achievement to make the effort to do so repugnant? Whatever the answer, his tennis scores were preserved intact, his life's work was not.

Cecil's collections were, I should say, comprehensive. He claimed and tagged everything he could lay his hands on. Having pickled the present, he began to cast a greedy eye on the past and future. When his daughter gave birth to his first grandson, he asked what the child's middle name would be, assuming as a matter of course that the last name would be DeMille. "The middle name will be DeMille," said Constance, laughing. It took a minute for C.B. to join in. When his beloved granddaughter Citci married an Egyptian in a mosque, the officiating mufti refused to accept Cecil as the proper male to give the bride away, and Cecil had to yield the place of pride to the girl's father. He was astonished and not a little chagrined. The bride, who adored him, was deeply amused.

It is not surprising that his abiding hobby became genealogy. He had the de Mille family tree carefully researched and to his great satisfaction was able to account for the unlikely right to use the names of Churchill and Blount, as well as the less known but equally honorable North Carolina names Bragaw and Cambreling. My father, believing Benjamin Franklin's maxim that "all blood is alike ancient," paid little attention to his brother's lineal preoccupation but casually hung the Blount crest (drawn and watercolored by me) on his wall, while the coat of arms and shield of wood, a handsome object, embellished his chimneypiece.

Cecil came to visit him one day and, not having been in his home for a long time, was surprised to note this decoration. "What are you doing with my crest?" he demanded. "Blount is my name."

"Well, Ce," said Father, "you're the one who is interested in genealogy, so you should know about primogeniture. I'm the older brother. The crest is mine. You belong to the cadet branch of the family—no crests."

Our house was a large, rambling wooden affair in three and a half acres of garden, including the largest bulb collection in Hollywood (every Easter we gathered clothesbaskets full of fleur-de-lis for our church). The furnishings were mongrel but comfortable, with a few fine pieces. There was a Steinway on which my sister and I put in long hours daily, and a mechanical organ. There were books. They were for reading. Life at our house was always vigorous and interesting. Mother and Father had a close circle of faithful and loving friends, and when I went to UCLA my group of professors and fellow students was added.

Father was an avid sportsman. He delighted in Saturday night poker, tennis every Sunday, and fishing when possible.

He had been a trout fisherman in the East. In the West he went after big game in the southern California waters, and served for years as the president of the Tuna Club of Catalina. Throughout his life, though, until he became too old and frail, his chief love was tennis. He played well, not well enough to attain national status but well enough to play with the best, and the best came to our court: three world champions — Bill Tilden, May Sutton, and Fred Alexander of the Davis Cup team — and others of ranking stature. Some came almost every Sunday and stayed for supper afterward. They stood at the core of Father's heart, even though they were interested in nothing but grips, angles, and bounces.

On Sunday after supper we always ran a picture for friends, and then my sister and I started proceedings. We played tolerably well, and then Father sang — not too well, I imagine (he never practiced). He sang good songs, however, and he invariably sang. He was relentless about this. Then the real musicians took over: Efrem Zimbalist, Alma Gluck, Edward Johnson, Geraldine Farrar, Rosa Ponselle, Reinald Werrenrath, Eva Gauthier. These brought their accompanists and performed enchantingly for our gatherings.

Father refused to have actors (except Chaplin and the Fairbankes) in the house, and he invited few directors, but he did welcome writers. Among these were Somerset Maugham, Rebecca West, Edward Knoblock, Elinor Glyn, Michael Arlen, and William Marion Reedy. There were personages from other spheres, too, such as the Anglo-Indian official Christopher Birdwood, Lord Thompson, who had entered Jerusalem on horseback behind Field Marshal Allenby when the city was delivered from the Arabs; Wilfred Grenfell, the explorer; and our navy commander, Benjamin Hayes Brook, who came to live with us whenever the S.S. *Pennsylvania* was in port.

At the end of every evening the talk was general. No one could compare to Pop in the role of conversational arbiter. He was witty, informed — my God, he was stellar. Cecil never came, because, I suppose, he could not be top man in his elder brother's house, and he could not lay down the law either to writers or to musicians. All in all, we were a very happy family, and Mother and Father shared the life in our house — overactive, even frenetic, and tearing to Father's nerves always, but stimulating and zestful. Here in his home, surrounded by admiring and enchanted friends, Father easily assumed the position of prominence he had held in New York, which he had come to think of as rightfully his, and which Cecil had abrogated in the studio and in greater Hollywood and in, yes, the world. Of course, it was Father's home aspect that I knew; to me he was the master artist.

Cecil's home consisted of two large houses built and purchased separately and eventually joined by a glass alleyway. They crowned a hill that had once been an arboretum of marvelous trees and flowers and that fell steeply in groves, sheltered paths, and pools to Franklin Avenue, lined by pepper trees. On the north side, open hillsides sloped to Los Feliz Boulevard and Griffith Park, a wilderness inhabited by coyotes and fringed with the truck gardens of Japanese farmers. On Cecil's estate there was a swimming pool (one of the first in Hollywood), a tennis court, and a circular rose garden. In this populous suburb the coyotes ululated every night, and snakes on occasion wiggled their way across the highways.

Cecil greeted a guest with ornate courtesy — as after my *Oklahoma!* success, when he hailed me by saying, "I see I'm not only the uncle of a beautiful woman, but a relative of a genius." As this terminated a long period of noticeable professional neglect, the remark rang with noteworthy effect. He then gallantly and with flourish ushered you into his large, open, flower-filled living room. Aunt Constance, soft-spoken, regal, trailing soft velvet or chiffon, gently made you welcome and comfortable. The square emerald on her left hand was enormous and nearly flawless, and she sometimes wore a rope of fire opals that hung to her waist. Her voice was halting but soft and had the modulation of a trained actress. Her humor was superb, though quietly expressed.

The big room contained a Steinway (seldom used), a gramophone, comfortable amounts of sofas, Cecil's rocking chair, a huge (eight by ten foot) Velázquez (colored print), a Rubens (dubious), and, over the mantel, a Willis Goldbeck (genuine). There was silver everywhere, highly polished, and there were splendid mahogany replicas. There was no color in the drapes or furniture; everything was subdued in tone, except for the flowers blazing on tables and piano.

About the house there were always the dogs, called Sloppy and Bougy (Salpiglossis and Bougainvillea). At night there was a German shepherd that went the rounds on a chain with the night watchman. Cecil himself always locked up; he had a light switch that lit the gardens near his bed and his loaded pistol within reach.

Every evening after dinner, if Cecil was not in active production, a film would be showing in the next house. Guests would proceed through the rich library (Cecil bought up whole libraries, mainly books of prints), along the long glass corridor to the second house, and into Cecil's home office, a rather romantic, quasi-Elizabethan room. Neighbors and friends would have gathered here to wait until he came from dinner with his intimates and honored guests. After the film he often asked for these guests' opinions (even the children's); he tabulated them and then pronounced judgment and said goodnight.

If he was in active production, he rose before seven, dressed, breakfasted with his wife in her sunny bedroom amid crawling grandchildren, and left for the office by eight, sometimes walking the three miles (his only exercise). By nine he was on the set, ready to put in a day that in energy and concentration rivaled a field commander's. The tension, broken only by a one-hour lunch, continued until seven. Then conferences commenced in his office: script, costume, scenery, budget, and business, unabating until ten or eleven.

Constance seldom went out in the evening. The children ordered their own social lives, while she held herself ready at home for Cecil's return. Family dinner was long since over and the servants had gone to bed, so Constance heated his food in double boilers and served it to him in front of the living-room fire, at a little table spread with the best silver and Italian lace. He sat in a rocking chair opening personal letters and sipping a glass of wine or Irish whiskey—one glass only. He and Constance talked over the day's work, sometimes conversing until early morning. After four or five hours' sleep, Cecil was up at seven.

He remained phenomenally healthy. This regime did not slack off in middle age or even later, as good habits often do. He kept himself a soldier.

The house bulged with people, pets, children, and projects, but unlike ours it was always serene, and this was Constance's contribution. There was never any emergency, any change of plan, any disturbing absence or presence, any business reversal —and Cecil lived through remarkable family stresses, through revolution and civil war in his business maneuverings—that could cause Constance to panic or cry out. She continued unchanged, above and beyond all. She loved him. She believed in him. He needed a quiet home, so she gave him a quiet home, as quiet and tranquil as an unstirred pool, and whenever Cecil looked into it he saw, as in a mirror, his own reflection. Whatever moved in the depths was never permitted to trouble him. She gave her life to seeing that it did not.

He was away often on weekends at his other home, his ranch, Paradise. Constance gave an interview once, saying that the secret of a happy married life was freedom, lack of possessiveness, and frequent separations, and that she herself never asked where her husband spent his weekends. The reaction of the American housewife to these bland remarks from one so squarely in the public eye surprised no one but Constance. She was abruptly requested by Paramount's public relations department to let it edit her professions of domestic philosophy. But she stood by her credo. Cecil went to Paradise whenever he liked; the family followed by invitation only.

Paradise was a wild tract of land in the mountain range north of the San Fernando Valley, difficult of access and completely private. For years there was no telephone. Although it was a real ranch (Cecil raised chickens and pheasants for market), the property was virtually an untamed wilderness, with mountain lions, coyotes, and deer drinking from the swimming pool and rattlers coiled under the dining-hall steps. Notwithstanding the environment, you slept on linen and dined off porcelain and crystal, and you dressed for dinner every night—if a lady, in deep décolleté and what jewels you could muster; if a gentleman, in the uniform Cecil had chosen, a czarist officer's blouse: red satin for an ordinary gentleman; purple for a director, government official, or head of a corporation; white for a producer. You could be your country's ambassador and not rise above purple. White was for producers and producers only. Never mind—red was by all odds the most flattering color, and many an ordinary male looked at himself in the bedroom mirror with astonishment and delight when he had donned the scarlet blouse the valet had laid out for him.

Then, all gay and bright and bejeweled, you gathered in the dining casino at a trestle table in front of a roaring fire. Ruby goblets winked in the light, and there you ate very well indeed, while an electric Wurlitzer pumped out Beethoven or whatever was requested. Paradise wasn't San Simeon, but it was a good pocket-size sample of the same thing, set in the sagebrush amid the cicadas, with the silent, soft-footed cougars coming around nightly to raid the chicken coops.

I went only once, to a party given in my honor on graduation from the university. No guest in the room was over twenty-two and our jewels were glass, but the faces above the Russian collars were burning with excitement.

"And now, gentlemen," said Cecil to his barely bearded companions, "you will see what you have always longed to see." The boys looked at him questioningly. "Women quarreling over jewels," he explained. The boys nodded sagely over their unfamiliar brandy snifters.

A table of costume jewelry, French perfume, feather fans,

powder compacts, and such was brought out by the houseboys, and the ladies—I and my schoolmates—were given dice to roll for first choice. When this was over (and I don't recall that we scrapped unduly for the goodies), we went out into the night feeling somehow that we had lifted the curtain an inch or two on debauchery and Roman splendor.

Somewhat later, but at an early hour, Cecil policed the houses to see that we were all stowed away exactly as we should be. I was sitting decorously by the pool in the moonlight with my boyfriend, not even holding hands. We were politely but firmly escorted by my uncle with a flashlight to our separate houses. Debauchery was over.

The next day there was archery, and Cecil sat on the porch signing $10 and $20 bills as mementos. He was signing the bills because he was vice president of the bank, and his signature made them legal tender, or so he told us.

A family treat of this nature was rare. On most weekends Cecil took his own guests, and what went on there, goodness only knows. No gentleman talked; Cecil's family never asked.

Constance when very young had said to my mother, "As long as I live, there will be no other Mrs. Cecil DeMille." There never was, but she had to accept much. When I was about twenty-two, Constance said to me, "You know, sex and love have nothing to do with one another. They are entirely different concerns in human life." I looked at her in amazement, and was filled with a great sadness. I had always been told by my mother that romantic love, especially dedicated, married romantic love, was the highest form of feeling and the goal of life. What was my aunt saying to me? What a wilderness of wasted passion and sterile effort this revealed! I turned my eyes away. I could not speak to her.

Gossip had it that the birth of Cecilia had been so painful and traumatic for Constance that she had determined to forgo further sex, but that being a fair-minded woman, she allowed Cecil complete freedom and apparently harbored no ill will toward the ladies involved. I did not learn about Cecil's mistresses until years after his death. They were Jeanie Macpherson, his scenario writer; Julia Faye, one of his frequently cast lesser actresses; and Gladys Rosson, his brilliant secretary-accountant. They knew about one another, working as they did side by side, but made no public outcry and functioned on all levels simultaneously. It was a seraglio. He kept them pacing in step and in tandem. I find this to be not the least wonderful of his achievements.

He was aided—more, he was supported—by Constance. She had the ladies for lunch and dinner. She had them nightly for the running of pictures. She pleasantly and graciously had them as companions on transcontinental trips and for many theater and opera and shopping expeditions, and no one ever knew what she thought. She endured them, but she yielded not one prerogative as Cecil's consort. Throughout everything she remained his recognized wife, and no one ever took her place at his side.

Mother refused to let the other ladies into her house, and she was outraged by Constance's permissive attitude. "She has let down the code," Mother said wrathfully. Well, it was true: Constance had encouraged scab labor.

I think Mother could not forgive Constance's permissiveness because she believed it influenced Father. Father had been so straitlaced that for years he had been known as the studio virgin. Then he began to imitate Cecil and the other men in his business and found that the liberal behavior was fun. It is difficult to overstate the temptations for casual promiscuity that offered themselves to directors daily. All the men with power in the studio had whatever they wanted. Women were common currency. Mother could not and would not accept a compromise situation; she was in no way like Constance. There had to be a total break. From the morning she walked out of Father's home she never spoke to him again. Yet she always loved him, and she remained to her death unmarried.

However, it was Cecil who was generally thought to be the ladies' man. I believe he was far too busy for casual liaisons.

He maintained his chosen three lovers, but it is unlikely that his attention and energy could have stretched beyond these. It must be borne in mind that his interests embraced much besides epics and the amazing intricacies of studio power struggles. He dealt in banks, real estate, ditch digging ("Did you know that I dug more ditches than anyone else west of the Mississippi?" he said to me once), racetracks, farming, oil, and of course stocks and bonds.

Father followed along to a fractional degree, but he had time to get into emotional trouble, and he did. His little brother, to his indignation, did not approve and had the gall to say so. "When a man has been married twenty-three years, he must not leave his wife," said Cecil finally and firmly. "Besides, I don't think your Clara Beranger is talented." Cecil told us this, not Father. The rift between them grew.

Father sired an illegitimate son by a studio writer who used the name Lorna Moon and who promptly developed severe tuberculosis. Having no way to keep the child himself, Father went to Cecil, who agreed to adopt the infant if both of the natural parents would permanently relinquish their parental claims and conceal their identity, which they did. The child was taken into Cecil's household as a foundling orphan and named Richard DeMille. He is, of course, my half-brother; he was brought up as my younger cousin, and he did not know who his father was.

What this experience cost Pop I do not know, because none of the principals ever spoke of it to me. Whether he loved Lorna, what giving up his son to Cecil meant — both men had wanted sons, but they legitimately fathered only daughters — whom he told, I have no right even to guess. Mother didn't know about Moon or about Richard's parentage. My stepmother, Clara, found out long afterward. It is an incontrovertible fact that four months after the birth of the baby, William de Mille and Clara Beranger started their love affair, and it was this love that resulted in Father's divorce and second marriage.

· · ·

Cecil talked about sex as though he knew more about it than anyone else. About sex he thought himself the ultimate voice, the pope. However, it seems to me that he was basically an aging juvenile, glued to adolescent eroticism. About dress he reverted to what had seemed highly desirable to him as a boy, the style and taste of the late 1880s and 1890s, the Sarah Bernhardt period. Sarah, whose signed photograph was on his mother's piano, lived in Paris in a hothouse of pillows, fur rugs, paintings, statues, bronzes, bric-a-brac, and potted palms. It wasn't that Cecil's choices were in bad taste or out of style. His taste was make-believe and inherited. But it worked. Cecil made hundreds of millions through following that taste.

His approach to history was, as one subordinate remarked, "liberal." Dates, sequence, geography, and character bent to his needs. At the same time he was a pedantic and undeviating realist about details. Harnesses, wagon wheels, pots, and weapons had to be exact, and the costume plates of museum accuracy. The designers who worked for him quickly caught on to the fact that every eyelash had to be drawn in a costume sketch, the fingernails and body hair put on each hand holding a spear. The spear had to be authentic, but the hair had to be there too.

Women's costumes had to conform to Cecil's idea of feminine desirability, which never changed, no matter what period. Right here authenticity went out the window, together with opaque clothing. For this reason he seldom used couturiers. With the help of Mitchell Leisen, an interior designer who became a director, and the designer Gilbert Adrian he invented his own fashion and actually set styles, which affected none of the élite but nearly everyone else. Millions of women who had never heard of Chanel or Lanvin wanted to look like Gloria Swanson and Hedy Lamarr. This is an interesting point: had Chanel dressed the stars, they might not have influenced so many. There was just that touch of vulgarity in all DeMille's clothes that appealed to the masses at this particular period—

and also that touch of sexual tease. Cecil skirted plain obscenity often in his work, but he always remained prudish in his speech before women, and thought Ernest Hemingway and D. H. Lawrence salacious. This was the considered judgment of a man who collected pornography and slipped photographs of naked women into his fine books.

He claimed he loved people and was interested in all their aspects. He kept insisting that he was bringing out the human qualities of his characters. But he showed those human qualities he himself saw, from which one would gather he had never met people, particularly people who were women. His heroines were either fighting-mad vixens, tomboys who had to be brought to heel (and loved to be) by sheer masculine brawn, or innocent beauties who went through dreadful experiences unmussed. They were in essence the daydreams of a prep-school boy at the turn of the century, complete with silk couches, silk robes, manicured feet (Cecil was fascinated by feet), jewels, sunken pools, rose petals, goblets, dim lights — golly! Never any humor, never any honesty or candor, never any companionability. They remained contrary, bewitching, unpredictable, and belligerent until the inevitable silken capitulation. This was very strange, because the women in Cecil's own family life — his mother, his wife, his daughters, his step-mother-in-law, and his sister-in-law — were strong, humorous, dedicated, loyal, and enchanting people, of considerable wit and presence. Obviously he longed for another kind.

His heroes were equally stereotyped: untroubled by doubts, though frequently tempted by sin. If they were true DeMille heroes, however, they repented, and after suffering intense remorse they recognized God in time. The mind divided, the mind doubting and lost, was not for the Boss. God always came through for him in the nick, right on schedule.

Pop, by contrast, had no eye; he cared little for dress and nothing for authenticity. "Women did not show their hair in the fourteenth century," I once stated, rather smugly and categorically. "Who is going to know?" was his only reply. He knew nothing and cared nothing for painting, sculpture, architecture, gardens, or furniture, except as it revealed character. But he had a fine sense of space in camera effects, of light and dark, of photographic quality. He knew a very great deal about cameras. And he had an ear! Every syllable was weighed, every word evaluated. He worked for a week on his subtitles and spoken titles and he wrote them himself, which was not customary among directors.

His favorite tale about titles was of Somerset Maugham, who authored one picture for him, *Midsummer Madness*, and supplied the following explanatory transition: "Not by accident they met Saturday night at his hunting lodge." Pop said it took him two weeks to shoot the three words "not by accident." This is a prime example of nonvisual authorship.

Father also gave us one of the first pictures with a soundtrack from beginning to end, one of the first all-talkies, *The Doctor's Secret*, in 1929. Now with the human voice restored, his popularity would be revived, one would think — but no, now the studios wanted Frederick Lonsdale or Noël Coward dialogue. Father was considered old hat.

As the years passed, Cecil made monstrous sums. He came through the IRS examinations of the 1930s unscathed, due to his lawyer, Neil McCarthy, and due to Gladys Rosson's extraordinary skill. In fact, her books were so remarkably well kept that the government officials complimented her on her job of accountancy.

Father had no such good fortune. As Cecil's financial power mounted, Father suffered failure, and his situation was complicated by his divorce. He discovered he had broken either the federal corporation law or the California community property law. His case made legal history. He confessed to me that he would never, in the whole of his life, be able to pay off his debt to his lawyers, and he developed a heart condition through stress and worry. The lawyers could not protect him, however, and he lost all his savings, every penny, to the government.

At the same time the vogue for his pictures ended and he found no studio willing to renew his contract.

Clara swallowed her pride and went to Cecil to beg for help, saying that she did not think it becoming that he should permit his only brother to suffer for lack of money and lack of work and that he must find a way to give him some paying job worthy of his very considerable talents. It cost her a great deal in humiliation to do this. Cecil did find Father a job, writing his next picture—the story of Mary, the mother of Jesus, a picture that was prepared but never made, partly because it was vigorously opposed by the Catholic church. Cecil paid Pop $150 a week, which was less than an assistant script girl received for sitting on the set and keeping track of camera angles. Father had never received such money, but he had to take this offer. There was no other.

Cecil had always been generous to Father with his yacht, with his car, with his tennis court, with tickets for all Hollywood functions, for racetracks, for tournaments, for benefits, for whatever big spectacle was afoot, but he would not share business opportunity. Father was a grown man and he should be able to take care of himself.

Clara then arranged for Pop to be dean of drama at the University of Southern California. She also assumed the major portion of his living expenses. Not all of them; Father took pride in stressing this point to me.

Father and Cecil grew further and further apart in their political and economic views. Father was a Jeffersonian democratic liberal, and Cecil was an old-guard Republican, believing in independent enterprise by no matter what confiscation of public rights. He believed in taking, not begging. His quarrels with the moving-picture directors and with the industry as a whole during the McCarthy era were notorious and did him no good in his profession. He phoned Father more than once at the University of Southern California to alert him about Reds on his faculty and order him to fire them forthwith. Father declined abruptly. They saw one another less and less frequently, but said nothing publicly except what was brotherly.

At Father's suggestion, Cecil made an endowment of $5,000 a year to the drama faculty at USC, but he retained certain rights over the management of the monies. By 1979, long after both brothers' deaths, the fund, which was greatly augmented, was renamed the William C. de Mille Faculty Development Fund. It was now sizable and was entirely derived from Cecil's original gift.

Father's contest with Cecil grew sterner with time. Father simply withdrew and held himself aloof. That was wise. He was not a success as Cecil was, a fact he acknowledged readily. What matter? But I think he got used to conceding. He began to accept failure on his own terms. Particularly after his divorce, he withdrew from the challenge of his work. He stepped aside from his own standards, and this was a tragedy. He lost his nerve.

Mother had been intolerably aggravating to him, but this is the vital fact: she was the spur in Father's flank, the gall under the saddle, and when Father was rid of her, when he had at last found peace from her exhortations, he sank into self-indulgence and never again made the grand effort toward his real work. He contented himself with the ready quip, with the apt, quotable remark, with the unchallenged comment; he got an instant laugh and lapsed back into complacency. He was happy with his small circle of friends and their expected response, happy with his daily cronies and the repeated stories. He no longer read. He never went to the theater or concerts. He followed his beaten track to his university classes and back without variance. He went on his nightly stroll with his buddy, the actor Frank Reicher. He never again achieved his possibility. He never again troubled himself to. But he was content, or nearly so, and he was kind, something he often had not been when young.

In the early fifties, Clara finally persuaded Father to take a world cruise with her, which she had been begging him to do for decades. The night before embarkation, Father had a stroke. He subsequently developed cancer of the throat and then of the lungs.

Cecil had been attentive to Jeanie Macpherson when she was dying of cancer, and he was faithful and loyal to Gladys Rosson; these deaths caused him pure grief, with no crossed emotions of guilt and need for revenge. Father's wasting and going must have tugged at his deepest roots, revealing poisoned memories. Finding them unbearable, he avoided them. During Pop's long and agonizing illness, he only went to see him twice—twice in four years!—and he only phoned him at times of crisis. Fortunately, Pop's other friends stood by.

At last Clara sent word that if Cecil wanted to find his brother alive, he had better get down to Pop's house quickly. So he came, and when the neighbors saw the great black limousine in the street they thought it was a hearse and ran out of their houses, crying, "Oh, Mr. de Mille! Oh, Mr. de Mille!" Pop's Filipino houseboy had to reassure them. Cecil had a final hour with his brother, and when he came from the bedroom he wept intensely, sobbing into his hands like a boy. At Father's death, Cecil phoned from Paradise and offered to come immediately. But it was too late. Clara refused; the widow had nothing to say to him. At the funeral he stood beside the coffin for long minutes, abandoned to grief.

Cecil B. DeMille lived at an ideal time for himself. Had he been alive today, his autocratic proclivities would have been inhibited by all manner of social and legal restraints. Had he been born earlier, his gifts for storytelling and drama would not have found their proper expression, for he was not a good writer. His ear was poor, but his eye and his sense of dynamics were supremely fine. He needed, therefore, a visual medium. The motion picture was invented just in time for him.

I think he has been both over- and underestimated. Hollywood has disdained him, joked about him, and overlooked him, but Hollywood owes its existence to him, and knows it. It was largely he who turned a small fruit-growing town into a metropolis and a struggling group of players into the fifth largest industry in the United States. Furthermore, Hollywood's neglect spells short memory. His early works were first-class, technically, photographically, and dramatically: *Carmen, Maria Rosa, Joan the Woman, The Whispering Chorus* — ask any of the veterans. Run these films again and see.

The extraordinary phenomenon Cecil presented was enormous craft combined with secondhand subject matter and an amazing lack of sophistication. Although not a great artist, Cecil was undoubtedly sincere, fervent even, as was a good part of his audience. But his aesthetics were faulty, his style and modes of expression spurious, and since he worked through an art medium, any taint in that medium violated the message. Great messages are voiced greatly. This is the basis and validity of the art experience. I believe with John Keats that "beauty is truth, truth beauty."

Cecil's approach to the religious message of his pictures may not have been inwardly convincing, but he was nevertheless the most popular religious propagandist in the world. He must therefore be considered as an expression of his times. He need not be considered, as he hoped, a great religious teacher. He was neither pure nor humble, and the people he reached were not touched at any depth. His Bible stories were never told with the simplicity of revelation. He knew that the singing of hymns and the torture of naked women, or the voice of God and a rape, was an unbeatable combo. But it was always the hymn, not the orgy, that closed the picture, and if the route to divine understanding had been a scenic one, where was the harm? He lost few traveling companions along the way.

Richard DeMille disagrees with much of this interpretation. "I do not think Cecil thought he was a profound biblical scholar," he says, "or any scholar at all. He thought he knew enough about the Bible to tell religious stories to ordinary people. It was a modest purpose, and he achieved it very well. Bible teachers don't have to be scholars, saints, messiahs, or even pure and humble. They just have to care about the Bible and know how to teach."

When Cecil dealt with what he really knew — with the battle scenes, with storming and conquest, for instance; with adventuring, with all matter of bravery and daring, with the mass movement of people under stress of agony or joy; with the contention of men, with hope and the struggle for survival — ah, then the ancient battle cry was heard, the thunder rolled, and heaven and nature were with him. This was his landscape, this his native country! He did not stop to analyze here, or talk about what the people wanted, or preach. He just damn well did it. And nobody has ever done it as well. Picture after picture, Colossal, Earth-Shaking, Moving, Mighty, Smashing, Resurrecting, Sea-Dividing, Law-Giving, Temple-Tearing, his life unrolled in film.

He fought to the end to preserve his power and place in the business. Hollywood knew depressions; studios failed, pictures lost money, producers grouped and regrouped, Wall Street interfered, panicked, cut off funds, the advent of talkies bankrupted many, the advent of television even more. There never was any enduring safety. Cecil fought on. He was imitated. When it was known he intended to redo *The Ten Commandments*, four Egyptian pictures were rushed through ahead of his schedule. He regarded the hubbub with grand amusement. He took his time; he knew his would be the best. It was.

The idea of stopping work, of retiring or resting, was out of the question, even after a thrombosis. Life for him meant work, and nothing else. He was well aware that his health was what the bankers invested in and that he could not be replaced. So he pretended he was well and strong when he was nothing of the sort, and went on planning with the financiers another great epic, this one to be about Boy Scouts, while the doctors warned and his family broke their hearts worrying. Every day he dressed and went to his office in the studio, until he literally could not walk out of his house. Even then he was up, dressed, seeing pictures, discussing business, locking up the house at midnight. "Let me do this for you, Mr. DeMille," begged his son-in-law. "I've done this for forty years; I can do it tonight," said Cecil.

But he very nearly didn't finish. His daughter Cecilia wept — one of the two or three times in her life she had been seen to weep. The doctors came and told him the truth: total bed rest or imminent death. He seemed surprised at the seriousness of his malady — almost astonished, like a child — and for once he became obedient.

Two days later his bed was found empty in the morning. He had disobeyed and got up. The distraught family went frantically searching. They discovered him sitting beside Constance, who was too ill to speak, possibly not even aware of his presence. He was quietly holding her hand and seemed to be waiting. On their arrival he went docilely back to bed, and there, his Bible by his side, a few hours later, very simply and in his sleep, he died.

These two men, William and Cecil de Mille, had the shaping influence over my character in my first nineteen years. Both were dazzling to me, but as my judgment matured and as the direction of their careers became evident, I had no wish to be like either. Cecil's taste was in no way mine. My father's professional path filled me with a sense of defeat. He had been first-class in his youth but grew steadily less so. He knew exactly the direction of his path; I saw this in his sad, beautiful eyes.

The lives of both men were enigmas. William I think aimed too high, too fast. Or did he? His troubles were compounded by his life — divorce and its attendant guilt and rages, and maybe, although I don't know, the heart-wrenching sense of loss in abandoning his son.

The contradictions in Cecil's life were equally blatant and tearing. He was the best-known moving-picture director in the world, decorated by many governments and blessed by the pope, yet he received only twice the most coveted prize his profession could give, the Oscar. The first time was in 1949, in general recognition of "thirty-seven years of brilliant showmanship," handed out as a sop to Hollywood's conscience, and a little late in the day for a man who had been worldrenowned for nearly half a century; the second, in 1952, was for *The Greatest Show on Earth*, his sixty-ninth and penultimate picture. Lesser-known directors have received the Oscar several times.

He was the terror of the Paramount lot; he was the darling of children. He could be the hardest and most terrifying man I have ever met, yet he sat beside many a deathbed, because in the last moments his voice, his strength, and his faith were needed for comfort. People called to him when they were dying. This is a fact, and it is unanswerable.

Father's house and garden went first. In the twenties the lovely garden was turned into commercial tennis courts, then apartments.

The Cecil DeMille house was maintained with all its furnishings (even some clothes and notepaper) until 1988. That October Cecil's grandchildren held a sale of the less choice objects at Christie's in New York, and netted just over $700,000. DeMille's desk, a plain American mahogany one, fetched $125,000. Most of the books were sold in Los Angeles, fetching $10,000; some furniture Christie's did not want brought an additional $30,000. Cecilia DeMille Presley kept the Doré book collection, the good Bibles, and assorted rare books.

Cecilia offered the house itself to the Motion Picture Academy Historical Society and other institutions, but Cecil's quarrels with these labor-related societies left his name in such bad repute that they spurned all offers, not wishing to encourage memories of their detested antagonist. Furthermore, the house was in need of fundamental repairs. The heirs sold it for $2

million. The purchasers have made the repairs and completely
refurbished its interior. It now sports gold cherubs on the living
room ceiling, has been dubbed "Design House of 1989," and
purports to be "C. B. DeMille's mansion." There is very little
of DeMille left, of course. The owners hope to realize $6.75
million in the eventual sale.

I remember Cecil and Constance having their quiet suppers
together late at night before the open fire in the big room —
how after supper he and his Gretchen (I don't know the origin
of this nickname, but Cecil acted in *Faust*, and I think he chose
the Faustian heroine for his true love) went about in gentle
connubiality seeing that every window and door was fastened,
speaking to the night watchman, locking up like any good
householders.

The part of the house that I took as my own province, by
formal invitation from Cecil and Constance, was his back
study, where he ran his pictures at night but where in the
daytime and late afternoons I was free to look at his marvelous
books — old prints of every picture in the Louvre gallery, the
prints of Doré, the color reproductions of geographical paintings, an 1878 edition of George Catlin's paintings of Indians
printed in Edinburgh, and the complete set of *Le Théâtre* back
to 1892, which held the treasures of the French theater and
most marvelous articles about Rachel and early nineteenth-
century stars. I was free to go into the still room where the
suits of armor stood in the corners, with the light of the afternoon sun firing the small-paned windows, firing the book-
case; the dark-red velvet curtains were glowing, the furniture
was glowing, the great books all around were open to my
touch, the unbroken quiet was marked with a distant filigree
of household noises that produced a friendly note of reassur-
ance in the background. Sloppy and Bougy came around, sniff-
ing out the interloper. On Cecil's large desk in the afternoon
sun was a bowl of ruby-red garden roses. His roses were every
shade of red, but the darkest and noblest were saved for his

desk, both here and in the studio. When people describe his office, they never fail to mention the armor, Du Barry's bosom, the shrunken heads, but I remember the roses in the afternoon sun, put there every day by a secretary who loved him.

Then I think of my dark, distinguished father, the central reason of our house: the sparkling presence, the commanding voice, the climax of all our days, and the fun. When I think of his wife Anna, my mother — Anna with her firefly humor flickering over all events; red-haired, curly-haired Anna; blue-eyed, white-skinned, tiny (size 1 shoe), impudent Anna, who tried with might and main to make everyone's life better and wouldn't let anyone rest until that person had made the effort to become better — when I think of Anna's house, our house, always bustling and busy and chaotic, with telephones and bells ringing, dogs barking, voices calling, and people doing things, I think mostly of the garden.

It was three and a half acres on Hollywood Boulevard, filled with lilies and all sorts of other flowers as well, old-fashioned flowers — English stock and lavender, primroses and daisies, lilacs and tulips, and even violets. I remember how I used to walk up and down the paths just before dusk, thinking, planning God knows what, looking forward to dinner, which would have fascinating people to listen to and also Mother's very good food, and Father sitting at the head of the table commenting humorously, incisively, on whatever topic was introduced. I remember how I stood among the darkening plants, which would give out ever more pungent odors as the light failed and the heat lessened. Father would be there. I knew that. What joy for the end of a schoolday! Father would be home, the dazzling host, the wit, the ladies' man, the charmer, the sportsman, the boon companion, the raconteur, the most quoted, the artist, the real one, the humanist, the one to imitate! He was ours, ours, our very own, to be with every night. Such riches! Would it last? Could it last? Wouldn't something break the happiness?

I waited.

The overwhelming honey of the camphor tree, buzzing with bees even after the sun had left; millions of flowers stirred under the impact of their wings, still humming, close to intoxicating; and lavender, musk roses, moss roses, all kinds of roses, a quarter of an acre of roses in the cooling air, breathing out, changing in the hush before the deeper change, waiting. I waited. Something would happen, something.

And then Mother's voice from the porch: "Come in, dearie. Come in. Your father will be home any minute now. Soon it will be dark."

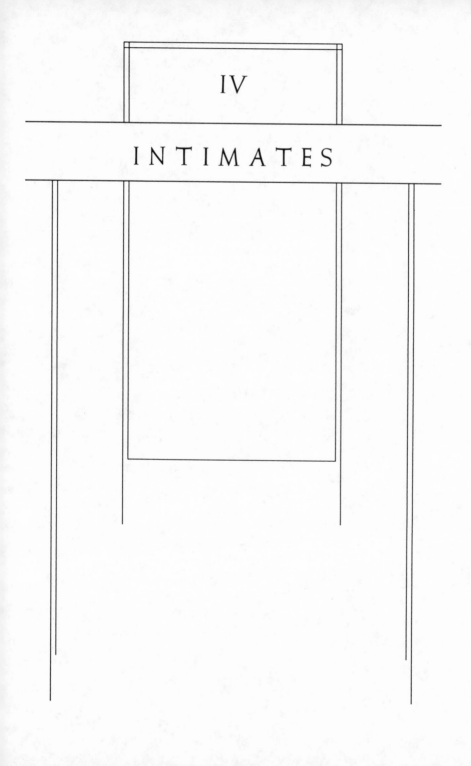

IV

INTIMATES

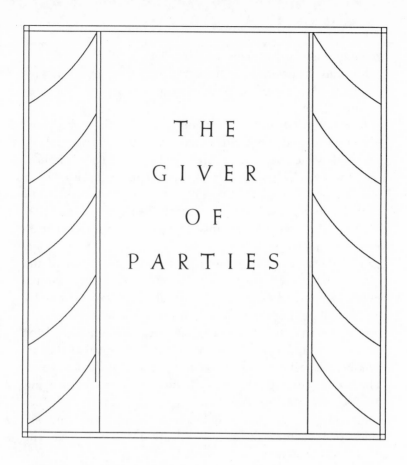

THE
GIVER
OF
PARTIES

MOTHER LOVED to give parties and all her life gave many, some of which were successful and quite a a few of which were obnoxious. The reason is not hard to find: the guests.

There was no other reason, surely. Our house was attractive, warm and flower-filled; the dinner service was exquisite; the food was good, and all homemade — I mean the jams and salads and condiments made by Mother in the kitchen, the cakes and cookies and jellies made either by her or by her cook from old recipes and with pure cream, pure butter, and real sugar. The liquor was excellent, with the exception of one lot during Prohibition, when Mother poured into her guests' glasses an unforgettable wine of her own vintage. She had never made any before and she never made any again, which may explain why she retained a few of her friends, even veterans of that noteworthy dinner.

As to the guests, many were famous, enchanting, glittering, but always — and here was the fatal flaw, Mother's compulsive flaw — they included two or three of what my sister and I called "bide-a-wees." These were her wretched protégés, either poor relatives or the unattractive but very sincere daughters of staunch Single Taxers who had given their life to the Cause. These misfits were of unblemished character, plain in appearance, retiring in deportment, and speechless. Mother always invited them secretly, without confessing to the rest of the family, and at the last moment, of course. They were always free to come, and they were always an embarrassment and a responsibility. I suppose people have rich relatives who are equally unattractive, but not equally helpless. They fend for themselves, and they do not have the unforgivable trait of making one feel guilty for whatever one personally does have. There was a cloying shame in meeting Mother's girls, in trying to hold conversation with them, in trying to find them other guests to talk to. They couldn't talk, being barely audible, unless one wanted a discussion in depth of the injustice of the present tax system.

That was one error I vowed I would never, never commit, and I never did. Mother had another weakness. She tried to organize her guests to enjoy themselves the way she thought they ought to, as she organized her family. Although she was tiny and went to infinite trouble, sparing no pains to make those she loved happy and carefree, she was unanswerable. Her will was unyielding.

For five days before Christmas, for instance, she commandeered my schoolmates and sat them around the dining room table cutting up dried glacéed fruit — candied grapefruit, glacéed cherries, pineapples, prunes, raisins, angelica. Then she set them to stirring the mixture in zinc washtubs placed on the table. When a fresh bowlful of cut-up pieces had been prepared she dumped them in, adding sugar and flour and brandy according to her great-grandmother's recipes until the mixture was too thick for a woman to stir and the broom handles we used for the task stood straight up by themselves in the almost solid contents; then the boys were asked to take over. Six or seven pans went into the oven at a time, all day for three days. The cake came out black and very nearly too rich for digestion. When the Christmas puddings were readied she sewed them up in muslin bags and garnished them with sprigs of native holly brought down from the hills. The cakes she iced white and decorated with red peppermints, representing holly berries, with angelica cut like leaves.

So far so good. In fact, the best.

One Christmas she thought of an added treat: she would have a Yule log, which she looked up in the encyclopedia. She procured an enormous log from the local lumberyard, then she pounded salts in a mortar with a pestle bought especially for the purpose. The salts would turn the flames to witchfire: bright blue, bright green, ruby red, savage orange. Then she tied a rope of ribbons to the well-salted wood. My sister and I were bid to learn sixteenth-century carols.

The sophisticated Christmas guests at the ensuing party were happily drinking Father's cocktails when Mother rushed quite unheeded to our mechanical orchestrelle and began pumping out a roll of Christmas songs. My sister, Margaret, and I hauled the log in from the kitchen, through the dining room and hall, and into the living room to our blazing hearth, bawling "Deck the halls" and "'Tis the season" and "Wassail, wassail" to a mounting din of conversation, which rose to screaming chaos in an effort to drown out our unwanted cheer. The guests were quite jolly enough as they were.

The clamor was topped by my father's voice from a chaise longue, as he suddenly called in his best director's roar, "Can't we have some quiet? Girls, stop singing. Anyone who wants a quiet drink, follow me to my study." He took three quarters of the party away and disappeared for the evening, leaving Mother and the two of us and one or two of her faithfuls crestfallen and silent. We watched the blue and green flames die down without a sound.

The evening ended with Mother in the kitchen, weeping. "I can't seem to do anything right." There was silence. "I wish I were dead." At that moment I learned that parties and party tricks can be just the powdered sugar one puts on the open sores of a festering life.

I learned one other very important lesson: one can't coerce guests. Of course, every theatrical performance is a coercion of sorts, and it takes all the skill and planning and intelligence that specially trained people can muster to produce the smallest amount of delight. How then can an amateur possibly expect to do the same thing spontaneously with casual spectators?

I never had bide-a-wees and I never tried to force the guests, but it turns out, remarkably enough, that my parties were disasters just the same.

Every woman's magazine each month is filled with recipes on how to give successful parties, how to occupy, feed, and enchant bridge guests, luncheon guests, dinner guests. I read these all carefully, having a curiosity about social customs. Since I was a busy person and unable to spend all day cutting favors or shaping cookies or making wastebaskets look like newly blown roses, I didn't try to follow the advice, but I brooded over it. We had a very good cook, and I gave her her head and bade her do her utmost. I got excellent, professional waitresses in to assist her. My dinner service was museum quality, the silver Jensen, the crystal Baccarat, and I always thought that interesting people would make interesting talk. That is true. They do — when they want to.

Well, this is a small sampling of what uncoerced, enchanting individuals behave like when let out to play!

I began with children's parties, because I thought that these would be easier and I could practice on them and learn how. Accordingly, on my son's seventh birthday I invited a few of his schoolmates to celebrate. The dining room was festooned and happy with crepe paper and balloons. Our Hungarian Erszi, the cook, had worked for two days preparing marvelous cookies cut in fantastic shapes, paper-thin sandwiches of cucumber and jelly, delicate meat pâtés, ice cream in amusing molds, and a birthday cake garlanded with sugar roses, my son's name, and squiggles of cream — and there was homemade punch. Dream food!

We no sooner had begun than a black-eyed eight-year-old pushed back from the table, tilted on the hind legs of a Sheraton chair, slapped her spoon down into her ice cream, looked at me from under her eyebrows, and leveled. "Mrs. Prude, I sure don't like your food."

"Well," I said. "Deborah, don't rock on that chair. I sure don't like your table manners."

"Why don't you give us decent things to eat at a party? Some party!"

Never mind that Erszi had spent days working in the kitchen, or that the table was enchanting. The children didn't care for it; in fact, they detested it. They threw pieces of cake at one another. They fed the sandwiches to the cat (that, at least, was fun). They spanked their spoons in the ice cream. They pulled the decorations to pieces. They gargled in the punch. They crawled under the table. One of them tried to crawl on top of the table. These were children who were going to Friends Seminary and getting good educational attention from advanced mathematicians and sensitive English masters at considerable expense.

I finally quieted the din and announced that we would have a moving picture.

"Well," said Jonathan Nathan very loudly, getting up and stretching. "That's something like. Where?"

My son was wide-eyed and silent.

Arthur Kleiner, who played all the piano accompaniments

for silent films at the Museum of Modern Art, had brought a projector and the film of *Robin Hood*, the original Fairbanks picture, which I had adored as a young girl. He was a first-class Viennese pianist and had been the head of the music department of Max Reinhardt's studio, and we had a Steinway, on which he played the original score, which I had learned to love so long ago. The kids disliked the music because they couldn't hear it through the din; then they disliked the picture because it bored them. Besides, it was silent, and they couldn't read the titles, let alone understand them. They began crawling around the floor, breaking my bibelots and playing tag or just jumping and screaming.

All their parents had withdrawn to the back bedroom and were having highballs with my husband, so they were having fun. I remained faithfully with Arthur, who played doggedly until the end, an hour and a half's worth, and then solemnly, without a word, rewound the film, collected all the heavy, valuable paraphernalia, and departed. I kissed him goodbye. Nobody else thanked him. Arthur didn't get in touch with me again for years.

Erszi sat weeping in the kitchen. "I thought they would like it. For three days I tried, and at night, even at night!" she cried.

The next day my son disconsolately said, "Two of the kids came to me and said that we were well off and why did we live like pigs."

"Do you think we live like pigs?" I asked.

"I don't know," said Jonathan in rather pathetic bewilderment. "I don't know how pigs live."

"What do they expect us to have?"

"Oh, washing machines and TV sets and fun food at parties."

"I don't know what fun food is," I said. "I must learn. But I don't think we live like pigs. And I'm very surprised they asked a question like this of you. Would you have gone to them and told them that their parents live like pigs?"

"No," said Jonathan. "It would hurt their feelings."

"Precisely. And speaking of pigs—their manners!"

I went to my friend Kitty Carlisle Hart. "What do you give children to eat at a party that will not make them violent?" I asked.

"Oh," she said, "I have a system. First I clear away all the valuable furniture, particularly bric-a-brac. Then I put down tarpaulins. Then I hire little tables and folding chairs, tough ones, and crockery, not porcelain, and mugs, not glass."

"And the menu?" I asked.

"I give them hot dogs, buns, all the fixings—that's important—and a great deal of ice cream and all the different kinds of sauces and trimmings."

"And they like that sort of food?"

"They won't eat any other."

So I learned.

Eight years later I saw these same young people at an eighteenth birthday party that Kitty gave for her son, which was also a very elegant supper–cocktail party for her own friends. For about five minutes the young men passed plates dutifully, then they sat down with enormous, overheaped dishes. Placing both elbows on the table, each one engorged himself, shoveling and gulping, his size-eleven-and-a-half shoes tapping on the floor while he hummed the latest rock song with a full mouth. Ten years after that I met these men again in the same room. They were well-mannered, exquisitely polite, and considerate, and they made delicious conversation. I do not know what happened.

"Children are rude," I thought, "because they're young and they haven't been trained. But my husband and I will give parties for grown-up, polite people, and they will be delish parties, full of enchantment. If one gathers together really fascinating, intelligent individuals in lovely surroundings with good food, it can't help but be a memorable success, sprightly, entertaining, and so forth."

I was living in Hollywood in 1954 when we made the picture of *Oklahoma!* One Saturday night, knowing we had a free day following, I asked what I thought was a fine selection of people.

The parties in Hollywood are famous; a happy few were wonderful to the degree of legend. I had been to some of the great parties in the thirties, when the era of competitive entertaining was in spate. Gladys (Mrs. Edward G.) Robinson and Tai Lackman vied for first honors, and we all witnessed a vast expenditure of imagination, care, and emotion. Gladys Robinson had Hollywood's first collection of great paintings —Degas, Monets, Sisleys—and she had money; Tai Lackman had money. They both took unflagging care of their guests. They competed for the privilege of entertaining Stravinsky; Gladys won. I remember Dolores del Rio bending over Louis B. Mayer, rubies the size of pigeon eggs swinging against her immaculate bosom, the bosom made famous by Diego Rivera. All the actresses buzzed about, and everyone crowded around the most powerful and the most celebrated and the richest in fearful, heady competition. They looked like tropical insects around fleshy carnivorous plants—the Venus's flytrap, for instance. The aftermath on the next day I remember equally well, when those invited and particularly those not invited took stock of their social and business standing and tried to gauge their current status by the number of invitations they had received or had not received. Some of those mornings were filled with cold despair.

Well, I had no such power, no such standing, no such ambition. I just wanted to give a party and ask the people I liked to be my guests for a nice evening. I got the name of a reliable caterer from my agent's secretary, who knew everything, and the caterer was more than efficient, providing tables, chairs, garden umbrellas, cutlery, china, napery, and extra edibles. The serious food, the actual meal, I reserved for my Erszi, who could not be bettered anywhere. The caterer's people simply assisted her and served. The guests included all the directing staff of *Oklahoma!*, many old friends, my husband's clients (who numbered world-famous names in music), and just a sprinkling of dancers to keep contact with the young. There were no actors, and I hoped there would be reasonable drinking and no scrambling for directors' or producers' attention, just an interchange of stimulating communication. In other words, a thoroughly nice bash.

My husband, Walter, told me that he had finally persuaded his client Gregor Piatigorsky, the great cellist, to come—a difficult feat, because his wife did not go out. His wife was Jacqueline de Rothschild, and she was extremely shy and hated crowds. She was also a chess master, and her mind worked in complicated and devious ways, but not socially. Chess masters as a class do not talk. She was a spare, tall woman of quiet, immaculate chic, with the stillness of a lizard. Her eyes saw—what? At our party, she did not move.

"Will you have a drink?"

"Non." Not "Non, merci." Just "Non."

"Then perhaps an hors d'oeuvre?"

"Non."

Her husband accepted both with Russian graciousness. No one else spoke.

Jacqueline de Rothschild Piatigorsky was a roadblock, a terminus. No conversation, no eddies of frivolous froth, could proceed past her. One could not divert, skirt, detour, interchange. The conversation ended. High above us her charming, extremely tall husband gazed benignly around, munching.

They were standing in our French windows, which opened to the lawn, where little tables were set out. The windows were the principal means of egress, and as the Piatigorskys remained close together, motionless and broadside, they forced the other guests to squeeze past them sideways, single file.

"Excusez-moi," said Jacqueline accusingly, stepping backward and treading on a young lady's satin slippers.

I shifted the couple forcefully. I tried again. "Where do you live?"

He named a choice spot in Bel Air.

"Do you? Arthur Rubinstein lives near there." Rubinstein was also a client of my husband's.

Piatigorsky surveyed me with a dreamy imperial smile. "The King of Pianists?"

This sobriquet had been given Rubinstein not mockingly but seriously by Olin Downes, the music critic of the *New York Times*. It was seized upon by Rubinstein's manager, Sol Hurok, and exploited on every possible occasion, to the jealous discomfiture of Hurok's other clients.

"I am a modest man." Piatigorsky smacked his lips deprecatingly. "I do not ask to be called King of Cellists."

"Surely Casals has earned that title," I interjected with blood-chilling tactlessness. Then I froze at my bluntness.

"But I would like"—here Piatigorsky took a large bite of guacamole—"I would like a title. Something lesser may be suitable. The Archduke of Cellists?" He smiled winningly.

A few proximate guests tittered and turned back to their rootless chatter. Piatigorsky sipped his drink and opened his large, expressive, mobile lips enthusiastically. He was getting wound up to discourse on his own worth and reputation.

Madame Jacqueline did not smile. She stood looking at— what? Ennui cloaked her like a fog. She had heard all of this more than several times.

"Oh, there's Dick Rodgers!" I cried, and fled to the haven of hostess duties.

The setting was beautiful. We had rented William Sistrom's old house, a 1922 mansion on a shelf halfway up a Hollywood foothill. It was two blocks above Sunset Boulevard, near Laurel Canyon and almost adjacent to the Wattle Gardens, which used to be one of the showplaces of Hollywood. Our lawn was wet from sprinklers, and the trees and shrubbery exhaled fresh odor, as always at day's end. The hill immediately behind breathed the acrid smells of sage, wild lilac, and wild mint. The lights below were starting to bloom like clusters of little flowers far away to the south. The day was no longer hard but luminous and intensifying. As the light died, the luminosity continued and stars came out sharp.

All the guests had drinks. They greeted friends and colleagues, admired the view, commented on trade news, exchanged compliments — oh, hell! They behaved like guests. The Piatigorskys did not move, but remained side by side.

"Help!" I grabbed my husband's arm.

"I told you," he replied sardonically. "Let's try food."

I found myself seated beside Piatigorsky (male) and Dorothy (Mrs. Richard) Rodgers, and then up came Walter with Piatigorsky (female).

"You can't sit here," I said. "You're the host and I'm the hostess. And the Piatigorskys are married. It won't do. Go to another table."

"We're sitting here," said Walter firmly, seating Jacqueline and handing her a glass of water, which was all she would accept.

"Take her away," I hissed.

Very low he breathed, "I dare not leave her."

Dorothy Rodgers was sprightly about everything. There was no such thing as flagging conversation in her presence. Silence was simply darned together with her pretty graces; solecisms eased away. But there came a silence longer and heavier than was comfortable. As a hostess I should have been up to the test. I failed.

Dorothy's Boy Scout ardor leapt into the breach. "This morning," she said brightly, breaking off a tiny piece of dinner roll, "I heard the recording of the full *Oklahoma!* song, with complete orchestra and chorus. It was really splendid!"

Jacqueline dipped a spoon into the cold fruit soup, touched it to her lips, and put it down. I had heard she was a cordon bleu chef, among other things. Well, so was Dorothy Rodgers, but she was also polite.

"Splendid?" asked Piatigorsky dubiously.

"It's marvelous what these technicians can do! Just think, Dick complained of one note being flatted in the flute, and they said they would get him a B-natural out of the vaults. Imagine! And for flute!"

"When I record," said Piatigorsky, "I won't let them change anything, even mistakes. This is the way Piatigorsky was — some very good, some faulty. But what you get is not a mechanical contrivance. I will not permit that. Ever. Ever." He added triumphantly, "You get Piatigorsky. Me."

Dorothy returned to her soup.

Walter finally tried. "Jacqueline, I've heard of a new opening gambit in the Russo-Austrian games."

Jacqueline rose. Then she spoke her first multiword sentence: "Show me."

The chessboard was in the master bedroom, upstairs. Walter walked briskly ahead of her, mercifully removing her from the table. He also removed one half of the hosts.

Dorothy looked at me, dazed. Piatigorsky ate. Dorothy went on making polite and pertinent observations automatically. Life had left the body some time since.

"Will you entertain each other while I be a hostess?" I said. Then I bolted.

I found Richard Rodgers standing stupefied in the living room, the only time I have seen him so.

"Well," he gasped, "I've just been given my comeuppance! I've never been brushed off like this!"

I looked at him round-eyed. One didn't brush off Richard Rodgers.

"I saw three of our dancers, and knowing how timid and shy young people are when in strange surroundings and meeting older and well-known, even world-famous, people for the first time, I offered to help get them some supper. And — just 'No thanks.' They turned me down haughtily and just flounced off."

"Astounding!" I said. "My God, foolhardy!" I thought. To flout brazenly the most powerful man in the American theater! It was historic effrontery. They didn't suffer for it, apparently, because one got solo roles on stage and screen (not in any Rodgers show, however), one got lead dancing roles on Broadway and later became an internationally known painter, and one married an Italian count, the maker of most of the pasta in Italy. They were beauties, of course, and could be expected to do all right. That night they did all right, because later I saw them seated with boy dancers, lost in giggles.

But I had Dick Rodgers and was leading him to solace. We fetched up on the back patio, beneath the swimming pool. There sat the director Rouben Mamoulian, who was holding his red-haired wife, Azadia, by the hand. Mamoulian had directed the original *Oklahoma!* and *Carousel* on stage and had naturally counted on directing the movie of *Oklahoma!* He wasn't asked. Fred Zinnemann, who had recently won his second Oscar, was. Fred was on the other side of the lawn, and I prayed he would stay there. It was gallant of Rouben to honor my party and to brave Dick and Oscar, who had so royally rebuffed him.

"Good evening, Dick," said Rouben politely but uncordially.

"How are you?" murmured Dick and wandered on.

I drifted back to problem no. 1. Dorothy had apparently come to the end of her repertoire.

"Those chess players must need food. I'll take them some," she said.

"If Jacqueline has captured someone on the other side of a chessboard, she won't release him all evening." Piatigorsky laughed merrily.

Dorothy rose and made dutifully for the food supplies. She took a full tray up to the bedroom and tried to break up the game. Jacqueline and Walter were now on their third, but Jacqueline's husband had been right. As soon as they finished one game, Jacqueline's hand came down like a trap on Walter's wrist. "Another," she said softly. She won them, all of them—a forgone conclusion.

So Dorothy, who found nothing to do, left dispiritedly, abandoning the untouched tray on the floor. Walter eyed it longingly.

"Your move," said Jacqueline inexorably.

I met Dorothy at the foot of the stairs. She shook her head. Arthur Hornblow, the producer, drifted by and chuckled with kindly benignity. "An adorable party, Agnes, simply adorable!"

One of the caterer's waitresses stepped up to me and in that joyously subdued tone that announces disaster said, "The cook, Erszi, says you are all out of meat, salad, and two of the vegetables, and people are coming back for second and third helpings. She says what should she do?"

I rushed to the kitchen. Erszi's white hair stood out in wisps all over her head. She was standing monumentally by the table, with empty platters spread before her.

"Mrs. Prude, what shall I do? Those young people, those dancers! They come back three and four times. They've eaten all the food. I have nothing more. They're still asking."

"Erszi, I told you to make four times the normal quantity when there are dancers. They eat the pattern off the plates. They eat more than their cubic contents."

"Ahhh . . ." Erszi made a guttural noise, then said something in Hungarian. She finally went into English. "But they're little and thin."

"Erszi, they're hungry. They're always hungry. They do not eat like normal people. They're carnivores."

Erszi sighed, very gloomily. "There's nothing more in the house. I've even opened tins."

"Make some spaghetti. Cook anything. Fill them up on roughage, anything."

Erszi flushed. "I've never served your guests 'anything.' "

"Erszi, you're the best cook I've ever known in my life, but these are not normal people. They're always hungry. Always. Always. I'll go out and see if there are any leaves or flowers." I rushed away. God knows what she gave them.

The chess master, Jacqueline, came down the stairs, cast a searching glance around the room, and went straight to the inner court, where her husband was conversing happily with Mamoulian. They were talking in French, which was her native language, so she quickly put a stop to it and marshaled Pia-tigorsky home.

A wan Walter followed her downstairs as though he feared to be intercepted. He was very hungry, he said. I laughed. I went to see Erszi. I found her in the kitchen in tears amid the empty dishes. She didn't want to talk to me.

All the guests left. It was early, ten-twenty. They rushed for their cars. Hornblow murmured, "Enchanting, enchant-ing!"

It is not a good idea to ask peers or rival artists. Famous people like to be the center of admiration. I once asked two great writers, Rebecca West and Elizabeth Bowen, to tea in London. No one else. I thought they would fascinate one another, as they were English stylists and stood at the very top of their profession and as they fascinated me. They canceled each other out. "A cold woman," said Rebecca West. Elizabeth did not venture an opinion, but she never came back.

There was the time a guest went unbidden into the kitchen, nearly blew up the stove, and set her hair on fire. There was the time a young lady who was falling-down drunk confessed to the family doctor that she made her living by playing a piano in a whorehouse; "Not true," I cried, "she can't play a note." There was the time the wife of an international star bragged that she could and did procure men off the street for her own pleasure for $10; the time two young daughters of famous fathers got into a screaming fight over the comparative de-merits of their parents; the time an amorous friend had to be forcibly ejected by my husband because of her unwelcome attentions to me.

The aforementioned episodes had to do with drink. Granted, there were others in cold sobriety. There was the time I gave a supper party for the Group Theatre and Tamiris, a dancer who was not a member of the Group, arrived uninvited and totally usurped the conversation for one hour, emptying the room. There was the time a young art dealer was brought in lieu of an invited art patron; he halted all conversation for twenty minutes while he baited me brutally about the value of my own work, until I appealed to other guests for support.

Then there was the unforgettable Christmas party that Sol Hurok graced, which came to a climax in charades. Sol turned over a chair and sat on the crossed supports twiddling his thumbs. We tried to guess his meaning for ten minutes before we gave up. *"Fiddler on the Roof!"* he screamed. We looked nonplused. "This is the roof." He kicked the chair. He twiddled his thumbs: "I'm fiddling." Oh Sol, Sol! The English language had failed him again. But he would not be mollified, so "Of course!" we cried. "How stupid we are." He stalked out, disgruntled.

Are there no successful parties, at the happy conclusion of which the hostess contentedly creams her face instead of weeping in the kitchen beside the weeping cook? Of course there are. Not given by me, however.

There have been unforgettable state occasions, with people enough, spending enough, protocol enough, importance enough, to ensure revelry—the Kennedys' party honoring André Malraux, the French minister of culture, for instance. Every available American artist was invited to the White House, most of them for the first time, and Thornton Wilder ran up and down the East Ballroom, spilling his drink on the parquet while calling out joyously, "Darlings, they let us in! At last they let us in!"

There was the American ambassador's party in Paris on the opening night of *Oklahoma!*, with *tout Paris* in their gorgeous couturier gowns strolling under the lofty eighteenth-century trees, indirectly lit among the great *jets d'eaux*. And the private party in Manila hosted by the Filipino whose title to his garden (in midcity) came from Philip II of Spain. All the exquisite small guests were immaculately sober, circulating around fountains of champagne (untouched) and tables groaning with tropical delicacies—guests like dolls in barongs frosted with embroidery, their ladies rising like flowers from panellas with butterfly collars and sleeves; and Walter in his embroidered

barong and I in my Maria Clara skirts and gauzy panella looked
just as fine. These were landmarks in our lives.

My father, a gracious man and one of considerable wit and
kindness, was a brute to my mother at family festivities. Why?
Well, he had stopped loving her and wanted desperately to rid
himself of family ties, so perhaps his case can be considered
outside of the normal pattern. But the others? Jacqueline Piatigorsky, a worldly, sophisticated sportswoman and artist,
went into a private sulk. Rebecca West and Elizabeth Bowen,
of international fame as writers, public speakers, and hostesses,
turned into mute, bad-tempered clods. Good-natured and intelligent children behaved like animals. Why?

One requires a gift to be a good guest. It takes a certain
humility, a certain graciousness, and always good feeling and
stamina. I think when people take the trouble to dress up and
go out to a party they feel they are owed a good time, and if
they are disappointed, they become angry and vent their temper without restraint. It has nothing to do with courtesy or
breeding. True courtesy began to ravel out after the eighteenth
century and the discrediting of the noblesse. In the twentieth,
it is indeed threadbare. We haven't the spare energy to make
the effort.

Of course, any time two or more people with the ability to be
amusing and friendly get together, there can be fun, but that
presupposes so much — a willingness to share the best of one's
heart and wit. It is extraordinary how often this is not evident
in gatherings. But it can exist, and it must be nurtured and protected, because it is precious.

In the words of Billy Rose's immortal song,

> A cup of coffee, a sandwich, and you
> A cozy corner, a table for two.
> I don't need music, lobster or wine,
> Whenever your eyes look into mine.

This was written for lovers. It could apply to friends.

My recipe for a party, then, is this, and it is simpler than
those in the ladies' magazines: the presence of something de-

lightful to share, something over which to rejoice. The operative word is *rejoice*.

Perhaps the happiest thing to do and the surest guarantee of pleasure is to go out privately with the person you love. My husband and I always did. We enjoyed these occasions the most.

ALLIE

ALL FOR LOVE

WE FIRST became aware of trouble when we woke at five-thirty in the morning to hear her sobbing. She was in the kitchen with Aunt Marie and their voices were muffled, but that Allie was crying hard was certain. Every one of us woke instantly. There were six of us on the porch, alert and terrified. There is nothing more frightening to a child than to hear adults weeping: if that fortress goes, we are all, of course, imperiled. So we lay without moving, trying not to breathe, so that we could hear better.

We cousins were all together in the magic forest of our family country retreat at Merriewold, staying for the summer with

Aunt Marie for a nominal fee in her very large summer cottage. In those days, most mysteriously, there were no mosquitoes, and we could sleep out at night with perfect composure and restfulness. So we used to bed down, five girls and a boy, in a row of cots on the large unscreened front porch, with the bats swooping over our heads from one pine tree to another and sometimes little animals like chipmunks running across the porch roof, and field mice around the floor. Otherwise it was absolutely tranquil. That one summer morning, however, just as day was breaking, we all woke at the same moment to hear Allie weeping bitterly, and Aunt Marie, the mother of three of us and the keeper of the summer clan, trying to soothe her.

"There now, Petty, have some coffee and try to stop crying. It surely isn't so bad."

"It's the end," sobbed Allie, "and I hoped this time . . . this time I felt surely it was a good thing. This time I believed I could count on him. Oh God!" She wept.

There were low, soothing noises from Aunt Marie. "Don't, darling; don't. Have some coffee, Petty, and keep your voice down. The children will wake."

The children were lying rigid, their heads a half inch above their pillows, their ears as distended as bats'.

Allie was our mother's slightly younger cousin, and we thought of her as middle-aged. I dare say she was at the time thirty-three or -four, but she seemed older, perhaps because she was so fat. She had been fat since she was a small white-skinned child, fat and boisterous and jolly — "a card," our mothers had said. She was quick with quips and teasing and little amusing gifts and impertinences. She made us gasp with her lack of respectfulness, but we always laughed. We counted on her to be funny on all occasions. In fact, she had become the family clown, spontaneous, original, and apposite. One always remembered what she said, and one always laughed. The little children shrieked, the teenagers howled, and the adults chuckled merrily.

Allie also listened to everybody, and she was discreet. Confidences were never repeated in common family gossip. Adolescents confided their anguish, children their rages, and adults their extreme bewilderment. To all, although she was extremely limited in personal experience, she gave counsel based on high principles. Chiefly she just listened.

She was darling with her tiny presents; "unbirthday gifts," she called them. "A little sumsing," she would say, pushing a very small package of gumdrops, a thimble, or an idiot pincushion into our hands. "You look as though you need this," she would say, handing a chocolate bar to a policeman on a cold crossing in midwinter. "Before I talk business with you," she would say across a Wall Street desk, "do have one of these cookies."

Allie seemed always happy and loving and full of curiosity and zest. If agony could lodge in all that mountainous, contented flesh, where was there hope for any of us?

We never expected her to get married. Strangely enough, she herself did expect to, and her sorrow at romantic disappointments scarred her otherwise tranquil life. It seemed tranquil to us, and very merry. It was not so to her.

"Oh God," said Allie that summer morning. "Why must it always be I who has to pretend to have no feelings? *You* can weep in public." She said this to Aunt Marie, a recent widow. "I asked him outright last night. I put it straight. 'When?' I said. And he replied—he replied—"

"Shh," said Aunt Marie. "There, now."

"—that he was not the marrying kind, and didn't I know that? Hadn't he made it quite clear?"

"That's strange, very strange. Here, hold your cup," said Aunt Marie. "He's been seeing you every day for months."

"Twice and three times a day," said Allie emphatically. "And special-delivery notes on Sundays when he couldn't leave his mother, and flowers on birthdays and all occasions, and the notes were love notes about how he needed me, how he relied on me—relied, mind you. This time I believed it would happen. This time I trusted."

"I don't understand," said Aunt Marie. "What happened? Is there another woman?"

"Nothing happened. Nothing ever happened. He said he was not the marrying kind. He said he would like things to go on and never change—to go on . . . as things . . . as we . . . as we . . ." She sobbed. "The same. He wants it the same. He won't declare himself."

"That you can't permit," said Aunt Marie.

"No," said Allie.

"Do you hear?" breathed Jane, without stirring in bed.

"Shh!" said Bea.

That morning we did not discuss one word of what we had heard, but for a wonder, we all assembled at the breakfast table on time, clean and neat and very attentive. Allie was not there. She had a headache, Aunt Marie said.

Allie came down to lunch, white and drawn. But she joked as always and teased Henry, Aunt Marie's son and the heir to Henry George's name, about his table manners. "Today you are going to eat facing the table? We have much to be grateful for."

We did not speak much lest we miss something. Allie ate hardly anything, but she kept joking. She talked a lot; jokes, of course. Aunt Marie kept talking about more helpings and keeping our elbows out of our plates and things like that. Once when she came back from carrying a heavy platter she patted Allie on the shoulder lightly, without looking at her. That was unusual.

Henry began his regular postlunch performance. He never wanted to help with the dishes. It was women's work, he said. Henry was eleven. He lay on the sofa clutching his stomach and moaning. He was the only boy among us and a great worry to his mother. This time Allie said she would deal with him; she'd like to.

"Now, Henry," she said as she sat down quietly and opened *Science and Health*, the Christian Science manual. "Stop that groaning."

He didn't.

"Stop that this minute. Pay attention. I've been reading this all morning and I think I know what it means. You try now. Hard."

Henry regarded her, amazed. "You're crying," he said.

"I am not," said Allie. "There are no such things as tears in God's world. Don't you know that?"

"Yes," said Henry doubtfully.

For the first time Henry Saw the Light in time to help us put the big plates on the high shelves.

After dishes, while we waited until it was safe to swim without getting cramps, we decided to watch the tennis tournament at the club. Allie was there, with Donald beside her —Donald, her la-di-da beau who wanted things to go on the same.

"Is that wise?" said Aunt Marie as Allie was getting out her hat. "I don't think you should do that, Petty. Don't see him today."

"Nothing more can happen to me," said Allie. "I don't want talk. People will think it queer if we're not together. I couldn't bear them to know."

"It's inhuman," said Aunt Marie. "Stay home and rest. I'll read to you. I'll read *Key to the Scriptures*."

"I can bear it," said Allie.

So there they were, side by side, and no one knew except all of us. We watched very carefully for a quiver or a break. Allie turned her lovely gray eyes under the white-gold lashes on him and smiled gently. She joked as always, but not loudly, and she only once playfully poked Donald, who was not laughing at all. He looked very uncomfortable and waiting and hot. He was overdressed as always in his stiff collar and laced boots. We thought him terribly swish, but he always laughed so heartily at Allie's jokes and kept his arm around her and stroked her fine soft white-gold hair. "Lovely hair," he would say.

"You shouldn't let him take these liberties," said Aunt Marie.

"Oh pshaw," said Allie. "He doesn't take my hair down, if that's what you're talking about. You have an evil mind."

"You shouldn't let him," said Aunt Marie. "It's not wise."

This time Allie didn't snuggle against him or pop gumdrops into his mouth or hold his hand and stroke his fingers. She just poked him once and made a joke without looking at him. He said he needed a glass of water and went away for a good while.

At the end of a week he left and went back to the city. We never saw him again.

Every so often in sheer bravado one of us would ask Allie, "How's Donald?"

"Oh, he's fine," she would say. But I don't think she ever knew, because I don't think she ever heard.

There were others. There was an elderly widower. Oh, quite old — with grandchildren. When he died she wept bitterly, and openly this time, but I don't think she ever loved him, that is, not to marry. He was a prop. He was just in case. He was the one man who offered her a substantial home. He was the only one not looking for a free ride.

Allie's sister got a divorce, the first in our family. Allie had to take care of all the emotional backwash of that, and the sister had a miscarriage, with Allie alone in the house and no help for hours.

When people died she was there, and laid out the bodies. When people were born she was there. When children were ill or failed at school or broke their engagements, she was there. As we began to grow up and became troubled about this and that, we took to going to Allie, who of course was not qualified to advise but who did anyhow. We couldn't talk with our parents, naturally; it embarrassed them too much. We took to going over to Allie's house to spend the night or to share hot chocolate or Saturday snacks and confidences. We could tell her anything because she was morally pure, being a virgin. Nothing embarrassed her because she really knew nothing.

She was certain that men wanted pure girls for wives, and that covered the entire question.

"Why do men have mistresses?" she would ask rhetorically. "Well, what does a mistress do? A mistress is always clean — absolutely dainty and clean."

"Aren't our mothers clean?" we asked.

"Your mothers are sometimes mussed," she said. "A mistress never is mussed and she is always glad and attentive. For instance," she said to me, "your mother sometimes sews as she listens to your father. It drives men crazy to have women doing something — little bits of sewing, little bits of knitting. The men want all their wives' attention. Every bit of it. And," said Allie, opening her gray eyes very wide, "they want it all the time."

"But she's doing it for him, she's doing it for us. She's sewing his buttons."

"It drives your father crazy just the same."

"If I fell in love with a married man and he couldn't get a divorce," I said — this was somewhat later, of course — "I'd have an affair with him."

"It would be better to die," said Allie and turned away.

"Mother said she'd understand."

"Your mother is losing her standards. I must speak to her. Sex isn't so much. Except lying in one another's arms — I've heard there was peace in that."

Our mothers began to be jealous of Allie and our fun and talks with her. "You'd better not come around for two or three days," Allie would say. She spoke very sadly.

I found letters of Allie's later. She used to walk the streets at night, looking into lighted homes, watching families at supper, reading together, playing games. She used to watch them setting off down the streets in the lamplight to the movies. She watched all her young cousins and nieces and nephews grow up and saw the mistakes their mothers made and tried to remonstrate and advise, but she was told to hold her peace. "You've never been married," they said. "You don't know."

"I've never been married," she said later over lemon pie in her kitchen, "and I've never had children. But I can tell when a boy is being spoiled, and Marie is spoiling Henry. And I wouldn't let your sister Margaret wear purple lipstick, and I wouldn't let Margaret take all the young men from the older girls"—that was me—"and flirt so outrageously with her father's friends"—that was very famous men in Hollywood. "Oh, if I had my own children, I'd bring them up differently, I can tell you."

But she didn't have her own children. She just grew fatter.

She was not college-educated and she was not really trained in business, but she picked up the rudiments of organization, and she had a wonderful way with people, as long as she did not get on their nerves. She lived with Great-Aunt Carrie George, whom none of the rest of the family could tolerate. Carrie, the older sister of Henry George, was an annoying little antique lady, forgetful, stubborn, interfering, proud, and suspicious. Allie's only common interest with her was the Christian Science church, to which they went on Sunday and for the Wednesday night meeting. But Great-Aunt Carrie complained of her bunions throughout and wouldn't declare the truth.

"They *do* hurt," she would say piteously. "I can't sit still, they hurt so."

"I'll not take you with me again," Allie would state in an unusually severe voice, "if you go on like that."

"All right," Great-Aunt Carrie would say. "But they hurt. I won't speak. But you'll know I'll be sitting there the whole time with my feet hurting something dreadful."

Father, who was kind to relatives, even Mother's, offered Allie paid employment as his receptionist. She sat in an outer office of her own, and part of the furniture was the unemployed actors who found her a soft touch. There was James Beard, later very famous as a culinary expert, who helped her in the kitchen. There was the Rumanian actor George Caliga—almost always there was George Caliga. He never had any jobs, but he always hoped for some, and as Allie was working in a key position for a big-time director, he found her very useful. He always found her comforting, and she was good for a home-cooked supper, snacks and chocolate after a movie (which she paid for), and long talks in the outer office while she sat at the reception desk. But whenever the director—that is, Pop—wished to enter his study, he had to pass by Caliga's long, pointed, black-and-white European sports shoes and freshly pressed white trousers (Caliga was slow in getting to his feet) and interrupt the thick continuous voice to make known any official need.

Allie had too little sense of self-preservation to realize that she was compromising her position with the hospitality she furnished on the boss's time. Pop scowled and snapped at her to bring her stenographer's pad and follow him. He didn't even glance at Caliga's oily black head.

"Oh, don't be such a grouch!" said Allie jovially, rising mountainously to her feet. "Have a Tootsie Roll and cheer up." She was not being impertinent. She was being cheerful.

"What I want is some peace and efficiency," the director barked.

"You know George?"

The director glared and went into his study.

"Wait for me. I'll be back," said Allie to George over her shoulder.

George waited, glad to. But then, unexpectedly, he got a job, and he did not come around so often.

There was the doctor, Carl Fisher. He was Allie's age or a little older, and well liked and very able. He had been on the staff of the Mayo Clinic, and therefore was very suitable. He became her constant companion. They went to concerts together, and to the theater and out to dinner, and he paid. He was always at her house for her small parties. We liked him very much, and we were glad he was there.

"Who gave you that ring?" said Mother one day, suddenly.

"Carl Fisher," said Allie promptly.

"Oh, my darling," said Mother, throwing her arms around Allie. "When did it happen?"

"Oh, don't be ridiculous," said Allie. "The ring belonged to Mama. I just never wore it before."

"But hasn't the doctor spoken?"

"No," said Allie, "not yet."

"He will," said Mother.

Allie was silent.

Then the doctor was forced to leave one doctors' firm, join another, and move his office. Just that, nothing more, as far as we ever learned, but he had a nervous breakdown. He stayed in Allie's house for a week and never went out at all. He lay on her bed, fully clothed of course, while she held his hand, and he went over every permutation and possibility of the removal again and again. She had to go outside and walk up and down in the grass to clear her head, but she would come back in, and he would cry a little in her pillow and fall asleep. Then he would wake up moaning and she would get him a cup of hot tea or some soup.

She endured this for ten days. She also helped him pack his books, did the work of secretary, nurse, and housekeeper, and helped him choose the new drapes, settle in the furniture, and order new stationery. We took Great-Aunt Carrie off her hands for two weeks so she was free to give her entire attention to the doctor's troubles. She absented herself from her own work and Father's all this time.

She got the doctor moved somehow, and he liked the new situation and cheered up. Then he came around to see her once a week or so, and sometimes (not often) he took her to the movies, and that was the end of that. No word of explanation was ever given, and the relationship never changed. Dr. Fisher of course was a homosexual, and something very emotional must have been going on, but neither Allie nor we suspected anything at all about any of that.

Allie grew fatter and more insistently jolly. Dr. Fisher begged her to have a metabolism test and assured her he could fix her up in a matter of months. But she refused pointblank, saying finally, "All I need is here," patting *Science and Health.* "Besides, don't you think I'm luscious as I am?" She laughed very hard. He never married anyone, so her weight wasn't to blame. In any case, she would not have the test. "I'd rather die," she said to us quietly.

"But that's silly."

"No, it isn't. It's what I believe, and don't for one moment think that's why Carl Fisher didn't want to marry me."

"Why didn't he?"

"He didn't need me after he moved offices. He never really needed me again. I served my purpose." She sighed deeply. "Probably he never needed me at all. That's how it is with some men."

Allie had loved Father closely and had delighted in his wit and his talents. She had been very harsh with Mother about her compulsiveness and possessiveness. When my parents' fight was over and Mother had been abandoned for a younger, more successful woman, Allie saw the agony of the dismemberment, went to her stricken cousin, and spoke out bitterly in protest. She spoke out to everyone. Father, who was supporting her, fired her from her job. She stayed just long enough to strip our home, pack the furniture, and prepare the house for sale. Father was living in it alone. Every day Allie opened all the bedroom doors so that he came home to a house of empty, reminding rooms, and every night he closed them again. They went through this silent ritual for four months. Allie continued to talk bitterly against him.

Mother, Margaret, and I came east after the divorce, and I started out to be a dancer. Allie followed, the old great-aunt having finally succumbed to a horrible, strangling spasm, after which her poor twisted little feet were tucked into her coffin and she was buried with the spare Christian Science rites. Allie stored and packed all her own belongings in suitcases, which she kept in different relatives' houses; she had a notebook saying what was where, but she had nothing substantial in storage —no furniture or trunks, just a suitcase of old letters, a few books, and the old clothes that she let out seam by seam every year.

During her free time she did publicity for me, the would-be dancer. Allie touted me as though I were Anna Pavlova. We never paid her anything. We gave her house-room and food. One never paid a pauperized female relative; we never thought to. It was all for love.

Gradually her interest in our beaux, her enthusiastic participation in our engagements, our weddings, began to give way to an absorbing preoccupation with our morals, in particular our sexual morals — and the morals of our young men. Allie laid down the law about what went on not only in our kitchen and parlor but throughout the world, and this became a kind of basis for faith. As other people believed in democracy, patriotism, brotherly love, art, primogeniture, or totem worship, Allie believed in monogamy and sexual purity. She personally lost face when a husband strayed. Our mothers had high sexual standards also, but instinct filled them with doubts, and although they trusted their daughters, they watched them like policemen. Allie permitted great latitude and freedom because she no more supposed we would neck than she guessed we would kill. She called necking "being foolish," but it was a form of evil to her, and there was no forgiveness in her plan for the universe.

We were all grown now. The objectionable Henry was a doctor, a good one, very, very kind and compassionate. Most of the girl cousins were married, some with Allie's approval, some not, but they were legally bound, so she was silent. Only my cousin Jane, Marie's daughter, and I had not found mates. In some kind of terrible companionship, I discovered that Allie was beginning to think of me as a sister, a virgin like her, a younger image. She identified with me in all ways. "You will find as you grow older," she said often, "that men will treat you as a . . . ," and her preview did not encompass marriage or sexual adventure of any éclat. "This won't hurt you so much later," she would comfort me. Or, as a variant, "You may think you can't stand it, but you can." Or sometimes, "Men are just an entirely different breed. They've been spoiled rotten." She would throw her great warm arm around me and hug me in a kind of horrible sucking way.

It was different with one serious beau. He wanted me; he wanted to marry me. The family—that is, Mother—was opposed, and I was caught in the middle of terrible stresses. Allie saw both sides clearly and sympathized with everyone. She took note of my exhaustion, my bewilderment and terror, as early symptoms of her own disease, the disease I most surely was destined to share. My mother was frantic lest I elope. I didn't particularly want to elope, but I looked at Allie and was afraid I'd better.

Then one spring Mother and Margaret went off on a short vacation to Europe. Mother sent for Allie and installed her in Margaret's bedroom in their absence, instructing Allie as my guardian not to take an eye off me, since the situation was perilous and I must be watched particularly this spring. Allie laughed very hard over that—"What does your mother think you are about to do?"—and slapped me on the back and winked. That I contemplated anything at all was unthinkable.

I was in a quandary. Flouting Mother and Aunt Marie was one thing. Destroying Allie, and I believed it would be just that, was something else. The young man, who was temporarily in Philadelphia with a theatrical job, wrote that I must make up my mind one way or another. He couldn't continue; his nerves, his peace of mind, his health, were wavering. I suffered. I used to lie in bed and literally tear my flesh with my nails.

Allie fell ill. She had grown gross and lay all day in bed, breathing heavily and singing Christian Science hymns in a wavering voice. Aunt Marie moved in to run the house, and Jane, still unbetrothed, came with her.

Allie decided that as she was suffering, she might indulge herself. She liked thick cream and chocolate. We did not give them to her, but as we all had jobs at different times of the day, she was alone for several hours and could order double malted milks and hot fudge sundaes from the drugstore and, from the Home Bakerie, layer cake with whipped cream, which she tried to eat fast so we would not know. Her face became puffy, her arms swollen. Her eyes almost closed, so that she could hardly read. When she rose from her bed to stagger to the bathroom, we were horrified to see that her belly was huge and bloated. She had suddenly become a monster, and she looked out from the pumpkin mask with little frightened watery eyes, the eyes of a small baby.

She sent for a Christian Science friend who lived in Philadelphia, the wife of a dentist, and this lady came by train and sat for hours, holding her hand and singing. We could hear their off-tune voices through the closed door. Then Allie would get up and stagger to the bathroom while Grace, the friend, went to fix her a thick eggnog.

It was full spring, violet time. Aunt Marie had to open her house in Merriewold, which was heavy work. She took me and Jane with her. She also took Allie—that is, Allie insisted on going—and Allie took her friend and supporter, Grace. It was a dreadful trip. The women sang softly all the way.

When we arrived, Allie rested on the black leather couch downstairs while Aunt Marie and Jane made her bed and a fire and I made the other beds. Getting her up the stairs was a nightmare, but we did it. I brought her a handful of violets and lilies-of-the-valley, their roots clotted with earth. "Thanks, Petty," she murmured. "Spring is beginning again." Then she put her face in the flowers.

Aunt Marie brought her some hot tea. "I want more sugar," she said. Grace winked at her. "In my luggage." In her bags were sugar, sweet cakes, cream buns. Grace fixed a plate and got a cup of rich country cream from the McCormacks down the road.

"I forbid you to take that in to her," said Aunt Marie, with a completely unprecedented show of spirit. "You may not give that to her."

"Marie," called Allie, "don't scold Grace. I asked her for

the cream. It's extremely kind of her to come and look after me."

"But Petty," said Marie, mounting the stairs. Her eyes had filled. "We're here, we who adore you. We look after you."

"You have no faith," said the pumpkin coldly. "You cannot help me. You can only hurt me. You bring malicious animal magnetism with you."

"Oh, how can you say such a cruel thing to me?" said Aunt Marie, covering her face with her hands and shaking her head as though she had been doused with water.

"You've lost your power to help," went on Allie with cruel persistence.

"Love can always help," said Aunt Marie, sitting down and taking the swollen, blotched hand. "Love reaches through anything, and I love you. I've loved you all my life."

Allie said, "Give me the cream."

Grace had to spoon it to her. She could barely sit up or help herself.

"Petty, darling," said Aunt Marie, stroking her hand as though Allie had bequeathed it to her, "we must get help. Let me call Henry, just to look you over. I beg you, let me call him."

"Never!" snapped Allie, and she almost sat up. "I'm fine. If you tell Henry, I'll never forgive you."

"Oh, Petty," moaned Aunt Marie, "it's tearing my heart out to be kept so helpless."

"My practitioner, Mrs. Lubkin, the head reader, is coming all the way from Philadelphia," Allie said. "It's marvelous of her to come. Agnes, take Marie out and cheer her up. She's depressing me. And tell Jane I'm furious with her for throwing out my cinnamon buns. You treat me like a child, and I won't have it! Now all of you, get out—just get out. I've got to get ready for Mrs. Lubkin."

Grace almost smirked as she closed the bedroom door. We held a council of war in the kitchen. But what could we do?

"Look what I found," said Jane, "in the broom closet." It was a package of dry ice, and it enclosed bottles of cream, ice cream, and butter. Allie had become a hoarder. "Grace hid these. She knows we search Allie's bedroom."

We opened the pantry door a crack. We could hear their voices from the bedroom.

"I can't stand it!" said Aunt Marie. "I just can't stand it! I won't take this responsibility. I'm sending for Henry, no matter what, and he can notify her brother-in-law, Travis. Mercy, we have two good doctors in the family, and she won't let them near her."

Mrs. Lubkin arrived; she was small, brown, elderly, taciturn, and brisk. She nodded to us and went directly up, shutting the door behind her. There they were, the three of them, locked inside for about an hour — sometimes singing, sometimes praying, and sometimes being perfectly quiet. Allie was fighting for a principle, and she was willing, as she had said, to pay with her life.

Mrs. Lubkin finally emerged to confront us. "Your cousin will come back with us to Philadelphia. She will live with her friend, Grace. I can see her regularly."

"She's too sick to travel," said Aunt Marie.

"She's nothing of the kind."

"This is very dangerous," said Aunt Marie. "Her brother-in-law and my son should know. The family should know."

"That would only make matters more difficult for her. She's determined. Arguing and quarreling confuse her."

The next day Allie appeared, more or less put together. Her hat was on the back of her head, her coat wouldn't button, and her legs were too swollen for stockings. How she got her feet into shoes, I cannot imagine. "This is kind of fun," said Allie. "I feel sort of drunk." Allie had never been drunk in her life, so of course she was guessing. She was leaning heavily on Grace, who looked grimly gay and quite strained under the weight. To me she said, "You can tell your young man, you can tell Robin, to look me up in Philadelphia if he likes." She was sympathetic to Robin only because his mother had at one time been a Christian Science reader.

ALLIE: ALL FOR LOVE / 235

As Allie descended the stairs, which was a major act of will, she became drawn and exhausted with pain. In her free hand, Grace held Allie's battered old suitcase, its clasp broken and tied round with straps. Allie giggled suddenly. "I think people will think I am pregnant."

"They may well," said Grace, snickering.

Allie looked at me penetratingly. Even in that ridiculous half-dressed condition, in her blown-up body, she could be arresting. "And don't you get into any messes."

She left. We kissed her periphery, and she left, escorted by her coreligionists.

"No one will think she's pregnant," said Jane. "She's too old."

"Oh, hush!" said Aunt Marie, weeping. "Poor thing! Poor lamb! Alone with those . . ." She couldn't characterize them, but blew her nose and put on her sweater to go to phone Henry in Philadelphia.

When she returned, she said, "Henry thinks she has dropsy."

In Philadelphia, Henry tried to reach Allie directly but was rebuffed.

I phoned every night. Sometimes she answered. She was making remarkable progress. Everyone was astounded. The friends and practitioners were kind beyond words. Stay away. Then for three nights only Grace spoke. I demanded to talk with Allie. She finally came. What was the matter with me? Didn't I believe her? And would I please not phone again. I was disturbing the dentist's household; he didn't like these nightly calls, and Grace had quite enough to do without running around answering our inquiries. Goodbye. Allie would get in touch with us when she wished to. Don't phone again.

We decided I should go to Philadelphia the next day, take the Pennsy and then the suburban train. I alerted Robin, and he met me. We went to the suburb where the dentist lived. It was about 2:00 P.M. We walked up together boldly and rang the doorbell. A maid answered. No one was in, she said.

"Miss Allie?" I demanded shortly.

"Oh, they've taken her away," she answered.

"Away?"

"Yes."

"Who took her?"

"The ambulance."

"I wish to speak to the dentist."

She shut the door in our faces and left us standing on the front mat. Robin put a supporting arm around me. After a while the maid came back. "He's at the clinic. He won't be back for an hour and a half."

So we walked in a field of deep, strong grass, blue with violets. We sat in the pale spring light and saw the new maple leaves, the trees Allie loved so.

"I'm so scared," I said, putting my head in his lap. "I feel something so evil and frightening."

"Don't be scared," he said. "This is the way Christian Scientists do things. I'll stay with you right through. I can talk to them. I know the lingo."

In an hour I went back and forced my way into the dentist's house. I had the maid get me the dentist on the phone.

He was very matter-of-fact. "Allie's all right. Don't worry. But it's my wife who must tell you about it. It's not for me to."

Grace would not return for five hours. The maid had no intention of letting us wait in the parlor, and we couldn't sit in the middle of the fields, no matter how many violets and strawberries there were. So we went back to the city and had dinner.

Robin was extremely kind and tactful, but time wore on, and he began to think that he also needed sympathetic understanding. He restated his case, somewhat forcefully, and what with the tension of absolute terror, the feeling of animal comfort and love he offered, the menu, the candlelight, and the sheer duration of the worry and fear, my feeling for the case began to blur and slide. But I could not give a definite answer. I just stared at him. I suppose what he saw in my eyes looked appealing. It certainly looked frightened.

At eight promptly I phoned. Grace was not in.

At eight-fifteen I called again. Grace was not in.

At eight-forty she was in. Her voice was cool. She could tell me nothing of Allie without the practitioner's permission.

Well, then, get the permission.

I was to call back in fifteen minutes to speak to the practitioner herself. I was shaking pretty badly by this time. Robin stood behind me at the phone booth, his ear against the receiver. Every so often he brushed my hair with his lips and put a hand on my shoulder.

At nine o'clock Mrs. Lubkin said in a quiet, steady, throbbing, distant voice, "Allie is where she can rest. She was doing better than we could hope. And then suddenly . . . well, you see . . ."

"I'm listening, Mrs. Lubkin."

"It isn't that Grace was inadequate or made any mistakes, or didn't try. It's just that it all got too much for her household, so it was decided that Allie should be taken to a hospital."

"Which hospital?"

"That I will not tell you. I will give you the number. Call and ask for Room 820. Goodnight."

I dialed, and soon I had Allie herself speaking.

"I'm coming to you," I said.

"No, no, you're not."

"Where are you?"

"The Philadelphia Homeopathic Hospital. They only took me in as a very great favor, on condition that no one would interfere with me or my treatment."

"Do you have a doctor?"

"Oh, yes."

"I'm coming over."

"You are not." Her voice was very frail and colorless and breathless. "There are strict rules here, and if I break them, they won't let me stay."

"Can I visit you in the daytime?"

"Yes."

"I'll stay the night and come over tomorrow."

"No, you will not stay the night. Where's Robin?"

"Here beside me."

"You go home. You go back to New York. You take the ten o'clock train home."

Then she sighed very deeply, and her voice faded. But she rallied and said, "What's happening to me is a miracle. Everyone is astonished! It's a real demonstration of right thinking. I'm so grateful to be able to experience this. It makes life worthwhile. It makes everything have sense and meaning. I understand the whole pattern now." Her voice suddenly hardened. "If you interrupt this, if you deprive me of this, if you tell one member of my family, particularly my brother-in-law or Henry, I'll disappear and you will never find me. Do you hear me? Do you hear me, Agnes?"

"Yes, Allie, dear."

"Give me your solemn promise before God."

"Yes, dear. Trust me."

"I will. Now you go home. The other promise I want is that you do not stay the night in the same city with Robin. I want this promise."

"All right, darling."

"Goodnight," she breathed, and hung up.

Robin put me on the train. "I'll see her," he promised. "She'll see me, I know. I've learned the password, you see. I'll keep in touch with you daily."

I broke one promise. Aunt Marie was waiting with apprehension. "I cannot take the responsibility alone," I said. "I must tell you where she is. But we can't tell Henry. We can't tell any of the men." So we clung together.

"I will pray," said Aunt Marie. "Although she doesn't think my prayers count anymore. I will pray." She slipped to her knees.

Robin phoned every evening at seven, and he took flowers to Allie. She didn't seem to get much better, but she was cheerful. Then one night at eleven the dentist's wife called and said in a thin, shaking voice, "Allie's gone."

"You mean she's dead?"

"She passed on, yes." After a minute: "Do you hear me, do you hear?"

"I hear. I suppose you want me to tell the family. At her insistence, you know, the family has been told nothing. It will be a shock."

I went first to Aunt Marie. I woke her. She sat up in bed. "Allie?"

"Dead."

"Oh, poor girl." Her voice was filled with awed grief. "All alone. We were not there. No one with her. She was alone."

We got there, all of us, two days later. The service was held in a mortuary chapel full of Chinese furniture and rubber plants. The dentist's wife was crying unheeded in a corner. The family, particularly the men, passed in silent, bitter outrage. The room crackled with hate.

I sat rigid with fear, my flowers on my knees. "I'm scared," I said. "I've never seen a dead body. What'll I do?"

Robin was holding my hand. "The quicker you get it over with, the better."

There was the final object—the coffin. Allie's sister was bending over the body, arranging flowers. She straightened. Her eyes were red, her face swollen. "If your mother had been here, if she hadn't been away, this wouldn't have happened. You are to blame—you."

It wasn't true. Should I tell her that it wasn't true? That Allie didn't want her to know anything, and above all didn't want her doctor husband to know? I let her hate me. I let her love Allie. I was silent.

I faced Allie. Mother had always told me that half an hour after death the hand of God goes over the face and smoothes out all signs of anguish. No matter what the suffering, no matter what the death throes, the face emerges serene, the very essence of the life, the very intent.

Allie looked like pink soap. She had been made up, and she

had eyelashes and fingernails—surprisingly, her own fingernails, and her straight, thick, pale eyelashes lay like little tooth-
brushes on her too-pink cheeks. But the mouth? Shut like iron,
shut like a fist in the face of fate. She died unforgiving. She
died angry. She died cheated.

We went to the crematorium. The outside slope was littered
with dying bouquets from previous services. The chapel was
absolutely barren, with the box on a slab. No music, no poetry,
no prayers. This was simply a sanitary exercise. As the coffin
started to descend, one of the male relatives spontaneously
began saying, "Our Father," and Marie, with trembling lips,
blurted, "Darling," and dropped a wilted bouquet of violets
on the disappearing box.

Out, out into the spring, into the world of grass, new leaves,
birds. We ran, we gamboled, we even went swimming. We
went to Bea George's house and she gave us a good big supper.
We were ravenous.

I grabbed Robin's hand as we raced. It didn't matter what
Allie had said. It didn't matter what Mother had said. They
talked all their lives. It didn't matter. There was only one
answer to that shut mouth. "Tomorrow," I whispered. "Tomorrow or the next day. But let it be in the woods, outdoors.
I want to see the sky."

C O R N E L I A

CORNELIA, AT FIFTY-THREE, suddenly proposed something so extraordinary that friends were frightened. Having lived the life of a well-to-do gentlewoman, replete with the usual pleasures and cares—usual in all ways except that hers had more illness than is customary and there was the early death of a beloved husband—she decided that with the coming of the first grandchildren she would do exactly as she liked for the first time in her life.

We had always treated her as one of us, a beloved friend, one of my parents' gang, but she was nothing of the sort. Her voice, for one thing, marked her apart; we all had good voices and

242 / PORTRAIT GALLERY

fine diction, but Cornelia's voice was very low-pitched, with clipped New England diction. Her intelligent, rippling laugh gave evidence of a fine heritage, what my mother termed "blue-blooded American," as did her appearance. She was beautiful in a classic way, with a very high forehead, a straight nose, and dark skin — extraordinarily dark when she was tanned, so that she looked like a Latin, or possibly even an Indian. Indeed, she looked as though she were carved out of mahogany. She had great dark eyes, dancing eyes, eyes that perused everything and appraised in humorous silence. She had a manner of attending and waiting while considering. Her smile was shy. From the time I first knew her (and I knew her when I was a very little girl), she bound her head with colored bands, which enhanced the Indian aspect. She was noticeable, all right, but not pretty in the Hollywood sense, and Hollywood was where we lived, Cornelia having emigrated there for reasons of family health. All her distinguishing marks and appearance, however, could have been accepted and assimilated, except that she was not one of us and we knew it, although we were told nothing of her hidden passion, her secret yearning.

No, Cornelia was different. She was grave, distinguished, and without in any way being haughty, she somehow seemed mysteriously aloof, like royalty incognito.

The hidden truth about Cornelia was simply that she yearned to paint. Cornelia had always wanted to paint. Against this willful independence stood her antecedents. Her grandfather had been the captain of the Black Ball line of New York-to-Liverpool packet ships, the first sailing ships to make regularly scheduled transatlantic voyages carrying freight and passengers. She belonged to a class and a generation that either got over artistic yearnings early or persuaded their papas to give them enough money to go to Paris and sign up in the atelier of some well-known artist, there to study until marriage, when they would abandon all thought of a profession and settle down, their husbands hoped, with, their husbands were sure, no regrets. Very few of the women students, mostly spinsters such as Mary Cassatt and Cecilia Beaux, made names as painters, and these were in a sense freaks.

Cornelia studied hard in New York at the Art Students League, painting with Robert Henri and modeling with James Earle Fraser, both of whom thought her work promising. However, family and environmental pressures were too great to be resisted — were in truth relentless — and she followed the traditional path by marrying a gifted young lawyer, Charles Runyon. She had no objection to marrying Runyon; she loved him. But she wanted to paint.

Family troubles, however, soon overwhelmed her. She and her husband had two sons, Charles Junior and Thomas Mercein. The baby distinguished himself when six months old by having a nervous breakdown, Cornelia told me, which necessitated constant supervision by a single person — herself. In addition, both Cornelia and her husband had long bouts of deadly illness, culminating in Charles's tragic death at the age of forty-eight.

By this time the family had long lived in Hollywood, where Cornelia now found herself a widow at forty-one, with two young children; well enough off, thanks to Charles's careful will, but quite alone. She was still comparatively young and vividly attractive.

She was a gracious and enchanting hostess. Let me hasten to say Cornelia was more than that: she had a rare, wonderful quality that very few people possess — the ability to listen directly and show no sense of age difference. She was wise, she was experienced, and she never under any circumstances condescended or patronized. Nor was she easily tired or bored or indifferent. No, even to us, the children, she was a respectful and understanding friend. It didn't matter what our sex or age or identity; if she liked us and if we wanted to talk to her, she was there to talk to.

All grown men found her fascinating, and for this reason their wives looked askance. Why didn't she remarry? they asked. Well, the money, of course; by the terms of her hus-

band's will she would lose certain rights upon remarriage. But
why then didn't she interest herself in what interested the
wives? Some of the husbands called on her without their wives
and had long, stimulating talks, which they found reassuring
but which their wives did not find reassuring. The wives, my
mother among them, were very uneasy.

The members of the moving-picture colony, including my
family, constituted the majority of Cornelia's acquaintances.
At the beginning of her western life they were unavoidable,
being at hand. Cornelia was devoted, but she didn't consider
them all-important, nor was she, contrary to their usual expectations, fascinated. The moving-picture colony was so self-
absorbed, so self-sufficient, so intent on making its identity
known, that it could not conceive of any other people having
equal fervor or lasting significance. Movie people were oblivious to outsiders, considering them of far less importance. But
there were other groups. Los Angeles had a rich and varied
community, and Cornelia was able to pursue her interests unchecked, unobtrusively and unqueried, and to deepen her curiosity about the arts.

In spite of her sons' developing lives and her flourishing
family, she became with time increasingly lonely. She thought
to remarry. Friends were dismayed. My father advised, "Don't
give up your security. You're a middle-aged woman. Why
marry?" He talked to a will-o'-the-wisp. She married and
moved to Brentwood with her new husband, but the marriage
proved to be a serious mistake. She had cast her lot with a
troubled and unreliable man, and after acute suffering, the
marriage ended in divorce.

In all the long interval since her first marriage, Cornelia had
never painted. That part of her life was seemingly dead, but
now, depleted and shaken by her recent venture, her faith in
her own judgment undermined, she found the courage, the
energy, and the will to make a totally new start and to risk
doing what she had suppressed for so very long.

She sold her house in Brentwood, moved to the wilderness,

and built a new home. It was finished just before the war, and
Cornelia moved into it directly before Pearl Harbor Day. With
the United States entry into World War II, Tom, her younger
son, became a pilot in the Ferry Command to North Africa.
He always maintained his home base at Cornelia's house, however, and made his military sorties from there.

The house was situated far up the beach past Malibu, in a
tract of land still unhoused and about to be called Zuma. This
was the last piece of untouched land, the primitive California
my grandparents had known. There were no telephones, no
mail, no police. One went miles to the local post office for
messages, and during the war the coast guard prowled Cornelia's beach four times a day with great police dogs on chains,
looking for signs of secret Japanese landings.

Built into the side of the hill along the shoreline and facing
west to the sea, Cornelia's house of pink sandstone, the exact
color of the earth, lay low and buried in a shroud of vegetation.
It was modern in design, economic and clean in line, hugging
the ground and fitting so nicely into the cliffs that one could
not see at first that any artifact had been placed there at all.

The rooms were always still and cool, the great mahoganies
of Cornelia's New England ancestors gleaming richly against
the pink stone walls beneath their fine stiff portraits. Around
about were pieces of driftwood. There were windows wherever possible, fitted with strong glass to withstand the wind, so
that when one looked west, north, or south one saw the breakers below, creaming, running, sucking, crashing, the wild surf
providing a thin and roaring barrier to the deep waters where
sharks and whales and enormous unimagined fish moved, and
where the sky rolled and spread all day, all night, while our
own domestic world turned back and went about its business.
Then, when one lifted one's gaze to the eastern wall, back to
the road and the mountains, there were clear skylights in a
high wainscoting so that from the bed, from the sofa, from a
chair, one could watch the hilltops as they changed in intensity
against the blazing Spanish sky. In the spring the steeps were

studded with flowers, bristling with white yucca or softly blue with lupine and lilacs. The flowers stayed longer on this slope than elsewhere, there being a sizable stream at the bottom, at which mountain lions drank.

Cornelia moved out there, sure now that she would be alone, uninterrupted, and free to work at last—free, free. Free for what?

My father and stepmother shook their heads and wrung their hands. "Cornelia, you are not young. You must not go away like this. You're moving into a wilderness. There's no doctor there. There's no telephone. You must not go off alone. What will you do? You will die of loneliness."

What would she do? She began looking at rocks wherever she walked and picking them up and bringing them into the house —the rocks that could resist the sea and the wind and the millions of years that had rolled them around on the ocean bottom. The best rocks were at the water line and had to be lugged up steps hacked out of sheer cliff, and for this she enlisted Tommy's aid, on his furloughs from plane-ferrying. Tight-lipped and sardonic, he carried some of the heaviest ones up the face of the bluff. When he got them to the top, Cornelia passed her hands over them in welcome and began to learn them in what was, as Anaïs Nin put it, "the opposite of an act of will. It [was] an act of creativity which remains rooted in nature, more like an act of giving birth."

Cornelia would take the stones into her bedroom and watch them at night, and see them change color and size at dawn— a hunk of rose quartz on top of Robert Todd Lincoln's marquetry desk, a chalcedon on the Sheraton table. When she felt she knew them, knew why they were the shape they were, and their color, and their tension, then she believed she could release the meaning that was inside.

One day she took a hammer and chipped off a piece. Suddenly she realized the truth: she was a sculptor.

Cornelia wished to work in gemstones directly, without making clay models first. She carved without pattern, not copying or enlarging, as most marble cutters do, but chipping directly into the substance, guided only by her inner vision. Error or accident could spoil months of work.

The great sculptor Isamu Noguchi says: "Stone is the fundament of the earth, of the universe. It is not old or new but a primordial element. Stone is the primary medium, and nature is where it is, and nature is where we have to go to experience life. . . . Stone breathes within nature's time cycle. It doesn't resist entropy but is within it. It begins before you and continues through you and goes on. Working with stone is not resisting time but touching it . . . Direct carving is a process of listening." Cornelia never heard these remarks, but I'm certain she would have agreed.

She had chosen to work in probably the hardest medium of all. Marble is the fourth softest substance used by stone carvers. Cornelia preferred the sea-stones and the semiprecious gemstones she found in the desert: blue calcite, howlite, rose quartz, aventurine, jade, jasper, basalt, obsidian, malachite, and granite. The rocks she was endeavoring to bring into shape had to be attacked with electric drills, sometimes gross ones, and sometimes with fine dental tools. She wore goggles like a street worker, and a wet cloth over her mouth, and the vibration and pull of the drill on her arthritic arms was painful and exhausting, so that spending more than an hour at work at a time was impossible. But the joy of bringing the hidden form, the latent power, out of everlasting stone, of sensing it emerge, was real, and she persisted all by herself, with a contentment she had never before known.

For five years Cornelia labored on pieces that she considered and judged with her own uncompromising eye, then quietly and resolutely pushed back over the cliff into the sea. She took no one's advice; she heeded no one's ridicule — and there was a great deal of that, even from the people she loved. She calmly went on chipping in the hot sun, wearing goggles, rubber boots, and rubber gloves, wetting the stone constantly with the garden hose to prevent friction and carrying the driving impact of a pneumatic hammer on a shoulder and back that long since had stiffened with disease. She worked alone. She cooked, she cleaned, she marketed alone. She asked only that she would be given enough strength for good work in the years left to her.

My stepmother was frantic. "She's going to make a fool of herself. You know, she's headstrong, and she's going to make an absolute fool. Oh, I suppose it does no harm, but why? She doesn't like to do any of the things women do. She always was very mannish and independent."

Cornelia wasn't mannish in the sense that she was unwomanly. What Cornelia had was the pure virile strength of real talent, uncompromising and direct. And so uncomfortable to people of little talent!

In time she had a one-woman show. She shortly had another, and suddenly her friends stopped patronizing her. Her pieces were selling for hard cash. Soon she was represented in major art museums. She was neither a freak nor a primitive like Grandma Moses, but a sophisticated and knowledgeable artist, acclaimed wherever her work was seen. Henry J. Seldes wrote in the *Los Angeles Times* on February 10, 1961, "Cornelia Runyon is a poet in stone." Anaïs Nin wrote, "Because she revealed the forms, moods, messages of nature without tampering with them, they retained their intense and vivid life and their mystery. Her lack of egocentricity is like that of cathedral builders who refused to sign their designs. Everything lies asleep until she touches it like some intuitive mother, and then it discloses its inner life which she has liberated."

At the time of Cornelia's show in the Pasadena Art Museum, which had just acquired one of her pieces, the novelist Irving Fineman wrote: "Slowly, like nature itself, she continues the carving [begun by] wind and water upon some stone cast down on a deserted beach; or brings to light the secret crystalline color and shape informed by fires and forces in the dark depths of earth. The results are like no other sculpture. They have at once the surprising freshness of newly minted coins and the timelessness of the classic subjects or of the natural creatures they suggest. I know of no other fine sculpture which I am not content merely to look at but must touch. . . . No use to say: 'Please do not touch.' In the gallery, one after another will stop to caress. It is intimate rather than grand sculpture, and yet deeply moving."

Cornelia's works were not realistic forms; neither were they abstractions. They were easily recognizable, evocative and often humorous animal, fish, mollusk, and human shapes. All of them seemed friendly, even the mollusks, self-sufficient and alive.

Now, in her sixties, Cornelia knew peace. She had time for work and privacy, and she had found her calling. She had a purpose.

She had sought the life of a hermit, but there were diversions. One day, paddling among the breakers looking for rocks, she noticed odd dark strands washing in the seaweed. They turned out to be human hair; she had hold of a drowned woman. She seated herself on a rock and wound her hand in the hair and called for Tommy to go the eight miles for the police. There was no carving done for the next five days. She was cooking for police and reporters.

One young boy who kept dropping in uninvited suddenly one evening ripped off all his clothes and went stark mad. As he was the only son of a beloved friend, this was particularly distressing. Tommy was once more routed out of his bachelor study, where he was trying to write a short story, and sent on another strenuous errand.

In due course, poor Billy had to be incarcerated in the insane asylum at Carpinteria, which is up the coast, near Santa Barbara. His father, Wilfred Buckland, who had been the great scene designer for Belasco and the early Lasky Company and who had created all of my uncle's fine sets and later the memorable sets for Douglas Fairbanks's *Robin Hood* and *The Thief of Bagdad*, then took to stopping in. He had been a lifelong friend, and he adored Cornelia. Now, since there was no one left of his family except Billy, and Billy was demented, he clung to her in his anguish. He always chose the coastal route to visit Billy's hospital, and he would stop off at Cornelia's and lay his poor bleeding spirits on her mercy. These were woeful visitations, forcing Cornelia to go to bed afterward.

Billy's condition worsened, and Wilfred finally withdrew him, took him to Hollywood to his home, and kept him there for a few days. Then, early one morning, after writing a letter to my father, he picked up his shotgun and fired a blast through the boy's head and one through his own. "I'm taking Billy with me," he had written.

Cornelia had to go away for a bit after that episode. But she returned and continued working.

Shortly thereafter forest fires swept the hills, as they frequently do in late summer, leaping quarter-miles from summit to summit. Cornelia and Tommy fought them, along with the rangers and the neighbors, and after five days they found themselves trapped in a canyon. There they waited out the night, praying for the wind to change. The sheriff sat at Cornelia's shoulder, a loaded pistol in his hands. Had the wind not turned, he kindly explained later, he was going to shoot the women first.

After that there was a lull. The landscape had been singed, and people felt chary about calling, but bit by bit they got over their timidity. Cornelia's house was on the coastal high road, and it was the best place for a meal between Ventura and Santa Monica, and most certainly the best place for conversation. Visits always entailed meals. Cornelia was a good cook and made wonderful salads (I remember some served in a small Tahitian hollowed log).

Friends needed Cornelia's wisdom and the rich sense of accomplishment that her place always housed, and although they may not have understood her intention, they had a sense of revelation and power as she passed her brown hands over the rocks and laughed. "She gives the impression that she is one of her own sculptures," wrote Anaïs Nin. "Her beautiful deeply tanned face is molded with finesse and strength to express wit and liveliness and something undefinably enduring, eternal as stone. Hers is a beauty sculptured by intelligence and quality.''

Cornelia's friends could easily understand her abiding love of work and her gratitude that at last she was doing what she had always longed to do. She was, in fact, a kind of vindication for life-patience. Those who could appreciate her point of view were deeply respectful, and the others felt that she had done her womanly duty, since her children were grown and she was beholden to no one. If she wanted to indulge herself at last in her old age, it was her privilege to do so.

Cornelia finally had to name days and hours for visits. She discovered what I have always suspected, that one visitor in a wilderness is a more demanding presence than processions in a metropolis.

As a further interruption to her work early in the war, my bridegroom and I went to her house on our honeymoon. My new husband was in the Aviation Ordinance and was stationed at Hobbs, New Mexico. Before going overseas he had been given a two-week leave for wedding purposes, and he came to marry me in Beverly Hills. We arrived at Cornelia's at sundown and stepped from golden afternoon to the glint and quiet of her beautiful living room. Cornelia was silhouetted against her window, the evening sea deepening and moving behind her, the sky aflame. That day her semblance to an Indian in color and serenity was heightened by the dark red scarf with which she had bound her brown head. Her silver jewelry gleamed in the dark as she moved forward. She put out her hands to us as she had put them out to me so often in my life, but this was the first time in sympathy with my happiness, and when she saw my face, she wept.

Her car was tactfully packed so that she could leave immediately. (Tommy had been banished God knows where, or he had just picked up and left. He did not like sharing his mother's guests.) But we begged her to stay for a bit, and she and Walter together cooked a turkey dinner. She also provided champagne, and when the coast guard came around she heard them outside, as always, for she was used to listening for them, having provided them with a shower and full bathing facilities as an ease to their monotonous and lonely patrols. She heard their boots in the sand and the rattling of the dogs' chains (the windows were sealed, of course, to prevent light from showing; Californians were afraid of sudden Japanese landings or air attacks), and she invited them in. The young men had never tasted champagne, but they took the crystal goblets in their great hands and nodded at us, and the dogs scratched and snuffled at the table legs and at our feet.

As she kissed me goodnight, she said, "I have no servant now, and I cannot arrange the luxury of leaving the music on while I go to sleep. Tonight you turn off the gramophone." She disappeared to her bedroom, and there was her house in our keeping — the fire crackling beneath the Rico Lebrun still life (he had been married on her hearth), the bottle of wine gleaming on a table before it, the portraits glimmering down, the great furniture standing richly about . . . and the sea around us. When all the lights were safely out, we could raise a shade and see the sliding shoreline coming and receding, to the north, to the south, lipping and lining the dim vastness of the west at the edge of the world. On this sea we leaned as on a sword, for it was to become a battle line. But all we knew at the moment was the strong moment of "now" — not yet the grim decisions, not for a while. Now was our time.

Cornelia tactfully went away next day in the morning. Five days later we walked the hills behind her house for a goodbye, and on the path carefully marked NO TRESPASSING Walter sprang three lion traps. Because he was not four-legged, and because I traveled more than five feet behind him, our bones were not crushed. Walter thought this rather piquant, but as the third steel bar snapped to with meshed teeth two inches long, I said, "That will do" and slid straight down the canyon wall, through cactus, spiders, sagebrush, and snakes to the brook and paradise below. There we picked Cornelia a bouquet of tiger lilies, roses, monkey-flowers, lupines, and simple pale long river lupines such as I had never before gathered and left it for her on the Lincoln desk with our hearts' love.

As we drove away, Walter stopped by the roadside and said quietly, "We will know much in our lives—all kinds of moments and experiences, maybe better—but not this, not just this—not ever again."

The war ended. The years passed. Tommy married and moved to his own house. Cornelia kept carving and was now represented in most of the good museums of the West. She continued always in her work industriously, quietly (as quietly as her many interloping visitors permitted), and very happily. But she very gradually, if surely, faced a terrible realization: she was going blind. Her sons and friends insisted that she find an easier abode, one in the heart of civilization, so she rented a small apartment—two rooms and a kitchenette—adjacent to the Old Soldiers' Home at Sawtell, and there she moved her lovely furniture and her paintings. Her sculptures, those not sold or in museums, were given to her family and friends; the rough stones were of course abandoned, pushed back. Her beautiful home was sold to Tommy, who moved there with his wife and two children. (Tommy and his wife owned and manned a restaurant made out of the old Malibu post office.) Cornelia was still independent, as she wanted to be, and she could still fend for herself, but in an extremely circumscribed and domesticated way.

Wherever she went marketing in the neighborhood, past the historic cemetery with the flower- and flag-decorated graves of Civil War veterans and World War I heroes, she collected a gaggle of neighborhood children who followed her, clutching bits of crayon and pieces of paper and begging her to stop for a minute, sit on a stone wall, and give her judgment on their latest drawings. She always did. They called her "C'nelia." They were no older than seven years and they toddled, but they were faithful, they were ardent, and she was making expressive artists of them.

Her eyesight worsened, as did her general condition, and

she flew to Washington, D.C., where her older son, Charlie, and his wife helped her settle in a good nursing home. Tom and his wife closed up the Sawtell apartment. Cornelia loathed nursing homes, but she went docilely. She loved her family, and she did not want to be a burden to them. Her doctors had diagnosed her ailment as a matter of age, and they really did not know any remedy for that. I believe Charlie wanted to keep her with him, but how could he, with a growing family? Further, Cornelia wouldn't have permitted it. She rose to the occasion with all her old charm. She was a lover of freedom, but above all of humanity. She would not let her free, striving soul crowd in on the young lives. Her last days were predominantly solitary and austere.

The nursing home where she now stayed was pleasant enough as these institutions go, situated on the banks of the Potomac, with a clear view, for those who could see, of the river from certain windows and a partial view of the gardens, trees, and a few flowers. But Cornelia was confined to her bedroom mostly, although permitted to use a few common rooms, including the dining room, and a parlor for meeting visitors. She was incapable of walking without help. One eye was sightless, the other dim.

When Charlie drove me the fifteen-mile trip from Washington to visit her, a nurse fetched her from the dining room, where she was eating alone. She wore a black patch over the sightless eye. She looked as smart as Lord Nelson and sat as straight as the admiral.

Charlie came to see her every day, she confided. "He is like his father—faithful, oh yes, faithful and chivalrous." Her one care was never to seem like an old woman to him, or to smell like one: "I have a horror of the old lady's smell." To prevent this, she whispered, she kept eau de cologne in her pocketbook. Her single complaint, and it was a bitter one, was that she could never see TV, because the TV in her bedroom, which she was compelled to share, was always on, and always with programs that did not interest her. Being gentle and noncombative, she yielded to the strident demands of her room companion, who had low tastes and no manners. Since she couldn't read, she was reduced to listening to her radio, using earphones.

She wanted to know about all the members of my family, about what I was doing, about her friends, her young friends, and friends younger than that. I told her all I knew. I asked her what I could send her. She shook her head and smiled the wonderful Cornelia smile, the one eye lit up with gentle luster. "If I could see you now and then—not too often, just now and then," she said. I promised and kissed her and held her in my arms, her frail, thin body erect, noble, so capable, so ready to serve, so ready to give, now rendered useless, as obsolete as an old tool.

Since she couldn't read and she wouldn't look at the TV programs that were offered her, what did she think about? What could she think now, shut in her box with old remnants, waiting to die—she, who found the confines of Hollywood with its gardens and hills and cocktail parties too close for endurance, she who had run away to the wild lands, she who had claimed her country where mountain cats roamed and seals came in to play on the shores?

I am sure she contemplated what lasted without change: the long, sounding shore where the Pacific waves rolled in forever, the sky torn with color, the streaming of the last conflagration of the light as it turned rocks into luminous entities; the great primitive enduring stone, the essence of the earth, the fundament, which she had been privileged to make her mark on and which she had had to leave too soon. I am sure she thought —oh, how often—"If I had started earlier!" But that was not the pattern, and because she believed in permanent, enduring things, she understood about pattern.

She had no time left. She had not had enough time. But all rocks meant was time. Rocks were time. This she understood.

AVOIR

DU

CRAN

"On va me tuer, Madame, on va me tuer."

Germaine was shaking. She sat up in the hospital bed, rigid with fear, resistant to my caress as she had been once before at a moment of crisis. Her coal-black hair started unkempt from her scalp; her black eyes stared wildly. Germaine was our cook-housekeeper, a great cook, and she gave us a peck of trouble.

Germaine had been in the United States thirteen years, but she refused to speak anything but Parisian French. Over the eight years she had been with us I had grown to believe she understood English pretty accurately and profited by her knowledge when it suited her. She had found, however, that it gave her a tremendous advantage, indeed the whip hand, if she spoke French fluently, even discerningly, while the masters of the house scrambled among tenses and nouns, becoming on provocation speechless with frustration. At that impasse, an evil, disagreeable smile would settle on her features as she waited for the pertinent verb. At these moments I nearly always launched into my own tongue, and I am vocal. But she was equal to rebuttal.

"Hein?" she would say as she compressed her thin lips and smiled pityingly. "Hein? Je ne comprends rien."

This was neither polite nor kind, and Germaine could be both, but only if there was cause. Now, in the hospital, she was in trouble and unexpectedly pathetic. Germaine equated all hospitals with the Hôtel-Dieu of eighteenth-century Paris, where one was sent to die.

"They are not going to kill you, Germaine," I said. "Now be reasonable. It is a difficult operation, but they are very skilled, and they've done this thousands of times. I know many women who have had hysterectomies."

The doctor came into her room and explained for the fifth time exactly what he was going to do, every step of the process. He added that the next day she would feel bad and be heavily sedated, but on the second day after the operation she would probably feel a great deal better. On the sixth day she could leave the hospital and work, but mildly. All of this I had to translate. Whether Germaine believed him or not, she grew quiet. Her needlelike black eyes ceased darting about. He patted her on the shoulder and left.

She was in a charity hospital, a brand-new, spanking new place—paint, windows, everything, lovely and clean. For this she didn't have to pay a penny, not a sou, to us ordinary American citizens or to those "charlatans," the doctors; this gave her considerable satisfaction. She was doubly complacent because she was not a citizen, so she had got the best of two governments.

Like most peasants, she retained cupidity and instinctive suspicion as her salient characteristics. Germaine never took out her citizenship papers in the United States but remained a French national largely, I believe, to profit by all the welfare she was entitled to at home as well as some she certainly was not entitled to here. She kept the two welfare accounts prophylactically separate. Ah, those little notebooks with the French sevens and the columns of figures! She spent hours on them in the kitchen, hours and hours daily, figuring how she could screw a hundred more, how Madame owed her $10 for this and Monsieur for that.

But although Germaine may have been mean, avaricious, scheming, and frequently disagreeable, she was scrupulously honest. She never once falsified an account or told a lie, except to the governments, French and American. These I think she felt bone deep were meant to be cheated, and anything she could do them out of was fair game. Any other course was blatantly stupid.

She never once in all her time with us (and this, I think, is remarkable) asked to borrow money. Almost every other servant I have ever had has done so, and not a few have defaulted. Germaine was independent and proud. She stood on her own feet, even if she occasionally trampled on ours.

In the hospital she continued in French, the language of intellectuals and noblesse. "When I die, I want you to take my body to France."

"Germaine, I can't do that."

"Madame, I have the money. I wish it sent to France so that my relatives may bury it beside my mother."

"But you hated your mother."

"She was a bad mother and I was a bastard, but"—her voice rose with pride—"I was acknowledged. I was recognized by my father. He admitted I was his child, although I could not bear his name. But I wish to lie beside her in a Catholic cemetery. This is very, very important to me."

"Why, Germaine? You hated her. There are Catholic cemeteries in the United States. And you never go to church."

"French soil!" she screamed. "French Catholicism! Beside my mother, where I should be!"

"She deserted you. She abandoned you at the age of ten. You had to go to work in Paris in a factory."

Germaine looked thoughtful. "Yes, I did. She was a beast!"

"Then why?"

Her voice shook with fervor. "I must be put into French soil. I have the money. It's saved."

"All right, Germaine, I promise."

Germaine continued with particulars. "Don't let my daughter, Geneviève, have charge of this. I don't want her to have anything to do with my burial. And I don't wish her to have my money, which I have saved so carefully. I want my granddaughter, Dorothée, to have it, and the house. Be sure."

"Yes, I'll take care of that, if I can. But have you put all this in writing? That's important. Your daughter is the next of kin. If you wish to bypass her, you must have that in writing."

"My lawyer knows everything."

"Who is your lawyer? Have you written all this?"

"His name is with my papers. I don't want that girl to get her hands on my money. Pas un sou. The granddaughter must have all. Everything."

"Okay, Germaine. But you're not going to die. You will be all right. Tomorrow you will feel simply lousy." Now, did I say that? No, I don't know the French word. I think I said "very poorly." "They keep you drugged so there's no real pain. Now go to sleep quietly. I won't come tomorrow. You won't want to see me. And by the way, Germaine, where is your daughter? She should be here. Her arms, not mine, should be around you right now."

"Sacré Dieu!" said Germaine. "Her arms!" She went into something that I could not follow but that I believe was not academic French.

The charlatans pulled her through. She came home.

I had been desperate when I hired her. At the time I was staging a major Broadway show and bringing a book through publication. A French girl who seemed to have proper credentials and was nicely spoken and neat applied for the job, but my husband took one look and said, "Too young." That was Geneviève, the hated daughter. But she asked to bring her mother. This woman was the right age, wore a neat and businesslike raincoat, and had black, bristling hair starting energetically from her skull, snapping black eyes, and a tight mouth: a Gallic face. She spoke not a word of English. Well, never mind; I could speak a sort of French, and I knew that my young son would be forced to learn the language—a very good thing, I thought. My husband did not like the idea, but he was willing to try.

"Do you mind pets?" I asked in my first interview. "We have two household cats, who are the special joy of my son. They're not an awful lot of trouble."

"I adore animals," said Germaine succinctly, "and they like me. We are good friends. I know how to handle them."

"That's fine," I said. "They are important to us all."

I asked for a reference, and she forked out of her smart raincoat pocket a very worn and tattered letter, obviously old, which had served for years. There was no date on the paper. The fact that Germaine had been fired from her last two jobs for insolence was a detail not mentioned. I, unwary, welcomed her, as did my family. Germaine moved in.

She cooked remarkably. She could have taken the position of chef in any great kitchen, except for her temperament, which revealed itself too soon as very nearly unendurable. She was sloppy (a bad trait in a cook), cantankerous, short-tempered, fierce—*farouche*, as her countrymen said—and inclined to quarrel.

At first we did try very hard to get along. She tried too. She was polite in the beginning. She did all the catering and planning, and she kept all the accounts like a bank teller. I had to stipulate nothing except how many there would be at table. This was of enormous service to me, busy as I was. But before many weeks were up, we realized that this smart, tart businesswoman in the kitchen was in reality a peasant, and that the cornerstone of her character seemed to be stubbornness. Still later I realized that the quarreling masked fear. Like any endangered animal, she attacked first and she attacked hard.

But she was also on occasion kind, even generous, and frequently tactful. She gave us presents: good French china, hand-embroidered French linen, and to my son on his graduation a louis d'or circa 1865. She also gave trifles in the name of "la petite Dorothée," her granddaughter. She was thoughtful when I was working late and concerned if I was grieving. Yes, she did try, but she lived in fear. She had reason; her situation was ominous. But what is important, I think, is that she could be salty, and appreciative of wit. Her verve, her energy, and her unexpectedness made life with her a possibility and sometimes, if not a pleasure, certainly an amusement.

She knew she was damn good at her trade, and like the expert she was, she loved to perform for company and responded with benevolent condescension to the praise that was always heaped on her after a meal. There was something almost regal in the way she sat in the mess of used dishes and accepted homage. When Igor Stravinsky came, she made a prodigious effort. I remember the maestro paying his compliments in French while Germaine sat exhausted in the clutter, getting her breath and mopping her brow. She didn't rise to meet the great man but beamed happily as on an equal and murmured elegant disclaimers. Then she quickly whipped out a set of his records, with pen and ink ready, and asked for his signature on each disc. These signed records would have monetary value later, as she well knew. The action surprised me the first time. After a while it didn't. There were many similar incidents, because we entertained the great musicians of the world.

Once we got a card from President and Mrs. Kennedy, inviting us to the White House for a dinner party in honor of André Malraux, the French novelist and then minister of culture. It was my first White House invitation and I was overwhelmed. I called Germaine and my son excitedly and showed them the card.

"Pooh, ce n'est pas grande chose," said Germaine. "I have one too." With that she went to her room and fetched an invitation signed by Charles de Gaulle and addressed to her personally. I was dumfounded. "I have some letters," she went on, and she produced a large folded square of linen notepaper which was, when opened, an order in French written in beautiful script, signed "L."

"Who is this from?" I said.

"Why, naturally, le roi Louis."

"Which Louis?"

"The Fourteenth, naturally."

"Ah. Naturally!"

She flourished Louis's letter. Why not? She had a right to it. She was a Parisian.

She wouldn't cook for just anybody. Us? Yes. We were her patrons. But ordinary friends? Sometimes with bad grace. We had one very nice supper party for several of our summer neighbors. I announced there would be another. "Aha!" she said with loud and ringing sarcasm. "The fiesta continues!"

On the day of the Kennedy assassination I went to her solemnly. "Germaine, I have something tragic to tell you," I said. Her face went white. "The president is dead."

Her face lit up like a lantern. It radiated pure joy. "Good!" she shouted. "Good. De Gaulle is dead."

"No, no, no! Not your president. Mine. Kennedy."

"Ah," she said and sat down in shock, "that is altogether different. That is terrible." Then, in admiration, with pride and reverence, she gave him the highest praise a Frenchman can accord: "Il a eu du cran"; he had guts. (The term signifies not just guts but nobility, chivalry, gallantry, and valor.)

Then we went together to church, Germaine in her smartest suit. She didn't believe in a Protestant God, but she did believe in Kennedy and mourned with me.

About de Gaulle she was unforgiving. She stopped seeing

her best friend because Berthe supported "le grand Charles."
Germaine threw her out of the house. Life chez nous was
always eventful.

In spite of Germaine's bravura, her bullying, her bad temper,
and her other unattractive social flaws, her sense of social tact
could be subtle and sympathetic. She appreciated good conversation. She knew that my husband and I liked to talk to one another above anything else, and that our cocktail hour and our
quiet conversations were precious to us, and she let us prolong
the cocktail hour past dinnertime to the imminent peril of delicious and delicate food. She didn't nag, she didn't scold, she
didn't summon; she humored us, and, miracle of miracles, the
dinner was never spoiled. She saved it and served it as a crowning achievement to the evening. This was remarkable. Ask anyone who has had a good cook; they are martinets, and they do
not accommodate.

One thing Germaine was incapable of: sitting down and
talking quietly through a problem, or, if she wanted something, asking quietly and reasonably. She delivered tirades, she
made demands and gave ultimatums. Every wish became nineteenth-century French drama, which she expressed with more
temper, fiery explicatives, gestures, sneers, imprecations mut-
tered under her breath, and stampings out of the room than
any French *farceur* would have permitted himself.

Her flaws became more evident. For example, Germaine not
only cooked superbly, she ate prodigiously, and demanded
portions equal to what our family of three shared. Once she
made a cake that was so extremely good that our guests and
the family ate it all, leaving nothing for the kitchen. She came
shrieking to me, "I had no dessert!" Well, I was very sorry.
"Make two," I said. "You cook very well and we loved it and
ate it all and it was greedy of us, but make more and keep one
for yourself." Ah, no, that was extra work! So the next night
we had a pie with a large piece cut from it before it was set
on the table. I didn't care for this and remonstrated. She

shrugged. The matter was closed as far as she was concerned. It was an important matter, though, and later led to dreadful consequences. (Should I have fired her? Yes. Why didn't I? It will become clear, or nearly, as this sorry tale continues.)

She seemed greedy, but she was really fearful, terrified of being deprived. Germaine had to fight for every favor, fight for every possible social advantage, fight for her place in the scheme of workers.

She had married a Belgian, who was taken prisoner of war during the German occupation in World War II and was released only at the end of hostilities, when he was free to reestablish his extremely ugly marriage. In the meantime Germaine's and his beautiful daughter, Geneviève, had matured. The father, the girl confessed, tried to seduce her, and he proved to be unsatisfactory in other ways.

Geneviève began roaming around with an American GI and very shortly found herself pregnant, a predicament that seemed endemic in the family. She attempted suicide. Germaine went straight to the American's commanding officer and named the boy. "Prove it," said the commander, and turned his back. So the little granddaughter, Dorothée, was born, and Germaine of course had to take care of both mother and child. After two years the baby was put into a foundling home; Geneviève had hated her from birth. She was a burden and a shame and she interfered with all Geneviève's hopes. Thus began Dorothée's heartbreaking odyssey.

The pretty and wayward Geneviève, with a chevelure of light brown curls dancing on her nape, took up with another American GI, this one a hillbilly on occupation duty. He was a decent boy, so he married her and took her to his home in the Arkansas mountains, where Geneviève discovered just how dreadful the life of an indigent American rustic can be. She attempted suicide a second time.

"Elle crève de faim," said Germaine, making her cheeks hollow to express starvation. However, Bobby, the hillbilly, was generous; they sent for the baby, now three years old, and the poor little waif came alone from Paris to Arkansas. Germaine showed me her passport: "Look, Madame, how sad she is! Oh how sad, at three!" The baby may have been short on food in Arkansas, but she had two years of mountain living in pleasant country, acquaintance with farm animals, and on the whole a grand good time before the three went to New York and began starving in the big city.

Germaine, who had left her husband long since and followed her daughter to America, somehow managed to get to New York and somehow managed to buy a small house and lot in Metuchen, New Jersey, for her little family. It was to be their stake in life, and it was all Germaine cared about.

And Germaine cared. She dearly loved her pretty, blond, blue-eyed granddaughter and hoped mightily for her. This was her core, her purpose, the reason she got up in the morning. She had besides strong, unbreakable ties with her wayward daughter, a dark admiration for her avariciousness and rebelliousness, and above all the root-deep French feeling for family. The three, mother, daughter, and granddaughter, were a unit and bled if one was disturbed. This bond excluded the hillbilly, whom they scarcely spoke to; the two women conversed in French only.

I have gone into this life in the kitchen in detail because it shortly became my own life, whether I willed it or not, and my husband's, and my son's. They didn't like the situation at all, but as long as Germaine was in the house, we were all dragged into her concerns. Dorothée lived separately with her mother and stepfather, of course, but they were always at our kitchen table, eating and conversing.

When I heard about the child, I invited her out of the city heat to our summer home. She had to come alone by bus. I first saw her when she was a six-year-old, with enormous blue eyes and flower-petal skin, a blond doll in a sweet little dress of pleated, soft material that was held at the shoulders with two large bows. She was playing around the back steps. I asked if she had been to our lake. She opened her eyes wide and shook her head silently. Germaine hadn't wanted to take her because it was a mile's walk, because she, Germaine, was an alien and could not speak to the neighbors, because Dorothée had no water toys to play with. So I got Dorothée a pail and a shovel, a little bathing suit and a cap, popped her into the car, and took her down to the playground by the water. She was shy at first but in no time was splashing with the other children, and she was happy. Then I took her driving to the farms around, where she helped buy vegetables and flowers and made the acquaintance of a domesticated yearling deer, which came to the car and put its long, soft, quivering nose on the window ledge and looked at us with enormous globular eyes under very straight, pale lashes. We stroked its nose, to Dorothée's astonishment and mine also, before it ambled off, casually nibbling two or three lilies and a phlox in the flowerbed on the way to the kitchen door.

Dorothée seemed happy, except that she was frightened of the raccoons that came every night for the food Germaine set out for them. They growled over the dishes and bared their teeth. Dorothée was under the impression that the older raccoons were trying to eat their young, and she had nightmares so intense that Germaine had to take her into her own bed and hold her close to keep her from shrieking with fear. This, I felt, was a curious and revealing dream for a child of six.

It was also a strange dream for a granddaughter of Germaine's, because Germaine was kin to all animals, domestic and wild. Her feeling for them was nearly uncanny, and their response was immediate. She never saw a creature but her hand went out, her voice changed, her eyes sparkled. She could communicate with all of them—with our domestic cats, whom she quickly made her familiars, and with the wild beasts in our forests, of which there were many. She would get them to feed from her—raccoons that would not approach any of the rest of us, porcupines, woodchucks, even the deer. If either of our cats was ill or hurt she became Florence Nightingale, inventing splints, inventing slings, inventing special little beds, and, oh my, inventing the most wonderful meals. They were always in her lap or around her neck or under her feet, and her news from this time on was equally divided between the well-being of her cats and the well-being of her granddaughter.

With the animals she was firm but patient, while always instinctive and kind; with Dorothée she was harsh and unsympathetic, her method of expressing maternal care being primitive. Discipline alternated with sudden, unlooked-for kindness. It was only the animals she could love with an untroubled heart. Yet Dorothée was the core of her life.

Dorothée grew to be a bonny girl, filling her grandmother with pride and her mother with jealousy. Then one day she fell and broke a tooth, and her mother began mocking her spoiled looks. Enormous tears formed in the child's eyes and rolled down her cheeks as she listened to the woman discuss how she had been beautiful and was now ugly. Geneviève wielded whatever power she had ruthlessly. Germaine never remonstrated; she, our lion, was intimidated too. Between Germaine's terror and Geneviève's irrational rages, Dorothée was doomed. Yet Germaine loved her.

As Dorothée grew older and more comely, Geneviève entered a program of deliberate denigration. Why? Because Dorothée had interfered with Geneviève's life, and because Geneviève was jealous of her husband's attention to the child. Germaine could do nothing because she had no rights. She expressed her distress in continued bad temper.

One day Germaine came to me and said with great emotion, "I've asked my son-in-law to come here and speak with you. He's walking out on Geneviève."

"It's none of my business."

"Do it. My English is not good enough."

We had an evening à trois, seated around the dining table. The poor boy was terribly embarrassed but quite firm. "I no longer love her. I can't bear her insane quarreling, her disagreeableness, and her mad jealousies. Why, she's even jealous of me and the baby. Every time I take Dorothée on my knees she throws a fit, and you know, Mrs. Prude"—he looked at me very soberly—"this will mean trouble for the little girl later on. She should have a father's love and care. She needs a man now."

"Yes, I know."

"I love that child and I want to take care of her. And Dorothée thinks I'm her father."

"Have you adopted her?" I said.

"No, I haven't, but I act like she was mine. I'm willing to take full responsibility for her, but Geneviève will not have it. She's unreasonable."

"But you did love Geneviève once?"

"Oh, yes, once I did, but now, no."

Germaine cut through all this chitchat. "Ask him if there is another woman."

"I don't want to ask him that."

"Do it!"

I apologized and mumbled the question.

"Absolutely not," said the young man. "No. I just have to get out of that house. I can't bear my life."

So he left, and then a few days later his voice was on the phone. "Don't let Germaine hear. Geneviève has taken the pills that she threatened to."

"Call the police. Go out into the street and get the neighbors—men, preferably. I'll call the police also."

I had to acquaint Germaine.

"I knew this would happen," she said quietly.

The police response was immediate. Bobby came with the little girl, as he couldn't leave her in the empty house and he couldn't leave her in the hospital lobby. He took us all to the emergency ward. There were four doctors working over Geneviève's stomach pumps, all the hideous apparatus purging the body of deadly poison. Germaine took one look and broke. She didn't dissolve, she cracked, and that's when I put my arms around her for the first time. Her body was as hard as a wall of bricks.

"She was so young! She was so beautiful! She was so hopeful!" We walked up and down and Germaine never yielded. She never softened or relaxed. The tears were squeezed out of her flesh, squeezed out of her eyeballs. They dropped like bullets.

So we left Geneviève there, the miserable little French girl, alone, with the stream of her light brown hair showing over the sheets and the serious doctors bending over her. I took Germaine, dazed and trembling, downstairs, and Bobby collected the small child, who sat with a comic book, bemused, amid the disheveled, bewildered, distraught, and frightened crowds of patients, and we three went back to my home in Bobby's jalopy.

The child was installed in Germaine's small bedroom, with the privilege of sleeping on our front sofa if she gathered up her sheets, blankets, and pillows in the morning and tidied them away neatly so there would be no trace of her during the daytime. I went out to find her a school and buy her a lunchbox, and she began to live with me, under the none-too-gentle care of her grandmother. They talked French like magpies in the kitchen. At least Germaine talked French; Dorothée answered in very ungrammatical English. She trotted off to school every morning with her little lunchbox, and when she returned in the afternoon, Germaine insisted that she stay alone in our apartment and not play with any other children in our lobby or in their apartments.

"Why not?" I asked.

"She's not of their class. She won't be able to keep them as friends."

"But now she's lonely."

"That makes no difference," said Germaine. "I do not wish her to associate with rich children."

If Dorothée disobeyed and went into other children's apartments, she was severely punished. Germaine punished her for nearly everything, and she punished her in the only way she could, by depriving her of food. Germaine was one of the best cooks in New York City and we did not stint in any way, but I think that child went hungry.

Geneviève got better and was released from the hospital. Dorothée went back to her.

Germaine spoke like Madame Rachel. Doom entered my room. "Bobby has a woman."

"I'm not surprised."

The next Sunday morning, when our forks full of Germaine's very good scrambled eggs were halfway to our mouths, Germaine came in with her raincoat on. "I've got to go to them," she said. An hour later there were open hysterics on the phone: "She's done it again."

I went into my litany. "Tell Dorothée to go into the street, get a neighbor," and so forth.

Germaine once more brought Dorothée to me. We resumed our sofa-lunchbox routine. My husband was frenzied.

"Can't we get rid of these people? Are we to be shackled by this sordid, depressing, deteriorating situation all our lives? This is not our concern. This is not our responsibility. Where is my peace and quiet? Where is the freedom of my home?" He was right, and I was ashamed. But these women were desperate.

Geneviève was now put into a closed psychiatric ward. I paid an outside doctor to visit her and give me a prognosis. He said, "She will not be well again for a long time. She cannot be released."

Germaine entertained the nineteenth-century view of insanity, which was that it was a shameful taint, a severe reflection on one's blood, worse than illegitimacy, worse than crime. How many of our great-grandparents' families had someone secretly hidden in an attic, about whom no one ever spoke? Germaine fought to deny that Geneviève had this mark of Satan on her. It meant that Dorothée would have it. It meant that somehow it was her own, Germaine's, fault. "My daughter is not crazy," she repeated over and over again. But in fact Geneviève was just that; she was, as Dorothée blithely put it, "quite cuckoo." Dorothée accepted this fact because it was the only way she could bear it. Germaine could not bear it, so she denied it.

Dorothée was a minor. Geneviève had total legal control.

At any talk of Germaine's adopting her granddaughter, Geneviève became uncontrollable. "Are you taking from me the one thing I have in the world, the only thing I have in my life, my little daughter?"

The doctors had reckoned without Germaine. In the middle of the central hospital lobby, in full view of about seventy-eight people—that is, nobody—Germaine delivered $1,150 cash to a doctor in charge, who put the money in the pocket of his white coat and released Geneviève into his own privately controlled clinic. She was discharged in a week without any reservations whatever, free to do as she wished.

Then she seemed to recover somewhat and took Dorothée back once more to the dreary, forlorn, and punishing regime that her home had come to mean. Geneviève even got a nine-to-five job, so Dorothée was left alone out in Metuchen.

Throughout this bizarre and unhappy interval my badly used husband continued miserable. He always referred to Germaine as Bijou ("Jewel"). We watched with a certain dismay her manipulations.

Germaine continued to be resourceful. She sent to France to get an old crone, a gentlewoman pushing seventy-five, whom she hired to come to America and keep house in Metuchen while Geneviève went to work, so that Dorothée would not be alone and would have hot dinners. The woman was fanatically religious; she went to mass twice every day and reserved her chief energies for turning Dorothée into a good Catholic.

Dorothée thereafter dutifully attended mass in preparation for her confirmation, but what progress she was making toward religious understanding it would be hard to say. Once, while the two of us were shopping, Dorothée and I found ourselves in front of St. Patrick's.

"Have you ever been into a great big cathedral?" I asked. She shook her head. "Then come."

We walked up one aisle and down the other and looked gravely at the chapels with the flickering lights.

"Who is the woman and the little baby who are all over this place?" Dorothée said.

"Has no one told you?" I asked. She shook her head. Evidently Madame Duval had overlooked a point or two.

Another item neglected was tooth-brushing. Dorothée never brushed.

"Madame," Madame Duval said to me, "Geneviève and her mother starve the child. They won't give her enough to eat. Dorothée goes through the garbage pails in the neighborhood, looking for something to eat."

When questioned, Germaine was indignant. She explained that Dorothée did go through the neighborhood garbage pails, but in search of returnable bottles for cash refunds. She laughed off all accusations.

The neighbors thought otherwise, and in due course a welfare officer called on us in New York. Germaine could not understand her, or pretended not to. I explained that Dorothée was a French national. "She is a minor," said the officer, a capable young woman, "and the people of New York have a concern for her welfare. Doesn't she get enough to eat?"

"What does she say?" said Germaine, standing with her needle eyes darting from me to the officer. "Tell me exactly what she says." I translated. Germaine went into voluble protestations, but she stood rebuked. Underscoring this humiliation was the undeniable fact that the officer was a black woman.

After she departed, Germaine gave full tongue to her rage and wounded vanity. "How dare *cette noire* question me!" Protestations, screams, expletives! "Dorothée is well loved," claimed Germaine. "She's a happy child. You should hear her when she's alone with us. She talks without stopping. She shouts with laughter. Look at all the pretty clothes I have bought for her." There they were in their cellophane wrappers, charming, *mignonne*, chic, as pristine as in a store — untouched dresses, a whole row of them, in Germaine's small closet.

"Why don't you give them to her?" I said.

"Her mother doesn't like me to give her anything. Her mother is jealous of me. She doesn't want her to be pretty."

Seeking only peace, Dorothée docilely said that she didn't want them, and Germaine was cut to the heart.

The little French caretaker, Madame Duval, even accused Geneviève of stealing the small presents that I gave to Dorothée.

"Stealing from the child?" I asked incredulously.

"Oh yes. And," Madame Duval continued, "they hit her." This Germaine categorically denied.

I asked Madame Duval, "Why doesn't the grandmother protect her from her crazy mother's tyranny?"

"Germaine is terrified of Geneviève."

"Germaine scared? Impossible."

"She is frightened of her. She has been frightened all her life."

I began to think she was right. Germaine was completely cowed.

My husband procured two tickets for the gala of four royal marching bands, the Black Watch and Massed Royal Pipers, at Madison Square Garden—a show he produced. Germaine and Dorothée were to have dinner out and go for a treat. Unfortunately, the morning of the appointed day Dorothée went with some schoolmates on some sort of junket and was late returning. Germaine waited, white with fury, her anger sharpened by terror of Geneviève's anticipated disapproval.

"Geneviève'll get over it in an hour," I said. To Dorothée I suggested, "Just be quiet and your grandmother will be sorry. She'll understand."

Dorothée stood at the window. Great tears slowly filled her blue eyes and streamed down her cheeks. "No," she said, "she won't."

And she didn't. When Walter got home at six to dress for the performance, the house was empty and silent. He made himself a sandwich and a glass of milk, then he heard a faint sound in the back bedroom. There he found Dorothée lying in the dark, alone.

"Why isn't the light on?" he said.

"My grandmother told me I mightn't have a light and I was to go to bed and stay there."

"Where is your grandmother?"

"She went to a movie."

"What about the Black Watch?"

"She's not going, and she won't let me go. She tore up the tickets."

"What about your dinner?"

"I'm not to have anything to eat."

"I'll get you something to eat."

"No, she'll see the crumbs."

"I'll clean up the crumbs. I'll clean up everything. You've got to eat." He got her a sandwich, then took her empty milk glass and plate away and washed them. Dorothée remained in the dark, alone and silent.

We were watching a small, lovely girl being maimed and warped in our own household. When a child has been thwarted and intimidated for years, she does not become a pouting Shirley Temple; she is damaged. Dorothée was becoming dazed and dull — as some said, "not bright" — the alertness and gaiety of childhood glazed over by a film of apprehension. She expected disappointment and was quite convinced she deserved nothing else.

I went to a lawyer and asked, "What can I do?"

"Short of legally adopting her, nothing."

"Short of adoption, can't we legally get her away from her mother?"

"It would be very tough. The woman is not certifiably insane."

I took Dorothée to a psychoanalyst. I took her to a dentist. Both entailed major expense, which neither Germaine nor Geneviève saw any need to share. They didn't mind if I was wanton enough to take sole responsibility.

I worried. I worried without cease. In fact, I was horrified. It was not in my pattern to sidestep trouble. My ever-present terror was of physical harm to the girl. Geneviève was mentally disturbed — insane, in old-fashioned parlance — and therefore legally forgivable, but aside from this mitigating fact and judging by her effect on other lives, she was the only truly evil person I have ever known.

If Germaine took any action on Geneviève's behalf, there were always pills that Germaine had not been able to find; Geneviève had a secret source, a hidden cache. A foster home or school for Dorothée seemed indicated, but both Germaine and Geneviève rose screaming at the suggestion, because of the expense and because they would lose their rights.

At this point Madame Duval returned to France. By way of notification, she phoned me from the airport, explaining only, "I can't stand it."

Germaine was abandoned without any help and with half the money she had advanced to the old lady unearned. Her rage was worthy of the seventeenth century. "*Cette bigotte!* What does she care about anybody, or her promise, or her obligations?"

Dorothée came back to our parlor sofa.

Germaine began thinking and planning again. She had relatives in France, and she arranged with one of them to take Dorothée, who was now eleven, and place her in a foster home in the heart of the French countryside. Very shortly the child was sent off to a land she had not seen since she was three, to relatives she had never met, who spoke a language she did not know. She went with a tag tied around her neck.

Germaine wrote her a long letter to read on the plane and on the bus. It was explicit and detailed, and, by God, in English, about arriving in France, about going through customs ("Is not this fun? Yes, this is fun. This is new and different and lots of fun"), about taking the bus to Paris and how to pay ("You now use francs and sous and centimes. Is this not fun? Yes, this is fun"). The letter continued: "In Paris Cousin Marie will meet you" (and *grace à dieu* Cousin Marie did—a child she had never seen). "Now you will go on a train from the Gare de Lyon. The train is different from American trains," and so on. "Now you will meet Madame Hatelier. She is very nice. She will take care of you," and so on.

Dorothée was met and was eventually installed in a home with eight other foster children of different sorts—some from Tunis, some from Algiers, some from the north of France; a mixed bag. On the fourteenth of July, Bastille Day, Dorothée, decorated with the tricolor, beat a drum in a parade through the town, and Germaine breathed easier. She all but broke open champagne.

Dorothée was happy. She had met a truly kind and good woman, Madame Hatelier. To this day Dorothée speaks of this woman as one of the four people who tried to save her. For the first time she was cared for with motherly understanding, without sudden scoldings and deprivations. She was surrounded with foster brothers and sisters, and she stopped being frightened.

But Germaine couldn't leave a good situation alone. In winter, just before Christmas, when Dorothée was making happy preparations, Germaine had a falling-out with Madame Hatelier—about money, of course—and decided to investigate personally. She forbade me, absolutely forbade me, to forewarn the French family. She descended on them without a word of advance notice, had a bitter quarrel, and accused Madame Hatelier of dishonesty. She said that Dorothée was living in an airless and windowless cupboard. (This was not true; my son had visited Dorothée to report.) Germaine placed Dorothée in a taxi, with the help of a man who acted like a policeman, and drove her away. Dorothée was crying and beating on the glass, while her foster mother stood in the street, wailing and shrieking, with arms extended, and the other children gathered weeping around her.

Then, by way of a Christmas present, Germaine acquainted Dorothée with certain facts of her life: for instance, that Bobby, whom she had always looked on and loved as her real father, was in fact not her father at all; that she was not ever again to speak to him, write to him, or see him; that he had deserted both Dorothée and her mother; that he was a no-good bum. Germaine then placed Dorothée in a French boarding school.

The next June Dorothée came back from France to spend the summer with Germaine and us in the country, and she could not speak one word of English, not one. "Hein?" she would say like her grandmother. "Hein?"

"She is faking this," said my husband. "That child could not forget her English. Why, it's her mother tongue. She is twelve years old. She has spoken only English for nine years."

"This is trauma," I said. "She is wiping out the American experience. It was too unbearable for her."

"Nonsense," said my husband.

In the autumn Germaine told Dorothée that she must stay in America with her mother, no matter whether she spoke English or not. This was obligatory. The girl immediately began speaking English. It seemed Walter had been right.

So now Dorothée had to live with her mother, because her mother was lonely, and because it was cheaper, and Dorothée entered a life of real duress and privation. Geneviève suddenly decided she could not bear to live under her mother's roof (even if Germaine was not often present), so she left abruptly. Since she had paid for the telephone, she tore the instrument out of the wall, cut the wires, and took it away, together with every kitchen and household appliance that could be moved. Dorothée was movable and was also yanked along.

Germaine's heart broke. She had made a tremendous effort, rescuing her daughter from the hospital, bringing the old-lady caretaker from France, sending Dorothée back to France and establishing her in a foster home, then arranging further French schooling, bringing her back here again, and helping to maintain the Metuchen home life the while. For the various enterprises she had paid out a good part of her life savings, and the result was that Geneviève shut her out completely and that her granddaughter did not love her, or dared not say she did. Her life had lost its purpose. She gave up all personal vanity, all interest, and retreated to her small, cluttered room, which was stuffed with bits of string, letters, empty perfume bottles, empty medicine bottles, spools of thread, golfballs, torn clothes, recipes, refuse, old French newspapers ("They will be a comfort to me in my old age"). They choked all space and were a fire hazard (Germaine smoked). She spent her time brooding over her lot, her cursed daughter and her hardhearted granddaughter. The row of beautiful little doll-like dresses hung untouched and immaculate in the filthy untidyness.

Germaine's entire emotional release was now restricted to the cats. But animals are short-lived, and during this forlorn decrescendo the beloved cats died. She took each loss with desperate sorrow, as though part of her life had been destroyed, and procured, at great expense, glazed photographs of them, putting them up in our garden as in a French cemetery. She also pulled up my best flowers and transplanted them to the graves.

She existed like a ghost, a very fat one, in the back room. She had started on a dreadful descent; she developed a bad hernia, cancer (hence the hysterectomy), varicose veins. She made a futile trip to France for treatment, against the American doctor's advice.

With deepening dejection she grew fatter. When she had first come to us she had been a comely woman, and when dressed to go out she had looked Parisian and almost dashing. Not now, not now. She had abandoned all physical pride along with hope. Her body was degenerating, and she didn't give a damn. She just ate. She ate unrestrainedly. She outgrew all the uniforms I gave her. We had to get her more. Then we had to get them made for her. They were always without buttons, ragged. Her uncombed hair hung in straggles. She didn't care. She had quarreled with all her cronies until there remained nobody she could go to see on her days off. Dorothée no longer came to visit. She herself never went to Geneviève. She was not interested in movies (unless French) or TV (unless French). On her days off she went back into her cubicle, closed the door, and made sorties only for food. She acted as though she were not there.

But of course she was there, and her presence in the house was pervasive, like something fetid and dying, a decay at the heart of our household, and ever present. If I was working quietly in my room up front, I knew she was back there, going over her notebooks, figuring how to make a little more money by buying stamps and selling them again, by buying coins cheap and selling them again, by buying some fly-by-night American stock—figuring, figuring.

"I must have some money for my old age," she said, "and I don't want Geneviève to get any of it. The house is not for her. I want Dorothée to have the house."

"Be sure you leave this in a will. Geneviève is the next in line to inherit."

"Never," she cried, "never! My life will be wasted if that happens."

"Leave it in writing. Germaine, would you consider dieting?"

She gave a short, bitter laugh. Oh, the bitterness of that laugh! "My life is no good." With that she went back in her room and shut the door.

She said over and over, like a litany, the answer to all, "Ma fille n'est pas folle"; my daughter is not mad. In other words, "It's not my fault."

Most wonderful to tell, she still produced meals of haute cuisine. We entertained the élite of the international music and theater world, financiers, statesmen, and friends from everywhere. Did any of our friends ever suspect that behind the façade of these polite dinners was a household crawling with grief and rot, working with decay like a maggot heap?

Germaine's unpunctuality grew maddening, her insolence insupportable. I would rebuke her, and she would simply raise her eyebrows, depart without a word, and go back to bed until there was something vital to compel her to leave it.

I began putting down her defaults in my diary. One day, to my astonishment and anger, I found written across the pages of my diary in red ink and in French, "This is not true. It is not my fault. None of this is true." She had read the diary, which was written in English; she had understood the diary; she took exception to it, and she had had the extreme gall to annotate it after her own fashion.

Why did Germaine do it? It amounted to an open dare. Did she want to be fired? Did she want to be forced from our house? Or did she want to humble me? I cannot answer, as I cannot explain now why I did not fire her. I was occupied twenty-four hours a day with another Broadway show, but to hell with that! My self-respect was in question, as was my husband's tranquillity. I cannot say. I am sure Germaine derived satisfaction from my silence and smiled to herself grimly at my weakness, the final verification of her pride, her proof that she was as good as I. Yet she was fond of me, I truly believe she was. She took pride in my successes.

"I'm sorry for her," I said as a vindication for keeping her. But that was not the whole reason, and everyone knew it.

"And Germaine is a superlative cook." But that was not the reason either. Certainly it wasn't a good enough reason to offset the extraordinary daily aggravation of the woman.

No. Germaine set up a constant challenge, a combat that somehow my spirit needed, a strong zone of struggle that was not in any heartbreaking personal area but more or less superficial, and in which I could exercise all my faculties without really jeopardizing my essential sensitivity. Somehow she imposed a penance on me which I felt obliged to pay. It was my festering spot, and Germaine with sure, black instinct had found it, as Geneviève had found hers.

Dorothée graduated from the Dickens period and entered her Victor Hugo era. She was left alone all day. She was forbidden to use the telephone, and to make sure she wouldn't, her mother put a lock on it. Then, believing that Dorothée had figured out how to pick the lock, Geneviève detached the phone from the wall. I was at our country place and managed to send Dorothée the change to call me collect from a pay phone. The calls often cost over $40. Then the mother not only locked the phone, she locked the apartment in the daytime, and Dorothée was forced to stay in the basement with oatmeal to eat. Forbidden to play with any other children, she invented imaginary friends and gave them little parties, at which she served them by dividing the cereal into three or four sections and then eating each section as a different character. When her mother came home from work in the evening, Dorothée was marched straight into the kitchen and told to get supper and clean the dishes. She was half-starved.

I arranged a method by which I could send her letters so that Geneviève should not know, and I enclosed cash so that she could buy snacks and phone me, and subway tokens so that she could go to her grandmother. Her mother would not let her come up to the country. "No," she said, "this is a hard summer for me. Dorothée has to take the bitter with the better. It's not fair that she should just have fun."

But in August, when the heat was at its worst and the summer was full, Germaine managed to get Dorothée away, and she came to the green woods, the streams, and the lake, and we welcomed her.

On the third night of her stay, my husband asked for a second helping of salad. Dorothée came from the kitchen to tell him there was no more.

"There must be," he said. "I picked the lettuce myself. There are bowls full of it."

"No," she said.

He threw down his napkin and went angrily into the kitchen, where Germaine was sitting complacently. "I want some more lettuce and I'm told there is none."

She started to protest, in French.

"Talk English to me," he shouted. "You understand perfectly well. Speak English. Where is our dinner?"

She smiled at him provocatively.

Then his temper broke. My husband was a Texan, and when he got angry he was formidable. His fury outdistanced anything Germaine could produce.

"You wicked, insolent, selfish, mean, conniving woman!"

he shouted at her. "You've made my wife ill with your aggravation, your perversities. You make my life, my personal life at home, unbearable. You've turned our household into something unclean. I won't have it. Get out of here! I give you until nine o'clock tomorrow morning to be out of here, bag and baggage. You will take the bus and go back to New York and we will settle up the business later. Just get out! Both of you!" And with that he grabbed her by the arm and shook her.

Then he came back to the table and with trembling hands served himself the rest of the lettuce. "Kiss me," he said triumphantly.

I rushed out into the kitchen. Both Germaine and Dorothée were standing shaking, without speaking. Dorothée turned and ran into the dark garden. I followed, put my arms around her, and held her. She was as rigid as Germaine.

"None of this is your fault," I said. "None."

"I know," she said.

"You have to be strong."

"Oh, yes," she said. "I must be strong." It was the voice of a fifty-year-old woman.

I went to Walter in his room. "Can't we do something?"

"I am so happy to get my own house back again, to get my own wife back. Find an English-speaking cook, and let's be done with Germaine. This has gone on for eleven years, and it's torture." All of which was absolutely true. He had been badly served. His home life had become abominable.

I went down to the little house in the woods where Dorothée was in bed looking at her stamp book, quietly, alone. I don't know what I said to her. What could I say? There she was alone, playing with her stamps. Germaine told me that Dorothée had stolen some of Germaine's best stamps to enhance her collection. Well, the poor child had to steal this and that. They let her have nothing of her own.

The next morning when I went into the kitchen, expecting to get breakfast myself, there sat Germaine cozily, with the kettle on and a stray cat in her lap.

"Where's Dorothée?"

"She's gone," said Germaine. "She took the early morning bus back to Geneviève's place."

"And you?"

Germaine said, "Madame, please sit down. Think of the years I've been with you." She started the most dulcet, heart-breaking, persuasive, extraordinary . . . well, in short, it was agreed that she would stay on, more or less on sufferance. She would no longer live in our house; she would live in her own house. The compromise meant that she would take another job, that she would come to us only for two days a week and then only in the evening.

Some time later I had a stroke. This was a major physical disaster, and it had me in the hospital at the point of death for three and a half months. Everything in my life and my family's life came to an abrupt halt. My husband ate not one meal at home, but dashed off in the morning to work and went from work directly to floor 18 of the hospital. He gave Germaine her notice.

She came to see me in the hospital, her arms full of her own garden roses: "Pauvre Madame Prude!" She had come to talk money, but it was difficult for me to talk to her because I'd had a massive cerebral hemorrhage and my French was now extremely halting, as was my English.

Germaine was bitter about having been given her leave "three months before her pension was due." What she meant by that, I have no idea. "This was not chic of Monsieur." Well, I'm sure he also hadn't a clue as to what she meant. I'm equally sure it had to do with cheating welfare.

Dorothée, now a teenager, was living with her mother in the hellhole she called home. A welfare officer investigated to see how she lived and found them in a small flat, very neat, the mother as always complaining. The officer tried to protest and could not get a word in. Geneviève cut her short and shouted, "If the girl doesn't like it, she can get out!"

Dorothée rose quietly. "I'm ready to go."

The welfare officer said, "You want to leave home?"

And she said yes and walked out the door. Geneviève was astonished but remained unmoving.

The welfare officer took Dorothée's hand. "Get your belongings, child, and we'll leave."

"I have no belongings," said Dorothée.

"You have nothing you want to take with you?"

"Not a thing." So they left.

Geneviève recounted this to me in indignation. "She is so mean and unnatural, she didn't even glance back at her cat, the cat she said she adored."

Dorothée went to live with a schoolmate, and the state paid for foster care. She ran away and gradually drifted onto the streets. She began running around with older men. She even played around with drink and drugs. But some deep self-saving instinct came to her help. One of her friends spoke of a Catholic home where they took in waifs and gave them an education. Dorothée went up to the house in Westchester, New York, and there she came under the supervision of a remarkable priest who had had training in psychiatric work. She poured out her heart to him: the long, dreadful summers, being forbidden to telephone, being locked away in the basement, being forbidden to have friends or to play. He understood. He helped. The whole school helped.

Dorothée studied quietly but, alas, not well. Along her dreadfully cruel way, she had lost the power to concentrate. Her attention splintered. Schoolwork did not interest her; jobs did not interest her—she was unable to stick to typing, to machine work, to clerical work, to clerking in a store. She had grown mentally listless—in popular parlance, "dumb." She didn't like any kind of work except, and this is curious, the care of retarded children. At this she was very good.

Then she fell in love with a schoolbus driver who had been living with a common-law wife by whom he had had four children, and whose hobby was seducing young girls. The driver tired of Dorothée in a couple of months. Reluctant to go back to school and refusing to go to her relatives, she took a wretched room in a northern town far from Metuchen, preferring a long series of bad and even dangerous jobs to life with her mother or grandmother.

Dorothée's yearning for affection led her into friendships with derelict girls and their transient lovers, and these last stole from her without scruple. She was neither surprised nor outraged. She expected to be rejected. She was no longer in touch with her priest, nor with any of her old schoolmates. In reality, she was out of touch with everyone.

She had grown into a svelte, lissom, fair-haired young woman with an innocent and honest face. Her voice was common, her speech coarse and ungrammatical but not low or foul. As she was quite pretty she was vulnerable. At this point she could certainly have gone bad. She could have started thieving. She could have started whoring. She could have taken to drink or drugs. She did none of these things. Throughout her long pilgrimage she remained scrupulously honest, although failing, unhappy, and alone; as honest as Germaine had always been. She maintained a certain primitive dignity. There were things she would not do. There were matters she would not touch. It was quite wonderful to behold, and to think about.

Furthermore, Dorothée, who was not quite smart enough to hold down a salesgirl's job, who had seemingly learned nothing, had acquired what Germaine only partially understood and Geneviève had no suspicion of: she had learned compassion. She got in touch with her stepfather, Bobby, and was invited to Arkansas, but out of consideration for his new family she stayed only a few days. She tried to trace her real father, learned he had a wife, and desisted. Madame Hatelier, her foster mother, offered her money and asylum, but knowing of the good woman's straitened circumstances, and with a heart overflowing with gratitude, Dorothée declined, although she was in dire need.

During this time, in all about seven years, Dorothée never received a word from her mother or grandmother—not a

Christmas card, not a birthday card, not any letters. As far as her family was concerned, she could have been dead.

Germaine was now alone, living on a pension with no friends, no TV (all TV was of course in English), no newspapers, no family, marketing only with great difficulty every third day, talking only to cats. How did she tell night from day? What could she participate in? What did she think about? She had no intellect. The dreary agonizing questions: Should she disinherit Dorothée or Geneviève, whom she hated? Why didn't Dorothée write? Hadn't she been good to her? Didn't Dorothée know she loved her? She caressed the cat in her lap. How much longer would she be able to clean the kitty litter? Or buy the kitty food? How much longer? Oh, Dorothée! Germaine was imprisoned in a seamless room, but she would not be the first to write. She had her pride. Pride was the reason that French peasants had withstood armies and revolutions and bad government and corrupt generals. It was rocklike immobility: they intended to survive.

One evening at our house in Merriewold the telephone rang, and to my astonishment it was Germaine. She was very sick and semiparalyzed, she said, and quite alone. Social workers were looking after her. She had just discovered that Dorothée had written postcards to her all along, but that her daughter had deliberately removed the addresses. Geneviève, wishing to break up all intercourse between the two, had also destroyed letters from Dorothée. Germaine now wanted to get in touch with Dorothée immediately. I promised to have Dorothée phone her that night.

I was very uneasy. Germaine's voice had changed. It was weak and colorless. There was that dark fraying that presaged doom. I called Dorothée and said, "Please go to her. Somehow go. Hurry." But Dorothée said she couldn't go immediately.

Two days later Germaine was found by the welfare worker lying dead on the floor beside her walker. She was quite alone when she died, hoping no doubt that Dorothée would get to her in time. The cause given was cancer of the stomach. The police notified Geneviève, who telephoned the news to Dorothée. It was the first time she had spoken to her daughter in seven years.

I told Dorothée to sit tight and that I would get her a good lawyer, who seemed to be the most needed person in this morass. The real property looked to be worth, we supposed, about $100,000, and there were in addition Germaine's caches of coins, stamps, papers, and goodness knows what odds and ends. These were unsorted but valuable, hidden under beds, hidden in boxes, hidden in fireboxes, hidden in the backs of closets. The police had put a seal on the house; no one could enter without a warrant.

I got Dorothée a very good lawyer from one of the top firms. He was young and French-speaking. Dorothée went to his office, a suite on Fifth Avenue that embraced three floors of Rockefeller Center, wearing sneakers and dungarees, with a clothesline around her waist and chewing gum. He got a police permit for her, and together they searched Germaine's house for a will. None was to be found. Germaine's lawyer, who was also Geneviève's, disclaimed all knowledge of any will. Indeed, he said that Germaine had never made one — which is, of course, a possibility, as it would have cost a little money.

Dorothée also found not a trace of any of the papers, coins, or stamps. Was it likely that Germaine, who squirreled away everything, would not have carefully guarded what was of real value? I had helped her every summer carry the boxes containing her treasures to the safe-deposit vaults in my bank, to be retrieved in the autumn and placed under her bed. Or had she sold them? And her will? Involved was her house and Dorothée's future. Not a trace? We felt certain she would have guarded that.

Dorothée said there was a secret back door to the house, not sealed, which led to the garage, and if one knew about it one could easily achieve entry. She suspected that Geneviève had been there immediately after the death. In any case, as there seemed to be no will, New Jersey State law would take effect automatically, and the next of kin—that is, Geneviève—would get everything.

In the meantime, Germaine's wasted body, no longer fat—she had been unable to eat—lay in a morgue, and no one was doing a thing about getting it out. At the last legal moment Geneviève recovered it and took it to a mortuary. There was a funeral, for which Dorothée came back to town, this time with her new boyfriend, who was forbidden to sit anywhere near the family. The mourners consisted of Geneviève and Dorothée and, adjacent, the young man.

The coffin was open. Germaine now weighed 118 pounds, she who had previously weighed 310. Dorothée said she would never have recognized the wizened little face, which retained no trace of the terror of our household. Germaine was sunk in her coffin, a pathetic, old, unwanted woman about to be buried in a local cemetery, a Frenchwoman who had longed with all her heart to lie in French soil, to go back to her mother, and who had saved up for this purpose; a woman who had wanted a peaceful old age with her granddaughter and a few chosen French friends with whom to denounce de Gaulle at ease.

The lawyer explained to Dorothée what she must do about getting some of the money, but the process involved a good deal of paperwork and telephoning, and Dorothée was occupied at the moment with another worry: she was pregnant, and she most certainly was not married. So Geneviève got everything, took everything, profited by everything. It turned out to be not so very much. Germaine had been quietly selling her possessions.

Dorothée bore her child with great ease. It was a son, and was baptized by Dorothée's beloved priest, with Geneviève in attendance (she brought one small, inexpensive toy). The boy was named Gérald, for Germaine. All Dorothée's worries and dissatisfaction seemed to drop from her on the instant. She and the young father struck up a household but did not marry, which proved more or less satisfactory, and in due course Dorothée had a little girl, whom she named Geneviève. The beloved Father christened her too. Madame Duval, the *bigotte*, would have been pleased.

Life had dealt hardly with Dorothée. She took her revenge on society in a perfectly legal way. She bred her children illegitimately; society paid for them through welfare, and she lived on this toll. I imagine there was considerable satisfaction for her in doing so. Nobody ever had done anything kind for her except in the way of charity. It was her right to demand the welfare, and she did demand it and did take it regularly.

Dorothée at last had come into her proper heritage. She had won out in the dreadful three-way lifelong struggle—she, the weak one, the helpless one, who asked so little and was given nothing. Her children will not speak good English and they will speak no French, and whatever else they know will be by accident, but they will be devotedly cared for. It is Dorothée who knows. Totally without bitterness, she knows how to love.

The Father told me this might happen.

OLD NEW YORK

MY GREATEST GIFT, I believe, is my memory, which is obviously long, but also accurate and highly visual. I learned to remember in color, and, what is much rarer, I learned to remember in sequence. The fact that I fitted words to my memories, that my parents were both highly verbal and my father memorable in his remarks, acted as a kind of preservative for very much of what happened, so that the New York of the early part of this century is quite real and vivid to me. The world of women in which I grew up, having a younger sister, female cousins, and many aunts and later being sent to a girls' school, was impressed on me in all its aspects. I shared in the exhilaration and the suffering and the risk of the century's tide.

I was born in 1905 in New York City, on 118th Street in Harlem, at that time a quiet middle-class white neighborhood. All our neighbors were white, different kinds of white. There were no specific black communities anywhere in New York then. Indeed, there were few blacks. The recent Jewish immigrants lived mostly on the East Side in the Bowery district, the Chinese nearby, strictly close to the Bowery, the Italians in the West Village, Germans and Hungarians on East 86th Street, and Irish Catholics everywhere. The Irish were servants or policemen, or, when affluent, ran bars or city government. There were lots of them, but there were few Latinos. Harlem was "pure" middle-class American, and our flat was close to Morningside Park, where we went walking in the mornings with our nurses and learned to hopscotch and roller-skate and where street boys played games in the dirt with extravagant multicolored marbles called aggies.

Above to the west jutted the rock on which stretched Morningside Heights and the Cathedral of St. John the Divine, not yet finished but well begun, with truncated towers and interrupted transept waiting. On the roof of the completed Lady Chapel an angel triumphantly blew her horn against the New York sky. She was high above us, and she was the last thing we saw against the darkening west and the first thing we saw each day as the morning sun gilded her wings and her raised trumpet. That angel was our guardian and our promise.

We lived in a railroad flat, rather dark, very long, and extremely ugly, but with conveniences — some quite surprising, some we don't have today: the dumbwaiter in the kitchen, for instance, which brought us milk, fresh milk, in nice glass bottles every morning, right up to the icebox, and all our meat and groceries right up to the stove and kitchen worktable. All deliveries were free, of course. The icebox was wood, with a zinc-lined chest at the top into which the ice man dumped, every other day, a large block which he carried, balanced and dripping, on a shoulderpad of a folded burlap bag. He wrestled this with large iron tongs into our box, chipped it down to size, and wedged it there.

We had three bathrooms, two very nice ones and the smallest for the maids. This was scarcely more than a sunless closet that contained the barest raison d'être and a tiny window giving onto a brick wall, admitting little air and no sun. At that, it was more luxury than the maids had ever known in the Home Country. Each room boasted electricity from a bulb hanging in the center of the ceiling—an execution light. There were additional globes, wired down to the sides by my mother for more kindly illumination. Every room also contained a gas jet, which we never used but which was there just in case, because about electricity you never could tell.

Just as you never could tell about the telephone. We had one, cumbersome and not always reliable. But we could call anywhere in New York City easily; Orange, New Jersey, after a little wait; Philadelphia after a longer wait. The western cities were out of the question, but to anywhere out of town it was more expeditious to send a telegram, which would be delivered within two hours—a neatly folded brown paper in an envelope, written in a florid but legible hand at a cost, I believe, of ten cents. Transcontinental telegrams cost a quarter. These telegrams were delivered by small boys in special Western Union or Postal Telegraph caps, caps that entitled the wearers to free subway rides and free entry into baseball games (the bleacher section of a ballgame cost fifty cents, the subway ride five cents). The owners of the caps may have earned only pennies, but they were members of the élite.

Mail was delivered two times daily; a letter cost two cents, a postcard one cent. A letter addressed within New York City usually arrived at its destination the same day, but without fail the following morning. In London a letter posted before noon always arrived the same day, and frequently the reply was delivered that very night. Of course there was no expediting machinery or computers to help in the delivery, and of course the postman's sons did not go to Harvard or Oxford.

Because my father was a playwright, young and unseasoned although quite successful, he was a man of limited means and precarious income. We were a family of four and could afford to employ only what was considered a very modest staff: a full-time live-in cook and a full-time nurse, a weekly cleaning woman, and a weekly laundress. (The washing was done in great tubs in the kitchen, taken to the apartment roof in fine weather, and hung there on lines. As a result, all the roofs of the apartment houses of New York were ablow with sheets and petticoats. In bad weather the laundry was strung out on lines in blind back airways and manipulated by pulleys from the kitchen window.) Mother helped all the time in cooking, household mending, marketing, family shopping, supervising, and minding the children. Mother kept very busy.

My father could easily afford all the necessary salaries, because the laundress received fifty cents an hour, the cleaning woman twenty-five cents, and the Irish cook and the Irish nurse $10 a week each for their full-time services. They were given their meals and their beds, and they had half a day off every week and a full day off every two weeks. As I recall, there was no summer vacation. I do not know about sick leave or sick pay. I do not remember their ever being sick. No doubt Mother ministered to them if they were. They were there and busy, and we always had hot meals, home cooked, and we children were taken out twice a day for walks and play, in hot or cold weather. We were given cold baths every morning and castor oil when indicated, in great tablespoons, with orange juice or root beer as a disguise (no help). We also got cod liver oil once a day, in a tablespoon, without cause, no matter what. And we had fresh air, fresh air, fresh air. My mother was insane about it. One could have fresh air then, even in the city. One came home all blown and healthy to the comfort of Service.

And one had fun. New York then was lively and picturesque and colorful. It is more practical now, as well as more astonishing and frightening, but it was more varied then. All the street noises were fun and more diverting then, not ear-splitting or mind-deadening. The fire engines, which now stop conversation or thought, then invited participation; they were drawn by live horses. These remarkable animals were trained at the first alarm to leave their comfortable stalls unaided and stand waiting in the traces of the engines until buckled into harness, as was explained to us when the Horace Mann School third-graders visited the fire station. The firemen slept upstairs, in the firehouse, we were told, and when the alarm sounded they dressed in a matter of seconds, because their pants stood ready in their boots. Then they slid down a brass pole to the ground floor, clapping their firehats on their heads and shouldering their big coats as they rushed to the engine. In less than a minute they were out and away. A little French boy in our class interrupted to ask, "But what if they were in the toilet?" We looked at him with wonder. He had dared to ask the unmentionable. We were all dying to know, but he had actually voiced it, I suppose because he was French. The fire chief smiled. "We have arranged for those situations," he said, and explained nothing.

But the glory of those engines and the accompanying pumper, which had to be manned by hand! I often saw the engines in action. Under the wheels of the engine and under the hoofs of the galloping horses ran a black-and-white dalmatian, a "plum pudding" dog. The dogs were also housed in the fire stations and had a soothing effect on the horses, I was told, and very possibly on the firemen. Beside the driver, who had to be unusually expert, sat a fireman with the rope of the bell in his hand, which he pulled rhythmically, sounding an alarm that superseded every other noise in New York. It was the sound of this tocsin that maddened the horses into a frenzy of superequine effort. They snorted and pawed the earth, and good Lord, how they galloped, insane to get to the smoke! There was a ladder truck, with the firemen standing on the running board and hanging onto leather straps, and a hose and pump truck, with firemen standing in back and hanging onto whatever they could. They went hell for leather, to find on arrival, very often, insufficient pressure at the fire hydrants, and in winter no pressure at all because the pipes iced over. I forget what they did then, besides curse and pray. The engines get places more quickly now, and buildings are seldom found on arrival to be in ashes, which is undeniably a good thing, but the process of saving them was certainly more entertaining then: four to six galloping horses and an engine shooting sparks! Wow!

The white wings, street cleaners, went down the streets twice every day in their white suits and with their little carts of rakes, brushes, brooms, and horse manure. They did not have a call or a bell; the horses could be relied on to provide them with work without notification. They were our city house cleaners, and they were as comforting to have around as any good domestics.

There were a great many street vendors of fruit and flowers and candy and drinks, and their calls and cries filled the air. And the knife-grinder! There were street organs, mostly turned by Italians, and their sound too could be heard. Sometimes the organ-grinders had monkeys dressed up with perky little hats, begging donations.

Occasionally came the sound of a piano through an open window, and this was a delight, because many people played well in those days, there being no mechanical music except now and then a player piano — but that was too vulgar for consideration. There was always something nostalgic and dulcet about personally made tunes, good or bad, heard at a distance and filtered through the sounds of busy street life.

There were other things to hear: trolley cars, with their bells ringing (on Broadway, Sixth Avenue, Eighth Avenue, Ninth Avenue); the rumble of buses, the fine two-deckers, and on Fifth Avenue the top decker, which was open to the sights and to the weather; the racket and banging of overhead railways on Third Avenue, Sixth Avenue, Ninth Avenue, and Amsterdam Avenue. These structures cut the light from all the adjacent buildings and, with their numerous iron supports, complicated the street traffic. But they did permit one to get downtown quickly.

And boys calling "Extra!" at times of crisis—they could be heard, always at the end of the streets, as windows flew up and heads appeared. "What happened?" "Who?" "Read all abaht it."

Fairly frequently from alleyways there came the unmistakable clang of a blacksmith's anvil and the clatter of a newly shod horse proudly stamping back into the streets. These sounds have completely gone from our life.

One could hear all this in the New York streets, to the end of a block, and although everybody complained, of course, about the din of the city, compared to today it was country silence. In addition, one came in from whatever noise there was to peace, absolute silence. There was no noise in the homes, none at all, there being no vacuum cleaners or Waring mixers or air conditioners or, Lord be praised, radio or TV. Indoors was quiet and restful, unless one made a rumpus oneself.

The stores then were different from the stores today, especially the food shops. To begin with, the shops were small and cozy—meat on one side, fresh and canned vegetables on the other. There were only a very few large stores of many departments, and these were situated way downtown at Herald Square, where Macy's and Gimbel's were, and they were truly marvelous. They had everything. They were Big Business.

That was where the *New York Daily Herald* was printed, in a beautiful two-story building, a kind of pavilion, designed by Stanford White, with ground-floor and basement windows of plate glass through which one could watch the late edition coming off the presses and being folded, gathered in piles, and stacked. Outside, two bronze workmen hammered a great bronze bell every hour, with reverberating and resonant clangs, deep and full-throated. All the busy pedestrians stopped to watch, and the bronze men never missed a stroke. They are still now, and this fine bell never speaks, but stands opposite a silent Horace Greeley, who, a perch for pigeons and hoary with their droppings, looks disconsolately at his dirtied shoes.

As to the uptown shops, the shops in our neighborhood, fruit and vegetables were not nearly so plentiful, certainly, nor so varied, nor by any means so exotic as we know now. Fruit was within season and it was limited geographically, and vegetables, except for potatoes, were limited by the season. All the summer vegetables disappeared with the autumn and were gone for months. Of course there was no frozen food. Look at the shelves of any supermarket and visualize just what this loss would mean. We used tins or home preserves, but preserved food was supposed to be not so nutritious, not even quite safe.

There was no nonsense about keeping merchandise out of reach. It was supposed to be poked, smelled, patted, even tasted, and to this end it lay invitingly open, uncellophaned and accessible to all, including small boys who thieved. And to flies. The shopkeepers took care of the children; long strips of sticky yellow paper hanging from above made a show of warding off the flies. The paper was soon as thick with black lumps as currant cake, but fresh ones were always zooming in.

The shops were redolent with the smell of freshly ground coffee beans (no tins) and tea, spicy and fragrant, in large japanned chests from the Far East (no dinky teabags). Standing around were great glass jars of candies and sugardrops (unwrapped).

Bakeries were good and plentiful, particularly the small shops known as home bakeries. Some of the big chains, however, had been established. Cushman's was worth the walk up to 125th Street for its charlotte russe, which I relished to the point of ecstasy (pale pink preferred). It was reserved as a reward for exceptional behavior.

Delicatessens flourished.

Butcher shops were forthright, the meat being hacked up in full view of passersby by fat-fingered men with bloody hands and bloody aprons. We were not so squeamish about the fact of butchery in those innocent but robust days. We ate flesh; we faced the fact. There was sawdust all over the floor and a great bloodied chopping block conspicuously displayed, on which the meat was cut according to individual specification and weighed carefully in front of each customer. For five cents extra one could get a large bunch of soup greens, and bones, including marrow bones, were free. There was no refrigeration anywhere, except in the stalls where meat was hung, and also occasionally for oysters. In the storage bins the meat was cold and preserved in good order, but once brought into view, it was on its own.

Mysterious and awe-inspiring drugstores displayed bottles and tins of unmentionables and castor oil, and enormous glass jars of colored liquid, in the windows outside, but few cosmetics beyond eau de cologne. They were beginning to have soda fountains, with little marble-topped tables and chairs with curly wire legs like musical signatures. Poisons were displayed quite brazenly on the counters. Arsenic, for instance, was used for cleaning furs. It was accountable for taking off quite a few curious juveniles.

Every block had one or more notion stores—shops selling ribbons, hooks and eyes, sewing thread, tape measures. This was because nearly every woman sewed, and most of the clothes were made at home. There were very few cleaning establishments; one had to walk quite a distance to find one. One did one's own cleaning.

And the dime stores! The five-and-tens, Woolworth's, were in fact five-and-tens; hardly anything in them cost as much as a quarter. What one could buy for an ordinary dime! I remember little bunches of red roses perfectly made, about five inches across. There must have been two dozen buds in each, all fashioned in New York sweatshops by starving tubercular girls, made beautifully, and sold to me for my grubby dime.

Just then, at that time, there was an influx of new Japanese stores. The market was flooded with cheap Oriental ware. For ten cents one could buy a spray of paper cherry blossoms, well made, and for fifty cents an entire branch. For a dollar one could obtain a small Japanese garden, with real moss growing for grass, ferns for bushes, dwarf trees bending over tiny pools, little bridges, miniature stone lanterns, and pagodas (these were Chinese, but who could tell the difference?). There were besides all kinds of paper fans and paper lanterns, even pretty paper umbrellas. The salesmen spoke hardly any English, but they knew how to sell.

A great many poor people, bums and vagabonds, crowded the streets, a good percentage of them with pockmarks — smallpox scars. Policemen in high hats and carrying billy clubs — the police never carried pistols — beat them up regularly and told them to get a move on. Street urchins built little bonfires in the gutters and were soundly thrashed by the officers' billy clubs, and the officers' boots stamped out the sparks of their fires. ("But Father, those boys are cold," I would say. "I think the police are mean." They were, too. "Get a move on," they yelled as they swung.) Not infrequently people fell down, dropping onto the pavement, and ambulances were slow in collecting them. The dray horses that pulled the great delivery wagons slipped on the icy streetcar tracks and fell too, dragging the carts over on top of themselves. Sometimes they had to be destroyed where they lay; sometimes they were goaded to their stumbling hooves with enormous trouble, curses, yelling, and lashings of whips and cries and the horrid scraping of iron shoes on the iron tracks. These sights burned themselves into memory.

The focus of any neighborhood was the church, whatever kind, and the spire of the church was always the tallest edifice in the neighborhood. One looked up to the cross or the spire or to the trumpeting angel. The skyline then consisted of blowing wash atop buildings, endless little smokes blowing out, and church spires — many, many spires. (In 1911 the roofs were black with people, as the population took to the top of the six-story buildings to watch the first airplane circle Manhattan.)

Has the weather changed much? It seems to me the seasons were more violent then. The winters were shrewd and hard to endure for all of us, rich as well as poor. Every day my mother dressed herself in her shirt; drawers; corset, which had to be pulled up tight, sometimes by one of the servants while

Mother held on to the bedpost; on top her camisole, at least two petticoats, and the big dress; and when she went out there was superimposed a coat or cape, hat, veil, gloves, bag, fur-piece, muff. We, the small children, were bundled up into a tremendous number of undergarments held together with buttons everywhere, smocks and sweaters and coats and hats and earmuffs and tippets, mufflers and mittens and gaiters, and then, all but immobilized, we were dispatched for a rollicking romp.

In their way, the summers too were fearful. In the summer all the nice apartments suspended green striped awnings on the outside of every window, which helped a little, but not very much. They were pretty, though. But oh, the heat! So many people collapsed from prostration. Every theater, every kind of public auditorium, was closed from Decoration Day to Labor Day. The theaters shut down totally, leaving the actors to rehearse in the dark, empty, fetid houses. Those actors who could took to the seashore or the Catskills. The others looked for jobs in department stores and similar menial positions.

The poor went out on the fire escapes and carried their bedding with them in order to live through the nights. Those who were domiciled close to the elevated tracks stayed indoors and raised the windows and endured the closed and used air, which became very nearly insupportable. Many succumbed. The ice wagons rolled constantly down each street, followed by a crowd of boys begging for slivers. On every block the police opened fire hydrants to allow the children to play in the water, while the wading pools and the reflecting pools in Central Park, not designed for swimming, were black with waders and splashers. The police did little to stop them, it being a question of survival.

Through it all the women buckled up in their corsets and petticoats and camisoles and long stockings. Why did they do this? There was no law saying they must. The doctors advised against it. The reformers fulminated. The corset manufacturers said they ought to in order to be modish — that is, attractive to men — but even the corset manufacturers were becoming cautious; whales were being decimated, and there was a marked shortage of balleen. The first result, as could be expected, was that corsets were becoming very expensive. Nevertheless, every woman had at least one or two pairs and endured the constrictions. The practice of compelling a woman to wear a corset on all occasions from the time she was fifteen was inhuman, but it persisted. Every woman also wore a petticoat, or two or three—even women who washed the floors, women who did the laundry and ironing, and these were backbreaking chores in those days of no detergents and heavy flatirons that had to be heated on the gas range.

And another thing: no woman had money she could keep. Even the floor washer and the laundress, who slaved for a pittance, could not call their meager quarter dollars their own. Their money became the property of their husbands. Their houses were not theirs, nor their clothes (not even their corsets), nor their children. My father used to call out to my mother, "Ann, come and blow your child's nose." This remark was considered very funny, and everybody laughed. Mother thought it unfeeling and unpaternal, but no one realized the full irony of the exchange. I in fact did not belong to my mother; I belonged to my father. I was my father's property.

Our lovely streets in Harlem are now neglected and festering. Morningside Park is today one of the most dangerous spots in this city, and after dark no sane person would venture into it, or even pass close by. The neighboring houses are broken and filthy. On occasion there have been tales of rats attacking the children. And of course the neighborhood is no longer middle-class. There is not a white face to be seen from one month's end to the next. The present inhabitants don't like the environs any more than we would. But they have to stay.

Street boys no longer play marbles or build innocent bonfires in the gutters; they mug old ladies and trade crack. All the police carry guns and use them.

The streets don't look the same, but this we expect. The fire horses are gone, together with the parlor maids, the white wings, and the ambulatory street, vendors, who couldn't be heard even if they were here and still trying. Gone are all the newsboys, the trolley lines, the double-decker buses, the els (they were torn down beginning in 1938, and the scrap iron was sold to Japan, which returned it to us in the bodies of our soldiers).

The church spire in any Manhattan neighborhood is barely visible, dwarfed and belittled as it is by business enterprises. These days one looks up to office buildings, and the towers of New York have nothing to do with intellectual or religious ideas. In fact, the entire island has become a remarkable conglomeration of stone monoliths, gravestones dedicated to greed.

Nothing is so picturesque, as pleasant-sounding, as personal, or as friendly as it was. We know we must expect changes; architecture and customs change with time. Always have. Must do.

On the other hand:

St. John the Divine is nearly finished. Because the church stands on a steep, rocky abutment, topography helps this holy edifice maintain superiority; its angelic trumpet can still aim at God's heaven and not into an office window. The angel still blows her challenge in triumph against clear sky. But in this St. John's is unique.

There are no laboring children on the streets, no delivery or mail boys. They are in school, learning it's hard to say what. People are older now, and healthier. The present generation has probably never seen a pockmarked face, for smallpox has been wiped out; tuberculosis, syphilis, meningitis, and infantile paralysis have diminished. Childhood disease is no longer rife nor fatal; the majority of children live. Although cancer, heart disease, and now AIDS seem virtually untouched, we have taken giant steps toward health. There are fewer one-armed or one-legged cripples. Most people, even elderly ones, have all their own teeth, something that was unheard-of in my youth. And there is no glint of gold when a person smiles. Only the indigent and the homeless smell. Most people can bathe. Even the poor have running water, generally hot.

The enlargement in the number of available drugs is spectacular, but active irritant poisons have been taken off the open drugstore counters, where they used to stand readily within the grasp of children.

As to enlargement of the variety of foods and nourishment: on the shelves of our supermarkets all the produce of the entire globe is displayed handily at the same time, year-round, despite the season. Most of the food is wrapped in plastic and is untouchable and sterile, and although the goodies seem devoid of attraction, there are no flies and no contamination. The fact of butchery is screened away as in an operating theater, and only the results are displayed, composed and laid out in their transparent shrouds. One does not now have to wait to choose and supervise the cutting and wrapping. This saves sensibilities and time. It also saves lives. Everything we buy is sealed up, protected, prophylactic. It's dull and frequently a nuisance. But we stay alive.

We have reached the moon, have broken the atom and harnessed atomic power. We have preserved the sound of dead voices and the look of dead people and their actions. Space no longer exists, nor time lapse. There is really no such thing as foreign or far-flung people. We see and hear instantly. Yet we have not succeeded in settling the basic, immemorial problem: our daily bread.

There are as many beggars on the street, as many indigent, hopeless, and insane people, as when I was a child. The need and the terror are the same. None of that has changed one bit. The drugged criminals frequenting Morningside Park are desperate people. I do not think they care particularly about the adventure on the moon.

"The poor ye have always with you." Was Jesus Christ, our savior, a profound economist or a hopeless pessimist?

But one group is better off, and the history of this century is distinguished chiefly not by mechanical or scientific advancement in medical research and the attendant blessings but by the emergence of one half of the human race from bondage. Women have come out of the closet—all women, poor as well as rich.

There are today only very few professions women cannot enter. They share in medicine, law, academics, government, building construction, weightlifting, policing, firefighting, garbage slinging. I do not know about cattle slaughtering.

Women own their own wages. They have first claim to their children and an equal voice in divorce.

Domestic service has been greatly reduced. In fact it has all but disappeared, discommoding the housewife, certainly, but eliminating the slave class. Servants today make a decent wage—better than that, a good wage. Devices for saving the mistress's knees and back have been invented (and notice that they were not invented until it was the back and knees of the mistress that were involved), so ladies can still have sufficient leisure. But so can their servants. This is new.

As a symbol of the great evolution, women have discarded their corsets, for the first time in three hundred and fifty years. For the first time in two thousand years they are choosing their garments for reasons of practicality—all women, not just day laborers. They have gone into pants. Considerations of comfort have won out over sex, which is as drastic a choice, as basic, and as difficult to achieve as though women had altered their skeletons—which as a matter of fact they have also done, finding slim hips more suitable to trousers than the wide pelvis of their grandmothers.

These astonishing changes have occurred in an unprecedentedly short period, historically speaking, and within my lifetime. Who made the revolution? Not wayward, militant, or flamboyant spirits, although they were present, calling attention to themselves and their triumphs. No, the revolution was made by those unknowns, with effort and patience, patience and endurance, with trying and with tears, by our aunts and our cousins, our nurses and teachers, our cooks, our mothers.

And by us, unceasingly, endlessly trying.

INDEX